# THE FRENCH INTERIOR

## IN THE EIGHTEENTH CENTURY

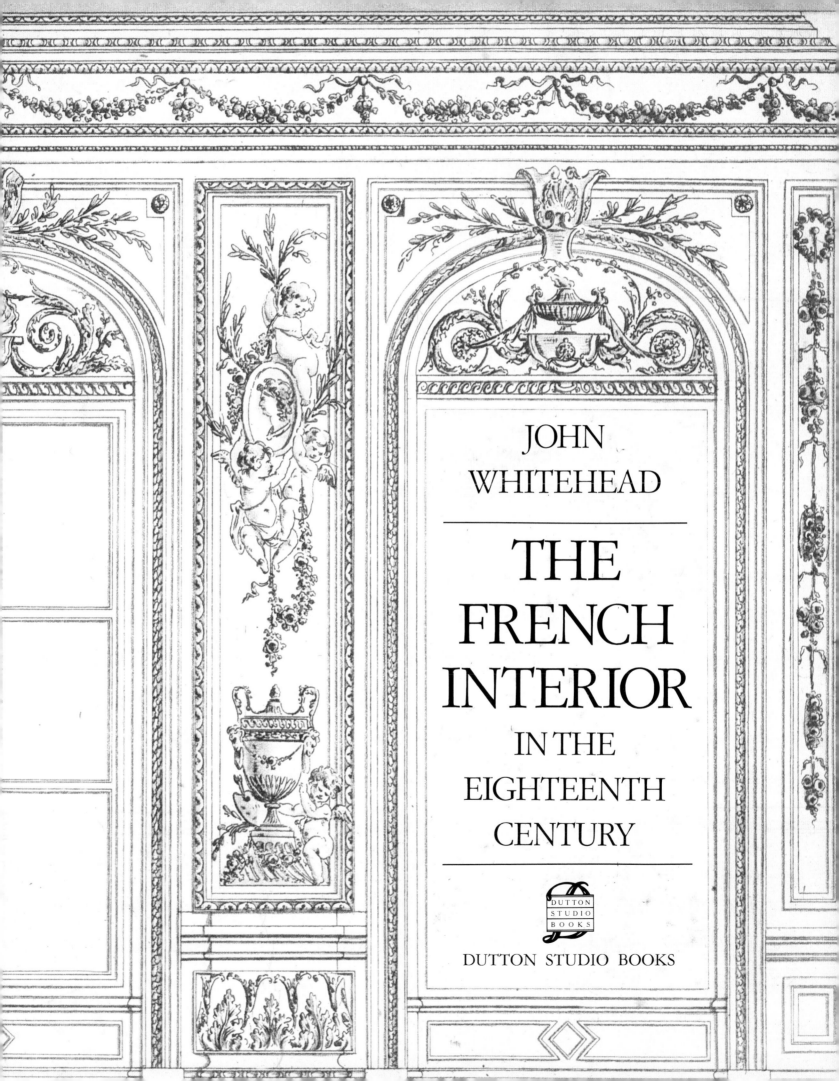

JOHN
WHITEHEAD

# THE
# FRENCH
# INTERIOR

## IN THE

## EIGHTEENTH

## CENTURY

DUTTON STUDIO BOOKS

*For Rebecca, Alice, James, and Edmund*

When embarking upon a book of this type it is easy for an author to
think that he is the only one whose work actually counts, but it
gradually dawned on me that without the skill, dedication, and, above
all, patience of my editor, Jacky Colliss Harvey, picture researcher,
Susan Bolsom-Morris, and designer, Richard Foenander, I would not
have got very far, and I thank them all.

DUTTON STUDIO BOOKS

Published by the Penguin Group
Penguin Books USA Inc., 375 Hudson Street,
New York, New York, 10014, U.S.A.

Penguin Books Ltd, 27 Wrights Lane,
London W8 5TZ, England

Penguin Books Australia Ltd, Ringwood,
Victoria, Australia

Penguin Books Canada Ltd, 2801 John Street,
Markham, Ontario, Canada L3R 1B4

Penguin Books (N.Z.) Ltd, 182-190 Wairau Road,
Auckland 10, New Zealand

Penguin Books Ltd, Registered Offices:
Harmondsworth, Middlesex, England

First published by Dutton Studio Books, an imprint of
Penguin Books USA Inc.

First printing, January 1993
10 9 8 7 6 5 4 3 2 1

Copyright © John Whitehead, 1992
All rights reserved

Library of Congress
Catalog Card Number 92-81946

ISBN: 0-525-93444-8

*Endpapers*
Silk damask, mid-eighteenth century.

*Frontispiece*
Detail of a doorway in the hall of a house in the Faubourg Saint-Germain,
remodelled by the architect P. M. Mouret in 1751. The carved stone cartouche
may be by Jacques Verbeckt.

This book was designed and produced by
CALMANN AND KING LTD, LONDON
Designed by Richard Foenander
Picture research by Susan Bolsom-Morris
Typeset by SX Composing Limited, Rayleigh, Essex
Printed and bound by Toppan, Singapore

# CONTENTS

# INTRODUCTION

*"Ôtez le luxe à la France, à sa capitale surtout, et vous tuerez une grande partie de son commerce; je dis plus, vous lui ôterez une grande partie de sa suprématie en Europe."* (Deprive France, and especially its capital, of luxury, and you kill the greatest part of its trade; I say more, you will have deprived it of much of its supremacy in Europe.)
The Baronne d'Oberkirch, 1782.

It is possible for us to envisage the fabled *douceur de vivre* of the *ancien régime*? The art historians of the last century had the great advantage of being only two generations away, but time, and great political, social and economic upheavals mean that we have enormous difficulty in piecing together an accurate picture across two hundred years, and believing what we think we see. There are visual clues: houses, furniture and objects, which, though we are hampered by their unknown rate of survival, can at least still show us what these things looked like. There are paintings and engravings, but as evidence these are seriously flawed because the artist's intention was seldom primarily to reproduce exactly what he saw; rather he sought to create an appropriate stage set for his characters. Finally there are documents. Wills, inventories, account books, newspapers, letters and memoirs are the closest we can get to a conversation with their writers, and they provide many answers, although we need to exercise great care when interpreting them. This book includes excerpts from many such documents, and they bring vividly to life the tastes and concerns of those who wrote them.

It also makes use of numerous photographs of interiors, wherever possible using those that are less well-known, or which have not been photographed before. Particular points in the text are illustrated with specific examples of furniture and objects, and once again an attempt has been made to use those which the reader will not already know. Many such pieces are no longer in France; even before the revolution foreign collectors had begun to appreciate the beauty of works of art produced in this period, and many are now preserved in private houses and museums all over the world. Paintings and engravings of the period have also been used to make detailed and important points.

The history of the French eighteenth-century interior is a subject so vast that few writers have dared attempt to cover it in full, preferring instead to focus on particular aspects. Many excellent studies have appeared since the second half of the nineteenth century, and some that I found most valuable are listed in the Bibliography.

The discussion of prices has been avoided. The subject is fascinating, but so complex that it would need to be entered into as a separate study. Similarly, a thorough investigation of the marks on porcelain, silver or gilt-bronze could not be undertaken here. The reader interested in finding out more is referred to the excellent specialist studies included in the bibliography.

No book of this sort can be written without the kind help of many *amateurs*, collectors, dealers and museum curators, and my heartfelt gratitude for a bewildering variety of useful advice and assistance goes to a large number of people, some of whose names are included here: Daniel Alcouffe, Armin Allen, Andrew Allfree, Pierre Arizzoli-Clementel, Tracey Avery, Christian Badin, Patrick Barbe, Christian Baulez, Jacques Bazaine, Geoffrey Beard, Michele Beiny, Sir Geoffrey de Bellaigue, Frank Berendt, Juan de Bestegui, Janine Bonifas, Anne Bony, Anthony du Boulay, the Duke of Buccleugh, Alistair Clarke, Alec Cobbe, David Cohen, Didier Cramoisan, Leon Dalva, Stéphane Dannet, Alan Darr, Kenneth Davis, Aileen Dawson, Ted Dell, Bernard Dragesco, Sara Elliott, Richard Falkiner, Kjeld von Folsack, Sarah Franklin, Simon Franses, Deborah Gage, Francesca Galloway, the Marquise de Ganay, Robert Gérard, Alexis Gregory, Olivier Goubot, Alain Gruber, Michael Hall, Antoinette Hallé, John Hardy, Jonathan Harris, Henry Hawley, Helena Hayward, Thomas Heneage, Lady Hillingdon, Judith Howard, John Hudson, Peter Hughes, Oliver Impey, Simon Jervis, William Johnston, Nicole Kolesnikoff, Clare Le Corbeiller, Genevieve Le Duc, David Legg-Willis, Sophie Le Tarnec, Isabelle Leven, Bruce Lindsay, Jean-Daniel Ludmann, Katherine Maclean, Errol Manners, John McKee, Sarah Medlam, Jean de Mézerac, Daniel Mingledorff, David Mitchell, David Moses, Edgar Munhall, Tessa Murdoch, Nicholas Norton, Olivier Odelin, David Peters, Alexandre Pradère, Tamara Préaud, the Countess of Rosebery, Baronne Elie de Rothschild, Baronne Guy de Rothschild, Kate de Rothschild, Alan Rubin, Louise Ruck, Carolyn Sargentson, Adrian Sassoon, Rosalind Savill, Julia Schottlander, Tim Schroder, Selma Schwartz, Martin Shopland, Tony Stevenson, Penelope Stiebel, Eric and Isabelle Turquin, Michel Vandermeersch, Sir Francis Watson, Lavinia Wellicome, Alex Wengraf, Robert Wenley, Judy Wentworth, Gillian Wilson, Timothy Wilson, Jayne Wrightsman, James Yorke and Ghenete Zelleke.

# 1
# CLIENTELE

One of the first steps taken by the Duc d'Orléans, upon becoming Regent after the death of Louis XIV in 1715, was to remove the Court and the seat of the government from Versailles to Paris. In doing so, he was merely continuing a movement which had been growing in momentum since the early years of the century. The military reversals of the old King, the increasingly stuffy atmosphere at Court, the rise of a super-rich financier class who did not attend Court, even the appallingly bad winters, had all contributed to shifting the focus of French society away from Versailles, the palace embellished by Louis XIV to serve as a temple for the worship of himself as Apollo, the Sun King.

The great Palace stood empty and little original work was to be undertaken there until the 1730s, after Louis XV's marriage to Marie Leczinska had finally provided an impetus to reactivate Royal patronage of the arts. For the first thirty years of the eighteenth century, it was in Paris that the finest, most luxurious interiors were created. The skills of the craftsmen who created lavish surroundings for the Regent and his circle had been developed in the second half of the seventeenth century for the specific purpose of decorating Louis XIV's vast palaces. All of Europe admired these and was busy copying them, while in Paris itself a new, independent, rich, less discreetly immoral society was clamouring for novelty. It was in the decoration of small, intimate, luxurious and harmonious interiors that the eighteenth century was to excel. Grand apartments were still made and finely decorated, but it is the *nids de rats* (rats' nests), as the Marquis d'Argenson disparagingly described them in his memoirs, that are the supreme achievement of the *dix-huitième*.

Versailles never regained its unique position as the fount of all taste. In the eighteenth century, decorations and works of art created for the aristocracy were to equal Court art, in contrast to the Louis XIV period, when much of the finest work was executed for the King.

PREVIOUS SPREAD
*D*etail of the *salon* in a Paris Hôtel, with panelling installed in the mideighteenth century.

*E*scalier du Roi at the Château de Compiègne, finished in 1785. The ironwork and gilt-bronze balustrade is the work of the *serrurier* (locksmith) Raguet.

## ROYAL PATRONAGE

### LOUIS XV

"Architectural drawings are the only way to keep the King amused," wrote d'Argenson about Louis XV; and surviving buildings, as well as the many now destroyed, testify to Louis XV's compelling interest in decoration. When the young King had returned to Versailles in 1722, the palace had not been touched since Louis XIV's death, and it was many years before Louis XV was to stamp his personality upon it. Among the earliest work to be undertaken was the completion in 1729 of the Salon d'Hercule, the room at the top of the Escalier des Ambassadeurs which was designed to act as *antichambre* to the Grands Appartements as well as to lead to the chapel. It was thus a component part of his greatgrandfather's project. Louis XV and Louis XVI respected their ancestor's work and the decoration of the Grands Appartements was to remain untouched, with the major and tragic exception of the Escalier des Ambassadeurs, which was destroyed in 1752 to enlarge the apartments of the King's favourite daughter, Madame Adélaïde. The Appartement Intérieur du Roi, the first-floor suite of rooms giving on to the Cour de Marbre, was gradually remodelled, and all the rooms from the Cabinet du Conseil through to the Cabinet de la Vaisselle d'Or are still decorated with the white and gold panelling carved by Jacques Verbeckt with *rocaille* motifs which was installed during Louis XV's reign.

Following the example of his great-grandfather, Louis XV continuously sought refuge from the bustle of the Court by creating private palaces in which he could enjoy the company of a few chosen friends. The first one, a palace within a palace, at Versailles itself, comprised the set of rooms above the Appartement Intérieur, in which the King gave his famous private supper parties in the company of his mistress of the moment and a few intimate friends such as the Maréchal de Saxe or the Duc de Croÿ. These rooms, known as the "Cabinets du Roi", were grouped around the Cour des Cerfs, the inner courtyard on the north side of the palace which had an abundance of trelliswork and aviaries, and a multitude of flowers. Access to the roof via terraces enabled the Royal party to stroll extensively after meals. Alterations were con-

tinuous; by the end of the reign, a small gallery which had been decorated in 1738 with gold-coloured lacquer by the famous lacquerer Martin and hung with exotic hunting scenes by Van Loo, Parrocel and Boucher, had changed in shape to become the *grand cabinet* of Madame du Barry's apartment, and acquired a large set of seat furniture, including a taller chair for the King's use, a dog kennel, and precious objects in lacquer, porcelain and rock crystal arranged on shelves.

Ange-Jacques Gabriel (1698-1782), a member of a large and distinguished family of architects, succeeded Robert de Cotte as Contrôleur of Versailles in 1734, and his own father as Premier Architecte du Roi in 1741. Louis XV held him in very high esteem, and with his help undertook all the great building and decorating projects of his reign. They were constantly to be found studying architectural drawings together, exciting the jealousy of courtiers, and drawings by Gabriel survive with extensive corrections in Louis XV's own hand. The châteaux of Choisy, La Muette and Saint-Hubert were among the subjects of their discussions. Built or redecorated by Gabriel for the King, they sadly no longer survive. At Choisy, bought by Louis in 1739, campaigns of redecoration and enlargement proceeded at such speed that in 1754 he decided to build a small château in the garden, where he could truly be alone with Madame de Pompadour.

## LOUIS XVI AND MARIE ANTOINETTE

"Louis XVI has simple tastes," wrote the Baronne d'Oberkirch after being taken on a tour of the King's private apartments in Versailles in 1782. "I found them beautiful but less elaborate than the Queen's."

Louis XVI's permanent preoccupation with economy was to distract him from building and decorating on the scale of his predecessors, and it is Marie Antoinette who, through the decoration of her private apartments at Versailles and the Petit Trianon, has become known as the principal patron of the *goût étrusque*. This is not to say that Louis was inactive. During his short reign (1774-93), with the help of his faithful Directeur des Bâtiments, the Comte d'Angiviller, he created new sets of apartments at the great châteaux of Fontainebleau and Compiègne, and acquired Saint-Cloud and Rambouillet.

One of the young King's first acts upon coming to the throne in 1774 was to establish a library for himself in the private apartments at Versailles. He was to retain his grandfather's decorations for the remainder of the rooms on the first floor overlooking the Cour de Marbre, contenting himself with renewing paint, gilding, and furniture, as well as filling the rooms with large quantities of the Sèvres porcelain

*M*id-eighteenth-century painting on a fan-leaf showing Louis XV and his family at table. The Royal family did not eat together at Versailles, so this must be a view of another château, possibly Marly.

*T*wo Vincennes porcelain plates (*assiettes à gauderons*) from the *bleu céleste* service bought by Louis XV in 1753-4. The shapes of this service, including those of the plates, were designed by Duplessis. The motif of overlapping gilded discs on the borders of the reserves may be an early neoclassical reference, recalling the appearance of stacked paterae (libation dishes) in the iconography of Olympian banquets of the gods.

*G*ilt-bronze profile portraits of Louis XVI and Marie Antoinette, in the style of medals. Signed and dated Lebrun, 1775, possibly for the *bronzier* Antoine-François Lebrun. Given by Louis XVI on the occasion of his *Sacre* (coronation) to the Indian prince Haidar Ali, the father of Tipu Sultan.

he so loved. The decoration of the library was supervised by Gabriel (it was to be his last job before retirement), and consists of white and gold panelling carved with edifying trophies and bas-reliefs, with incorporated bookcases, and doors built to look like bookcases with false bookbindings. The white marble chimneypiece was carved with putti by Boizot and mounted with gilt-bronze by Pierre Gouthière. It was not new, but had been removed on Louis XVI's order from a pavilion built several years previously for Madame du Barry at Fontainebleau – a surprising choice considering his puritanical attitude towards his late grandfather's favourite. Louis filled the room with objects which bear witness to his personal taste. The chimneypiece was surmounted with a garniture of five Sèvres vases decorated with flowers in reserves on a blue ground, and two Sèvres biscuit figures of huntresses with hares, deer and partridges. On the commode sat a pair of gold candelabra protected by glass cases. A Sèvres vase, also in a glass case, stood in the centre of a large round mahogany table by Jean-Henri Riesener. The vase had a white and gold ground, with handles in the shape of satyrs' heads with garlands of flowers, also gilded; it contained white porcelain flowers, and was surrounded by six Sèvres biscuit figures from the series of the *Grands Hommes* of France, commissioned by the King from leading sculptors. Each *Grand Homme* stood on a base of gilt- or patinated bronze or marbled wood. A pair of globes were supported by figures of Hercules, in plaster coloured to look like patinated bronze. The mahogany library steps, a small writing desk also by Riesener and a shagreen-covered telescope completed the ensemble.

Louis XVI shared with his grandfather a craze for hunting, and was happy to see references to this pastime in decoration carried out for his use. In 1780, the finest painters at the Sèvres factory transposed onto porcelain the cartoons for the *Chasses du Roi* which Jean-Baptiste Oudry had painted for the Gobelins fifty years previously, replacing the face of Louis XV with that of his grandson. These were hung in the dining room of the Appartement Intérieur; it was this room that was

used for the yearly exhibitions of the Sèvres porcelain factory's production, an event in which the King took an inordinate interest.

Until the death of Louis XV, it was the king's mistress who had been the leader in fashion and extravagance. With Louis XVI's accession to the throne, however, this role was to be taken over by Marie Antoinette. Brought up at a court almost as magnificent as the French one, she lost no time in ordering for herself the finest that was available, in a highly capricious and impatient way which was to lay the foundation for her subsequent appalling and largely unjustified reputation.

As with Louis XV, most of the work carried out for Marie Antoinette was intended for intimate apartments which were never seen by the majority of courtiers, giving rise, through ignorance, to the same accusations of unspeakable extravagance that had been levelled against him. The Queen's aversion to the stifling etiquette of Versailles, which was in marked contrast to the relaxed atmosphere at Schönbrunn, where she had been brought up, can largely explain her desire to retreat into her private apartments at Versailles, the Petit Trianon, and Fontainebleau, whose astonishing jewel-like richness and fineness provoke the

*J*ewel cabinet *in situ* in Marie Antoinette's *chambre* at Versailles, made for her in 1787 by the *ébéniste* Ferdinand Schwerdfeger, with painted panels by Lagrenée and figures modelled by Boizot. The model for a rejected project is illustrated below.

*R*ejected model for Marie Antoinette's jewel cabinet. Made in 1787, after designs by Dugourc, and submitted to the Queen by Bonnefoy Duplan, the Intendant of her Garde-Meuble.

question of how much she personally intervened in the decisions about their decoration and furnishing.

Common strands run through the work executed for the Queen. A passion for flowers, ribbons and drapery is reflected not only in the textiles she ordered from Lyon and in the elaborate upholstery created for her, but also in the marquetry of her favourite *ébéniste* Riesener, as well as in the gilt-bronzes with which he decorated the commodes, secretaires and tables delivered for her use. The cynosure of this taste is to be found in the *mobilier du treillage*, a set of seat furniture executed by Georges Jacob in 1787 for the Queen's bedroom at the Petit Trianon. This was carved by Triquet and Rode with imitation trellis and basket-work, and garlands of ivy, flowers and pinecones. Painted by Chaillot in naturalistic colours, it was upholstered in white silk embroidered with multicoloured flowers, supplied by Desfarges of Lyon.

At the Petit Trianon, given to Marie Antoinette by her husband within weeks of his accession to the throne, the Queen was to create her own charming world, both in the gardens and in the house. It was there that she gave several fêtes, including those in honour of her brother Joseph II, the Holy Roman Emperor, in 1781, and of Gustav III of Sweden in 1784. The Swedish King was enthralled, and lost no time in commissioning a Swedish artist resident in Paris, Nicolas Lafresen, to produce a gouache of the Temple de l'Amour showing the illuminations. Inside the house, Marie Antoinette was slow to change the decoration, originally conceived by Gabriel in the late 1760s, and already in the neoclassical style. Her architect, Richard Mique, a former protégé of Marie Leczinska, designed new panelling for her boudoir in 1787. Delicate arabesques and garlands of roses were carved around the edge of the panels, and painted white on a sky-blue ground (see overleaf). At night, similar panels slid up from the floor to hide the windows. Mique was principally employed on other projects; he built a theatre for the Queen at the Petit Trianon, as well as the famous model farm, which consisted of buildings with rustic exteriors and exotic interiors, including a *cabinet Chinois*.

The relative lack of activity displayed by Louis XVI can be accounted for by his interest in what was to become known as the "Grand Projet", the plan to rebuild Versailles on the entrance side, providing vastly enlarged apartments for the King and Queen, as well as a truly grand staircase to replace Louis XIV's Escalier des Ambassadeurs. Marie Antoinette enthusiastically supported this, since it would have resulted in the replacement of her very cramped private apartments. To act as a temporary residence during the rebuilding works, the château of Saint-Cloud had been purchased from the Duc d'Orléans in 1785, and was itself redecorated for the King and Queen. Louis XVI was in no hurry, as is proved by his one partly executed commission for the Grand Projet, the splendid Sèvres dinner service with mythological scenes in reserves on a richly gilded dark blue ground, which he ordered in 1782 and which was to have taken twenty years to complete. Production of the service was discontinued when political events overtook the unfortunate monarch, and the architectural aspect of the enterprise remained on the drawing board.

For the whole of the eighteenth century, such schemes were overseen by the Bâtiments du Roi and the Garde-Meuble de la Couronne, two administrative departments within the Royal household which carried out most of the decorating and furnishing.

*M*arie Antoinette's boudoir at the Petit Trianon, with panelling designed by Mique, 1787. The panelling that slides up at night to hide the windows incorporates looking-glasses in gilt frames. The fine set of chairs now in the room was ordered from Georges Jacob by the Comte de Provence in 1785 for his mistress, the Comtesse de Balbi.

*The Garter*, by Jean-François de Troy, 1725. An interesting mixture of fashionable and traditional furnishings can be glimpsed in this realistic interior. The chairs and the bookcase with its clock by Boulle are clearly some fifteen to twenty years old, while the console table is in the latest fashion. The wall-covering clearly testifies to the inefficacy of the ban on printed cottons.

## THE BÂTIMENTS DU ROI

The post of "Directeur et Ordonnateur général des Bâtiments, Jardins, Arts, Académies et Manufactures Royales" was described as early as 1771 as a sort of minister of the arts. The extent of the Directeur's responsibilities was considerable. As well as supervising the architecture, upkeep, and decoration of all royal buildings, and being in charge of the royal gardens, he oversaw the Académie Royale de Peinture et de Sculpture and the various factories enjoying royal ownership or patronage, including the tapestry workshops and the Sèvres factory. It was his job to propose new projects to the King, and to select the artists and craftsmen who were to undertake them. Many of these artists were given lodgings in the Louvre, at the Directeur's discretion.

The Bâtiments were responsible for the major, fixed part of the decoration of royal houses. The King would discuss his intentions with the Directeur, who consulted with the Premier Architecte; they then reported back with detailed plans, which were often altered before being finally approved. The Premier Architecte could call upon teams of designers, who were usually junior architects, and work was put out to tender among the builders and craftsmen. This involved wall, ceiling, floor, fireplace or stove and wall decoration, in materials such as marble, stone, wood, painted surfaces and mirrors.

Louis-Antoine de Pardaillan de Gondrin, Duc d'Antin, a son of Madame de Montespan, was appointed Directeur by Louis XIV in 1708, and remained in the post until his death in 1736. D'Antin seems to have been no connoisseur of the arts, and he neglected the Académie de Peinture to the extent that the annual Salons were abandoned and only started again in 1737. D'Antin was nevertheless responsible for the revival of the Savonnerie carpet works, placed under the care of Robert de Cotte in 1708. In his caustic *Mémoires*, Charles-Nicolas Cochin accused d'Antin of sending to the Académie de France in Rome not the artists who had won the annual Prix de Rome, but those who had managed to ingratiate themselves with him. Boucher, the winner in 1723, had to wait until 1728 before he could afford to go. It was not until 1735 that d'Antin, finally recognizing his qualities, asked him to paint four grisaille *Vertus* for the ceiling of Marie Leczinska's bedroom at Versailles. D'Antin's work was diverse and intense at first, involving, for example, visits to Fontainebleau to report on holes in ceilings, but after Louis XIV's death, when the new King was a minor, his duties were much less arduous, and it was at this point that he built for himself the magnificent but short-lived château of Petit-Bourg.

Philibert Orry de Vignory, d'Antin's successor, was an extremely

*The Declaration of Love*, by Jean-François de Troy, 1725. The giltwood moulding which borders the wall-covering has been designed to harmonize with the back of the sofa and the upper part of the pedestal, as has the frame of the painting. The correspondences at this time between textiles used for clothing and those used for interior decoration are beautifully illustrated by the man's coat, which is in a very similar material to the curtain, and the lady's dress, which goes with the printed cotton cushion.

able civil servant, who, as Contrôleur général des Finances (finance minister) at the same time, was well aware of the connection between art, commerce and prosperity; he was an active follower of Louis XIV's minister Colbert in this respect. (Colbert, through his policies of reconstruction and protectionism had laid the foundations for French prosperity in the eighteenth century.) It is characteristic of Vignory's policy that he supported the order of silk from Lyon in 1737 for the renewal of the upholstery of the King and Queen's apartments, with the intention of helping the Lyon silk weavers, who were suffering from lack of work. His dismissal in 1745 was the result of his rivalry with the Pâris brothers, financiers who supported Madame de Pompadour.

Charles-François-Paul Lenormant de Tournehem, a prosperous *fermier-général* (tax farmer), owed his appointment to his support for Madame de Pompadour. Not only was he the uncle of her husband, Lenormant d'Etioles, but he may also have been her father. D'Argenson, in his memoirs, clearly disapproved, stating that Tournehem *"n'a ni goût, ni économie"* (had no notion of taste or moderation in spending). That this judgment was at least partly unfair can be seen through Tournehem's tireless activity. The competition for a great square in Paris in honour of Louis XV in 1748 (now the Place de la Concorde) was his idea; the architecture was eventually executed by Gabriel and the equestrian statue of the King by Bouchardon. In 1747, Tournehem established a new kind of competition for painters: eleven artists were invited to submit entries, which were to be judged by officers of the Académie de Peinture. In the end, they were all purchased by the King.

Abel Poisson, Marquis de Marigny, was the brother of Madame de Pompadour, who selected the post of Directeur as a suitable appointment for him, and sent him on a Grand Tour to Italy in 1749, so that he might acquire the necessary education. When Tournehem died in 1751, Marigny, then only twenty-four, succeeded him, and his sister lost no time in forcefully recommending to him the correct course of action: "Come straight away to thank the King, who has placed you at the head of his Bâtiments. This position is akin to that of Petronius. You will need to be an arbiter of taste, and encourage the fine arts. But you will therefore need to study them, and refrain from believing those little flatterers who will besiege you because of your post with praise for qualities which are not yours."

Marigny's tenure coincided with the rise of the neoclassical style. Indeed his Grand Tour companions, Cochin and the architect Soufflot, were neoclassical pioneers. Soufflot benefited from his association with Marigny, being appointed to oversee the work of the Gobelins and Savonnerie. Marigny's competence can be judged from the fact that he maintained his post after his sister's death, being dismissed only in 1773. He was briefly replaced by the Abbé Joseph-Marie Terray, a politician who, as Contrôleur général des Finances, was as effective as he was unpopular.

Charles-Claude Flahaut de la Billarderie, Comte d'Angiviller, when appointed to the post of Directeur général in 1774, decided to concentrate on a few important projects only, in an attempt to stem the seemingly endless flow of money from the royal coffers. Louis XVI's new library was, however, followed by a deluge of orders from Marie Antoinette, including those for the Cabinet de la Méridienne and the *cabinet intérieur* in her private apartments. The new Premier Architecte was Richard Mique, and d'Angiviller found it difficult to surmount his personal antipathy to him. In a letter to Marie Antoinette, he

*D*esign for a gilt-bronze candlestick, mid-eighteenth century. One of a number of designs commissioned by the Garde-Meuble, and bound together in an album in 1752. It contains designs for upholstery, furniture and gilt-bronzes by Slodtz, Lajoue, Chevillon and others. Now in the Bibliothèque Nationale, Paris.

complained that Mique, who (as the Queen's personal architect) could execute work for her without d'Angiviller's approval but at the Bâtiments' expense, was poisoning the Queen's mind against him.

D'Angiviller's correspondence with the director of the Sèvres factory and the Savonnerie show him to have been a careful and positive administrator with an attention to detail; he repeatedly expressed interest in the execution of individual commissions, for the King and Queen as well as for other clients. Rambouillet, bought from the Duc de Penthièvre in 1783 because of the excellent hunting in the surrounding forest, was a project for which d'Angiviller was made personally responsible, and he successfully converted the estate for use by the Royal household by enlarging the outbuildings, as well as providing plans for a new château to replace the old one, which Marie Antoinette had disparagingly referred to as a *"crapaudière"* (toadhole). The revolution was to prevent this project from being executed, but d'Angiviller meanwhile had supervised every detail of the building, in 1786, of the famous Laiterie de la Reine (Queen's dairy) in an attempt to reconcile the Queen to Rambouillet. Designed by the architect Thévenin, the Laiterie comprised a small temple flanked by two outbuildings, one of which contained a circular dining room with grisaille overdoors by Sauvage and carved "Etruscan" furniture made by Georges Jacob to designs provided by Hubert Robert, who had already been employed by d'Angiviller to design the gardens at Compiègne. Inside the temple was a circular room leading to a grotto containing a large marble statue of the nymph Amalthea and her goat, by Pierre Julien. The room itself was domed and contained Sèvres porcelain vases and bowls of shapes and decoration designed by Jean-Jacques Lagrenée, reputedly using as inspiration the collection of ancient vases bought by Louis XVI from the Baron de Non.

## THE GARDE-MEUBLE DE LA COURONNE

Founded by Louis XIV in 1663, this body was responsible for supplying the King, his family and household with the movable elements of decoration, including textiles, furniture, lighting accessories, table- and other silver and carpets. At its head during the eighteenth century were first three generations of the Fontanieu family, and then, from 1784, Marc-Antoine Thierry de Ville d'Avray, whose other post, that of Premier Valet de chambre du Roi, also guaranteed him instant access to the King.

The Garde-Meuble dealt with the makers and dealers from whom furnishings were obtained. Long-term relationships were established with suppliers; the *tapissier* (upholsterer) Pierre-Germain Lallié was succeeded by his partner Claude-Germain Sallior in 1736 after thirty-five years of work for the Garde-Meuble. Sallior himself retired in 1754. The *ébéniste* Jean-Henri Riesener supplied over seven hundred pieces of furniture during the first ten years of Louis XVI's reign, and although Thierry ceased to employ him in 1785 in an ineffectual attempt to reduce costs, he continued to sell furniture to Marie Antoinette through her own Garde-Meuble, which was run by her servant Bonnefoy Duplan.

The enormous quantity of textiles supplied to the Garde-Meuble has unfortunately largely disappeared, along with the braids and other trimmings that are tantalizingly recorded. Many of these had been designed by artists in the Garde-Meuble's employment, such as Alexis

*M*id-eighteenth-century design for a decorative panel, perhaps to be executed in painted silk. From the Garde-Meuble album in the Bibliothèque Nationale, Paris.

Peyrotte and Jacques Gondoin. Peyrotte, described as "Peintre et dessinateur du Roi pour les meubles de la Couronne", had varied duties including designing upholstery fabrics and their borders, and painting motifs directly on silk and velvet. Such a set of four paintings on silk, 11 *pieds* (3.57 m) high and 8 *pieds* (2.59 m) wide and consisting of *fleurs, ornements et animaux*, was made for Louis XV's dining room at Compiègne in 1768. Peyrotte also executed designs for furniture.

# ROYAL MISTRESSES

## MADAME DE POMPADOUR

The Marquise de Pompadour, Louis XV's acknowledged mistress from 1745 until her death in 1764, played an essential role in the development of the arts. She was constantly seeking new distractions for the King, and this was to lead her to create at Versailles and at her splendid private palaces surroundings of great comfort, intimacy and artistic accomplishment.

During the nineteen years of her "reign", she built, bought or rented many houses, including Bellevue, Crécy and Champs, and Ménars, which she was to bequeath to her brother. Indeed she must have been a compulsive builder and decorator, for when she bought the Hôtel d'Evreux (now the Elysée Palace) in Paris, she wrote to her

friend the Comtesse de Brezé: "Have you heard that I have just bought the Hôtel d'Evreux? I really had to have a house in Paris, but I'm going to have it knocked down, and build another one more to my taste. Everyone laughs at such building mania, but as far as I'm concerned I fully approve of this so-called madness, which feeds so many paupers; I get much more pleasure out of distributing gold than out of hoarding it."

Madame de Pompadour used the finest artists, designers and craftsmen to create interiors of which we can have a vivid impression today, thanks to the *livre-journal* of the dealer Lazare Duvaux, and to her own posthumous inventory. Through these it has been possible to identify surviving objects, which invariably testify to her infallible taste. She was possessed of a sound business judgement, and although she did receive gifts from the King she supplemented them considerably through her own investments, such as a bottle factory established on an island on the Seine below the Château de Bellevue. It was to a site adjoining the gardens at Bellevue, in the village of Sèvres, that the Royal porcelain factory was to be moved from Vincennes in 1756, and it is no coincidence that Madame de Pompadour was one of the factory's principal clients, to the extent of having a vase named in her honour.

## MADAME DU BARRY

When in 1768 Louis XV took a mistress thirty-five years his junior, who had been little better than a common prostitute, the general reaction at Court was one of horror. Yet Jeanne du Barry's name is of considerable importance to the history of French decorative arts on two counts: her patronage of the *marchand-mercier* Simon-Philippe Poirier, and her role as a promoter of neoclassical taste.

From 1768 to 1774, Poirier and his fellow dealer Dominique Daguerre supplied Madame du Barry with Sèvres, Chantilly and Meissen porcelain, lacquer, gilt-bronzes (including clocks, wall lights, lanterns and mounts for vases) and furniture decorated with marquetry, lacquer, or inlaid with Sèvres porcelain plaques. Sèvres-inlaid furniture was Poirier's quasi-exclusive speciality, and Madame du Barry was to be his biggest client, buying many of the models created by him for general sale, as well as four extremely elaborate pieces which may have been designed specially for her, and which were never repeated: two commodes with large plaques, one painted with pastoral scenes after Pater, Lancret and Van Loo, and two tables with plaques representing a *sultane* in an exotic interior.

Claude-Nicolas Ledoux designed for Madame du Barry a small Pavillon in the gardens of the Château de Louveciennes, which Louis XV

had given her. This was built in 1771, and marks the complete flourishing in France of the neoclassical style. Madame du Barry had owned furniture and objects in this style, but the pavilion's unified and harmonious character made it a landmark. To Ledoux's designs, the *bronzier* Pierre Gouthière made the gilt-bronze bases and capitals for the pilasters in the dining room, as well as the door and window handles, the wall lights and the ornaments for the fireplaces. The chairs by Louis Delanois, visible in the watercolour by Jean-Michel Moreau (Moreau le Jeune) of the first reception given there for Louis XV in September 1771, have oval backs and turned tapering legs and match the remainder of the classical decoration, including that of the *surtout de table* (table centrepiece, see page 224). Madame du Barry's rejection of the rococo is clearly shown by her decision to replace almost immediately a set of four paintings she had ordered from Fragonard for Louveciennes by another set commissioned from Joseph-Marie Vien, a pioneer of neoclassicism. The subjects remained, however, broadly similar, including the aptly entitled *Amant couronnant sa maîtresse*.

*L*acquered bronze and silver sugar-casters, circa 1745-50. The figures may be the work of the Martins, who are known to have produced lacquered figures of Chinamen to support clock cases. The bronzes bear the crowned *C* mark. Their original owner, Madame de Pompadour, entrusted them to Duvaux in September 1752, as recorded in his *livre-journal*: "to clean and repair two figures carrying sugar-canes, and polish the sugar-canes and flowers" (*remis à neuf & rétabli deux figures vernies portant des cannes de sucre, fait reblanchir lesdites cannes d'argent & fleurs*).

*T*he *Marquise de Pompadour* by François-Hubert Drouais, 1764. This portrait, finished after the sitter's death in April 1764, shows Madame de Pompadour seated at her embroidery frame. She may have bought this from Lazare Duvaux; Duvaux at any rate sold a similar one to the Dauphine in 1751: *un métier à travailler en vernis vert poli à relief en or, garni de ses ferrures dorées d'or moulu* (an embroidery frame of polished green lacquer with raised gilt decoration, with gilt-iron fittings). The *goût grec* marquetry table containing the embroidery wools is certainly by Jean-François Oeben, in its original bright colours.

# PRINCELY AND NOBLE CLIENTS, FINANCIERS AND FERMIERS GÉNÉRAUX

The household of a prince or great noble could include a permanent department concerned with architecture and decoration, modelled on the Royal departments but on a smaller scale. Artists and designers used titles which indicated that they were working or had worked for a prince. Thus, Gilles-Marie Oppenord proudly proclaimed himself on the title page of a book of decorative engravings to be Directeur général des Bâtiments de Son Altesse Royale Monseigneur le duc d'Orléans, Régent.

*Charles-Alexandre de Calonne* by Elisabeth-Louise Vigée-Lebrun, dated 1784. At the time the portrait was painted, Calonne was Louis XVI's Contrôleur général des Finances (finance minister). He does not seem to have felt the need to adhere to the newest fashion; he sits upon a Louis XV *fauteuil à la Reine*, and the gilt-bronze frieze round his desk is from a model by Joseph Baumhauer of circa 1770. Moreover, the inkstand dates from the Régence.

*O*val *salon* on the ground floor of the Hôtel de Soubise, designed by Germain Boffrand and completed in the late 1730s. It formed part of the Prince de Soubise's apartment; an identically-shaped room immediately above belonged to that of the Princesse. There all the carving in the panelling is gilded, and paintings replace the stucco spandrels by Adam and Lemoyne.

Princes and important noblemen required magnificence around them, and built lavishly, while lesser aristocracy in Paris were content with lodgings which, while they might be on a smaller scale, were often equally finely decorated. The Faubourg Saint-Germain, the newly fashionable quarter on the left bank of the Seine, boasted a great many houses in which the principal reception floor consisted of four or five rooms, a telescoped but still recognizable version of the suites of rooms of larger and more important houses. The Palais-Bourbon, at one end of the scale, faced a square, the Place du Palais-Bourbon, in which were houses of few rooms, but decorated in part by the artists working in the palace, such as the decorative sculptor Jean-Baptiste Boiston.

The Palais-Bourbon, owned by Louis-Joseph, Prince de Condé, was to epitomize building projects of the period. When the Prince, head of the second most important branch of the Royal family after their rivals the Orléans, decided to enlarge the Palais-Bourbon in 1764, he proceeded in a royal fashion, asking several of the leading architects of the day to submit plans. The winner, Barreau de Chefdeville, began work immediately but died within a year, thereby missing a building and decorating campaign that was to be practically continuous until the revolution. Indeed, the Prince never lived in the palace, having bought and redecorated the Hôtel de Lassay next door while the work was in progress. He adopted a less tolerant attitude to the extravagance of

*T*op of a snuffbox with gold mounts by Louis Roucel, with a view of the *chambre de parade* in its *mobilier d'hiver* at the Hôtel de Choiseul, circa 1770.

BELOW LEFT
*M*iniature *en suite* with the preceding, now bearing a false signature and date and remounted into a nineteenth-century box, showing the same room in its *mobilier d'été*.

Both miniatures were probably painted by Louis-Nicolas van Blarenberghe. The *chambre de parade* was also used by Choiseul as a *cabinet de travail*. His bedroom, a different room, is depicted on one side of the winter box. He could, however, get dressed in the *chambre de parade*; the summer box shows a valet ceremoniously placing Choiseul's *cordon bleu* (the *Saint-Esprit*, the most important of the French Orders) and coat on the bed. The decoration of the room, in white and gold, dates from circa 1730. The profile bas-relief portrait of Louis XV above the fireplace is appropriate for a formal reception room. The paintings on the walls have been represented so accurately that their twentieth-century whereabouts have for the most part been identified. The paintings are not all the same on both miniatures, so Choiseul must have rearranged his collection from time to time. The furniture is set out in a traditional way, with chairs against the wall. The only chair in the centre of the room is the *fauteuil de bureau*, which is caned, but has a loose cushion matching the remainder of the upholstery. On the winter box, a chair is being advanced for a lady to sit on. The wall lights are placed as close as possible to the looking-glass so that their illumination is reflected back into the room. The matched pair of secretaire and bookcase are in the early neoclassical style of the workshop of Jean-François Oeben. The figure on the right-hand piece is under a glass dome. These were common in the eighteenth century, but rarely survive today. The commode to the right is decorated with red lacquer.

This is probably the only surviving pair of pictures showing the same room with its *mobilier d'hiver* and its *mobilier d'été*. The winter furniture consists of a rich blue damask with gold braid, and the summer set of light-coloured silk with flowers. Some of the chairs and the *lit à la Polonaise* are upholstered *à châssis*, enabling the material to be changed. The bed, the walls, the chairs and the firescreen are all upholstered *en suite*. The door and window curtains are also made of the same material. On the summer box, the Louis XVI *bergères* to the left are differently upholstered, and have antimacassars (*tetières*). The floors are not the same on the two boxes. The summer miniature shows an ordinary parquet floor, of diagonally-laid squares, while the winter box shows a marquetry floor of some magnificence. This disparity would seem surprising were it not for the description of lot 215 in Choiseul's posthumous sale in 1786: "Inlaid parquet floors, from the former Hôtel de Choiseul. 215. Three parquet floors of different shapes and designs, inlaid with tulipwood, rosewood and others, which can be adapted to any desired shape". (*Parquets en ébénisterie, provenant de l'ancien Hôtel de Choiseul. 215. Trois parquets de différentes formes et dessins, composés de bois de rose, pallissandre et autres, qui sont susceptibles d'être mis à toutes les mesures que l'on pourra désirer*).

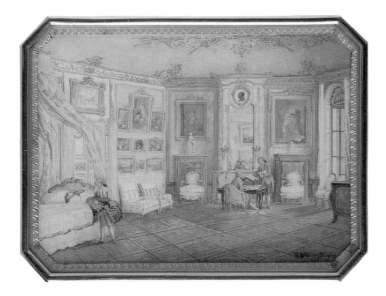

others, for Bellisard, the architect from 1773, was dragged before a court by the Prince in 1783 for using craftsmen working on the Palais to execute decorative work for his own apartment, including mirror frames and wax models for gilt-bronze wall lights.

Vast new fortunes had been created in the late seventeenth and early eighteenth century, some as a result of the financial upheavals caused by John Law, the Scottish banker who briefly became Contrôleur général des Finances in 1720; and the new rich of this period sought to establish themselves in society through the acquisition of offices, marriage into old families, and the creation of magnificent surroundings. Many families of the old-established aristocracy continued to have members who held offices at Versailles or served in the army, thereby preserving their status, but few of them possessed means on a sufficient scale to indulge in expensive decoration; much of the best at this period was created either for the *noblesse de robe*, who supplied magistrates and members of the *Parlements*, or for the newly prosperous financiers.

Men such as the Crozat or Pâris brothers demanded luxury as a means of asserting their wealth and position. The set of seat furniture made by an unknown *menuisier* for Pierre Crozat circa 1715-20 (see page 117) was a typical commission. The suite was made for the *galerie* at the Hôtel Crozat in Paris, which had walls covered in crimson damask, hung with paintings and tall mirrors; against the walls were four marble-topped giltwood tables, two Boulle cabinets and several Boulle pedestals, on which stood marble busts and bronzes. The suite, consisting of twelve armchairs, two sofas, two benches and four stools, was arranged between the other pieces.

The Marquis de Marigny, as Directeur général des Bâtiments for twenty-two years, was perhaps more concerned with interior decoration than most. It is revealing to see him engage in a long correspondence with his *ébéniste* Pierre Garnier in 1779. He asked Garnier for furniture such as an elaborate secretaire for the bedroom of his Paris house, and, when Garnier admitted that he had none fine enough, thanked him for his honesty in recommending one belonging to a colleague, and requested him to ask that colleague to replace the white marble with *griotte d'Italie* to match the fireplace and the top of the commode. The two also discussed altering and embellishing furniture, including some from England: "have you any ideas about how to embellish my English dressing table?" They argued about style, Garnier evidently favouring mahogany while Marigny preferred ebony: "ebony and gilt-bronze furniture is much nobler than mahogany furniture, especially in a white and gold library."

# COLLECTORS

"And you must stuff [rooms] fuller than they will hold with granite tables and porphyry urns, and bronzes, and statues, and vases," wrote Horace Walpole to the Countess of Suffolk in 1765. Walpole's comment about Paris interiors refers to a particular type of house: that of a collector. French noblemen were not as avid Grand Tourists as their English counterparts, but there were nevertheless in eighteenth-century Paris a substantial number of people for whom the decoration of houses and

the acquisition of works of art were full-time occupations. These *amateurs* or *curieux*, as they came to be known, frequently opened their *cabinets* to the discerning public, and descriptions of them appear in a number of almanachs of the period as a result. The lists are formidable, and show the extraordinary variety of collectors and their tastes. Princes, dukes, soldiers, *fermiers-généraux*, priests, scientists, artists, doctors and art dealers collected paintings, sculpture, drawings, engravings, old furniture, porcelain, hardstones, bronzes and books, as well as more exotic and unusual objects such as ethnographica, shells and natural history specimens, and scientific and medical instruments.

Among the most famous collectors was Augustin Blondel de Gagny (1695-1776). Descriptions of his Cabinet confirm his voracious tastes: as well as Italian, Flemish and French paintings ("*peintures des trois écoles*" as they were known) he amassed sculpture, both modern and ancient, including "a bronze by Le Lorrain, of Andromeda tied to the rock". In furniture he enjoyed Boulle marquetry and gilt-bronze: "two commodes in marquetry with gilt-bronze mounts, made by Boulle". Exotic and unusual furniture, including lacquer, was also to be found in his collection: "a tortoiseshell coffer made in England, with copper strips, on a carved and giltwood stand" and "two cupboards of lacquer with relief decoration of figures and fruit in soapstone". "A small lacquer *vide-poche* table with its top of French porcelain" registered his interest in modern furniture. Gagny was one of the shareholders in the Sèvres porcelain factory so there is nothing surprising in his owning such a table, probably made by Bernard van Risamburgh. The lower shelf of the table held "a pot-pourri vase of antique lacquer" and on the

*P*alissy ware ewer, second half of the sixteenth century, mounted in gilt-bronze in Paris circa 1765. An extremely rare example of early European ceramics mounted in gilt-bronze in the eighteenth century. Horace Walpole bought two Italian sixteenth-century majolica vases with gilt-bronze mounts of the same exceptional quality in Paris in 1765-6.

floor underneath it was "a vase of antique porcelain" (the description "antique" normally meant Oriental). Porcelain was everywhere: Meissen and Sèvres as well as Oriental, some on *consoles* (brackets) of giltwood or gilt-bronze. There was porcelain mounted with gilt-bronze, including "a small vase of antique green porcelain, of a very beautiful colour, and very well mounted". The *garniture de cheminée* in one room consisted of "in the middle, an alabaster vase on a foot of gilt-bronze; two bottles of antique porcelain with small necks and lizards and two boxes of antique red lacquer on their feet of gilt-bronze." Gagny's two sales, in 1776 and 1777, were among the more important of the century.

The sale of the collections of the Duc d'Aumont in 1782 was another event of note, and the chief purchasers were Louis XVI and Marie Antoinette. But it was the composition of the collection that was surprising. It held practically no pictures, consisting almost entirely of decorative arts, and many of the objects were new, having been made for d'Aumont himself. He had employed the *bronzier* Gouthière to mount a quantity of vases and other objects of marble and hardstones, as well as porcelain; some of these were unfinished at the Duc's death and Gouthière had to borrow money from the estate to enable him to get them ready in time for the sale. The auctioneers Julliot and Paillet, in footnotes, state that some of the porcelains had previously had different mounts. Of two blue and white bottle-shaped vases with gilt-bronze mounts: "These two bottles have belonged to the Duc de Tallard and to M. de Jullienne, as well as to M. de Boisset; they were once mounted with elaborate footrims and collars of silver-gilt, which shows how the best pieces of this fine porcelain have been valued." Quality or ownership by previous prestigious collectors had clearly not deterred d'Aumont from commissioning fashionable new mounts. The Baronne d'Oberkirch called him "the most eccentric and the dirtiest man in France". As one of the four Premiers Gentilhommes de la chambre of Louis XV he had been in charge of the Menus-Plaisirs (the Royal department responsible for Court occasions and festivities) for one year in four, a position which brought him into contact with artists decorating the great fêtes given by the King. He happened to be doing his turn of duty when Louis XV died, and thus became entitled to remove certain objects for his own use, including notably the great commode by Antoine-Robert Gaudreaus with mounts signed by Jacques Caffiéri, delivered in 1739 for Louis XV's bedroom at Versailles, and now in the Wallace Collection.

# LES FILLES

In 1759, Mademoiselle Deschamps moved into her new house in the Rue Saint-Nicaise, decorated at the expense of her lover at the time, the Duc d'Orléans. It contained ten rooms on one level, reached by a monumental staircase of polished oak. On one side were the *antichambre*, the *salons de compagnie* and the dining room, and on the other the sleeping apartment with *garderobes* and *cabinets*. The principal *salon*, which had three windows and four doors, was hung with crimson damask in three shades framed with giltwood mouldings, and all the upholstered furniture was covered in the same damask. Above the doors were paintings in frames carved with palm branches. Fine gilt-bronze firedogs and wall lights competed with marble-topped tables on which sat Meissen figures and Sèvres vases. Another smaller *salon*, for the winter, was hung with painted silk. Behind this room was a small library, and finally came a boudoir in pink and silver, whose ceiling, including the alcove above the *ottomane*, was covered entirely in mirror glass. The *ottomane* held down-filled cushions edged with gold braid.

*M*odels of *Les forces mouvantes* in Bonnier de la Mosson's Cabinet de Physique, drawn by Jean-Baptiste Courtonne the younger. Bonnier, who died in 1744, assembled the finest *cabinet de curiosités* in Paris. Here, the objects sit on shelves supported by palm trees, and are surmounted by an allegorical painting by Jacques de Lajoue, who also painted the overdoors with fanciful views of the Cabinet.

*I*nterior with a dog on a bergère, watercolour signed by Antoine-Louis Sergent and dated 1783. It is summer, since the fireplace has been blocked by a board with the owner's monogram.

The dining room panelling, which was painted and varnished, incorporated groups of figures and birds amid bushes and bulrushes, all in relief; around the room were bronze figures holding four-light candelabra, and pouring water into marble basins. The bedroom, decorated with pilasters, sported a *lit à la Polonaise* upholstered with crimson *Perse*; the chairs were covered with the same material, and on the walls as well as on the furniture were candelabra carrying over fifty candles. Two *cabinets* were reached from the bedroom, one a *lieu à l'anglaise*, the other a *cabinet de toilette*, containing a bathtub of solid silver decorated with *point d'Angleterre* lace.

The owner of this most elegant residence was well known as a particularly rapacious prostitute. She occupied a place in the chorus at the Opéra, which unpaid position enabled her not only to be exempt from arrest for soliciting, but also to show herself to potential clients. When she went bankrupt in 1760, her sale attracted a large gathering. Her notoriety was such that when Diderot, who strongly disapproved of Boucher, wanted to explain the expression of a goddess in one of Boucher's paintings he claimed that it was "borrowed from la Deschamps".

Mademoiselle Deschamps's position was some way up the hierarchy of which the summit was firmly occupied by Mesdames de Pompadour and du Barry. Ladies of questionable virtue abounded, hardly surprisingly in an age where noble marriages were almost invariably dynastic and couples often had little affection for each other. It would seem to be no coincidence that the fashionable quarter of the Rue Saint-Honoré, where the *marchands-merciers* mainly operated, should also have been frequented by a substantial number of prostitutes, since the clientele was broadly similar. The New Year presents given by prostitutes to the police inspectors often consisted of objects they had received from their clients in payment for their services.

Mademoiselle Villemont de Beauvoisin's posthumous sale in 1784 clearly indicates that she had managed to retain many of the presents she had received from her lover, the enormously wealthy Baudard de Saint-James. Among the lots were: "fine porcelain from Sèvres and elsewhere, candelabra in alabaster vases and celadon porcelain, mounted with gilt-bronze, on marble columns, figures and groups of marble, terracotta and Sèvres biscuit, barometers, thermometers, wine coolers, monteiths".

When *les filles* did not receive in their own houses, their clients entertained them in exquisitely decorated pavilions on the outskirts of Paris, of the type described by Dufort de Cheverny in his memoirs, or by J. F. Bastide in *La Petite Maison*: "Mélite . . . utterly forgot that she was in a *petite maison*, and that she was there in the company of a man who had sworn to seduce her through the very things she was looking at so carelessly, and praising so openly."

# FOREIGNERS

Europeans came to Paris in droves during the eighteenth century. Art and decoration were among their principal preoccupations, both for their residences while in France, and to take back to their native lands. Others employed French designers and craftsmen without travelling themselves. Foreign craftsmen came to Paris to be trained, such as the Swedish *ébéniste* Georg Haupt, who worked for Jean-François Oeben before returning to his native country to become Ébéniste du Roi to the francophile Gustav III. A *tapissier* working in Stockholm in the 1740s was described by the Swedish Count Carl-Gustav Tessin as having been "apprenticed here [in Paris] with the king's [upholsterer] in the Rue de Cléry". Tessin, the Swedish ambassador to Paris from 1739 to 1742, was advising his wife on the choice of an upholsterer in Stockholm: naturally one who had worked in Paris would be more fashionable. French-born craftsmen travelled also; Charles-Louis Clérisseau (1721-1820), after travelling in Italy from 1749 to 1767 and working there with

*G*ilt-bronze and red morroco coffer bearing the Braganza arms, 1750-60, now in the Museu Nacional de Arte Antiga, Lisbon. The interior is fitted to contain a *toilette*, and it was almost certainly supplied by François-Thomas Germain to King John V of Portugal. Its fine decoration suggests it must have been intended for display.

*S*and-box, circa 1775. The Empress Catherine the Great commissioned an elaborate inkstand to celebrate the Russian naval victory over the Turks at Chesmé in 1770. This sand-box, which is of the same form as that on the inkstand, may have been ordered with it. The figures were stated to be the work of Houdon.

Robert Adam, visited England in 1771, and went to Russia from 1778 to 1782. His speciality was the design of neoclassical interiors in the "Etruscan" style. The *bronzier* Etienne Gastecloux and his family also went to Russia, to work for Catherine the Great. They made small-scale gilt-bronze objects, such as *surtouts de table*, as well as casting in bronze life-size copies of Antique sculptures for the gardens at Pavlovsk.

The Empress Catherine the Great was a voracious patron of French art, and persuaded many French artists to come and work for her, as well as ordering works of art in France itself, including vast services of silver and Sèvres porcelain. When Catherine sent her son and daughter-in-law to tour Europe in 1782 (under the apt incognito of Comte and Comtesse du Nord to avoid the massive complications of etiquette which would have been caused by a state visit), contact with French art was one of the most important aspects of their journey, and they re-

turned to Russia with quantities of furniture, gilt-bronzes and porcelain, some of which they had bought and some they had been given by Louis XVI. The Baronne d'Oberkirch, travelling with them, described visits to the Sèvres factory, and to the dealers Daguerre and Granchez. They also visited the houses of notable *amateurs* such as Beaujon ("the house is magnificently furnished, with wonderful antique furniture and *Vernis Martin*") and Grimod de la Reynière ("we stayed there two hours and we didn't see half of it").

Other royalty supplying themselves regularly in Paris included Louise Elizabeth, Duchess of Parma (Louis XV's eldest daughter), King Charles IV of Spain, and at the end of the century the Prince of Wales, the future George IV. In each case they retained the service of an agent on the spot. The Duchess of Parma used the financier Claude Bonnet, the Prince of Wales the dealer Daguerre, and Charles IV employed the clockmaker François-Louis Godon, who supplied the large number of French late eighteenth-century clocks which survive today in the Spanish Royal collection.

Noblemen were able to travel more easily than royalty, especially as ambassadors. Such was the case with the English Dukes of Bedford, Richmond and Manchester, Count Tessin and the Spanish Count

d'Aranda, to name but a few. The Duke of Bedford, in Paris from 1762 to 1763, brought with him a large household staff, and moved into an Hôtel in the Rue Saint-Dominique. This he proceeded to furnish with the help of various dealers, including the upholsterer Belache, who also rented him some furniture for the Hôtel he had to take at Fontainebleau when the Court moved there for its yearly *voyage* in the autumn of 1762. Objects as diverse as commodes, chandeliers hung with Bohemian crystal drops, suites of chairs, firedogs, clocks and artificial flowers were purchased, many of which returned to England with the Duke.

Ambassadors frequently took home gifts for their sovereign, as well as the objects they had bought or been given for themselves. Tessin, in a letter to his wife, described some of the presents from Louis XV to the Sultan of Turkey, taken back there by the Ambassador Saïd Mehemet Pasha in 1742: "A mirror and its pair, fourteen *pieds* high . . . silver figures weighing several *marcs* (these were life-size), carrying candelabra . . . A table with twelve place settings, made by the renowned Germain, and like all his work, ridiculously expensive . . . A jug and its

Louis XV marquetry cabinet, in the style of François Delorme or his better-known son Adrien. This was probably also among the presents given by Louis XV to the Ottoman Sultan. The description of the presents includes: "Two very large *nécessaires* of exotic woods, mounted with gilt-bronze, and filled with silver vases for coffee, sorbet and jam; and with a microscope, a telescope and two opera glasses with gold mounts, and with all sorts of instruments for surgery, clockmaking, mathematics and gunmaking" (*Deux Nécessaires très grands de bois des Indes, garnis de bronze doré d'or moulu, remplis de quantité de Vases d'argent pour le Caffé, le sorbet, les Confitures; et encore d'un Microscope, d'un Téléscope, de deux lunettes garnies d'or et de toute sorte d'Instruments pour la Chirurgie, l'Horlogerie, les Mathématiques et l'Armurerie*). Now in the Topkapi Museum, Istanbul.

basin, in rock crystal mounted in gold, with on the lid an oriental hyacinth the size of a fist . . . Several Savonnerie carpets". The registers of the Présents du Roi, a department in the Ministère des Affaires Etrangères, supply further details about some of these gifts. The mirrors, for example, were in fact 15 *pieds* (4.87 m) in height and had gilt-bronze frames designed by Gabriel and made by Jacques Caffiéri, incorporating attributes appropriate to the Ottoman Empire: trophies both martial and evoking "the riches of the sea". Countess Tessin, writing many years later, visibly disapproved: "These carnival embassies are expensive and of no real use." She was echoing the feelings of George III, who had an equally negative attitude to the gifts with which his diplomats returned, no doubt in the knowledge that he would be expected to reciprocate with similar munificence.

Among the many Englishmen abroad for pleasure or on business were the Duke of Kingston, who bought silver from Meissonier; Horace Walpole, who sent advice back to England on how to arrange rooms in the French style; and William Beckford, who during the height of the revolution was commissioning carpets from the Savonnerie factory, plates from Sèvres and silver from Auguste despite the enormous risk of being there: he was a member of the Parliament of a country at war with the revolutionary authorities.

Most foreigners purchased principally movable furniture and objects in Paris. Tessin, writing to his architect Hårleman in Sweden in 1740, asked him to "send me the measurements of the places in my new house [in Stockholm] which you consider might be appropriate to hold decorations, such as overmantels, commodes, marble tables, corner cupboards, overdoors, beds for alcoves . . . Please be so kind as to give me the measurements for upholstery materials, including width and height of walls, and number of rooms." He also ordered fireplaces: "we will have to decide on the height of the chimneypieces; I would like these to be of marble so that I may be broke more quickly".

It was not every kind of foreigner that could understand and appreciate French decoration. The American John Adams consigned the following to his diary during a visit to Paris in 1778: "I was wearied to death with gazing wherever I went, at a profusion of unmeaning wealth and magnificence." Thomas Jefferson and Gouverneur Morris (Gouverneur was his name, not his title) did not, however, share their fellow-countryman's feeling, and both purchased extensively during their visits to Paris in the late eighteenth century.

*S*et of silver-gilt dessert cutlery for twenty-four place settings, with serving pieces, by Jean-Henri Huré, Paris, 1785-6. The fitted leather case records that the set was "Supplied to Lord Spencer by Auguste, goldsmith by appointment to the King. 21 March 1786" (*Fourni à Milord Spencer par Auguste, orfèvre ordinaire du Roy. 21 mars 1786*). Lord Spencer was a major client of Daguerre's in the 1780s.

# 2
# DESIGNERS, GUILDS AND DEALERS

**M**any different kinds of artists and craftsmen were involved in the creation of the fine interiors of eighteenth-century France, and their work was normally coordinated. The architect who built or remodelled a house usually designed the interior, and then oversaw the work of the craftsmen who were employed to execute the fixed elements of the decoration.

The architect might also provide designs (not necessarily his own) for elements such as wall lights, firedogs, console tables, chairs and sofas, thus achieving a strong sense of unity and harmony. For example, the carving, painting and gilding of the panelling of a room could match that of the console tables and chairs, with the gilt-bronze ornaments *en suite*, while the upholstery of the walls could be the same as that of the seat furniture, and the marble of the chimneypiece could match that of the tops of the console tables, commodes and pedestals. Variation would then only occur at the level of the interpretation of the designs by different specialist craftsmen.

In many cases, however, clients resorted to specialist dealers, often

*P*aris porcelain, marble and gilt-bronze model of a galleon, late eighteenth century. A decorative object combining the work of several craftsmen, and therefore likely to have been sold by a member of the guild of *marchands-merciers, grossiers, joailliers*, which bore as its arms *trois vaisseaux équipés et les voiles enflées d'argent, voguant chacun sur une mer de même et portant une bannière de France au grand mât et un chef d'azur chargé d'un soleil d'or* (three ships, fully fitted out, with bulging sails of silver, each sailing on a sea of the same and flying a banner of France from the main mast; in chief azure, a sun or).

*D*esign for a *girandole* by Jean-Jacques-François Le Barbier, circa 1770. The inscription suggests that Gouthière was to execute it in gilt-bronze. Its depiction of a Bacchic feast would have made it a suitable design for a *salle à manger*, as one of a set standing on torchères around the room.

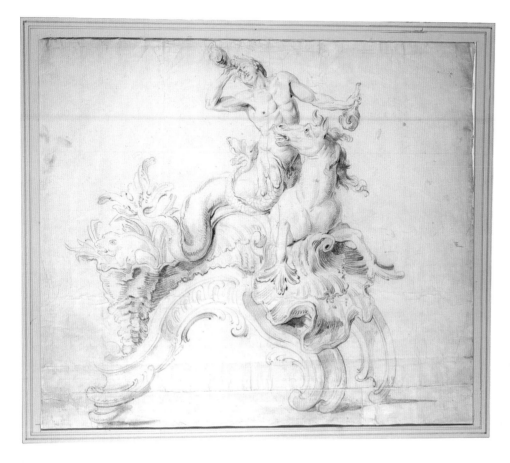

*D*esign for a gilt-bronze *feu* (firedog), perhaps by Lambert-Sigisbert Adam. The base is in the fully-developed version of the *rocaille* style, but the triton and sea-horse are sculptural elements associated with the Régence, so the design probably dates from no later than 1740. Adam was a member of the Académie Royale and one of his brothers was a *bronzier*.

known as *marchands-merciers*, who, as well as being able to provide some of the basic elements mentioned above, also stocked fashionable furniture and decorative objects, designed and made by specialists in their employment. Occasionally the architect or designer may have had a hand in selecting the dealer's goods.

Such coordination was born during the reign of Louis XIV. Charles Le Brun and Jules Hardouin Mansart, as well as providing designs themselves, brought together the work of the junior architects working for the Bâtiments du Roi and that of the various skilled artists and craftsmen decorating the King's palaces, to create a single harmonious style. This type of unity was to remain important throughout the eighteenth century.

# INTERIOR DESIGNERS: ARCHITECTS AND OTHERS

For many of the large building projects of the eighteenth century, particularly those undertaken for the Crown, one or more draughtsmen worked under the supervision of the architect, providing designs which he then ratified. This has led to confusion about authorship, since these draughtsmen in turn often became architects themselves. They were usually widely competent, being able to design outdoor architecture, garden parterres and decorative sculpture as well as inventing ground plans, ironwork, wall, ceiling, door, fireplace or stove and floor decoration, fittings such as furniture and gilt-bronzes, and in a few cases also providing drawings for paintings. Some of the drawings could be life-size: panelling designs, for example, might be drawn on the bare walls for approval. Tracings could then be made which would be stencilled on to the wooden panels for carving. Gilles-Marie Oppenord and Jean-Démosthène Dugourc provide two splendid examples of the variety of talents an architect could be asked to display.

Gilles-Marie Oppenord (1672-1742), whose father, an *ébéniste*, had worked for Louis XIV, was trained as an architect, visited Rome, and became Directeur général des Bâtiments to the Duc d'Orléans in 1708. He published numerous designs for architectural details, interiors, clocks, obelisks, gravestones, trophies, ironwork, fireplaces and panelling, some of which record the work he undertook for the Duc d'Orléans at the Palais-Royal. His masterpiece there, the *salon à l'Italienne*, named thus because it rose through two storeys in the grand Italian manner, was in marked contrast to the more advanced decorations he undertook for the other rooms in the Grand Appartement, as well as for the suites of smaller rooms in which the Regent's famously dissolute parties took place. Here the panelling was strikingly innovative, abandoning completely the traditional rectilinear form, and adopting instead a much freer style in which delicate scroll and leaf ornament intermingled with exotic fauna in an early example of the rococo style. It is thought that

Design for a chimneypiece with *feu* and *girandoles*, signed by Dugourc, late eighteenth century.

J. D. Dugourc, invent.    1re Cheminée arabesque pour un Sallon.

Oppenord may have been the designer of the great medal cabinet, now in the Bibliothèque Nationale, which the Regent's son commissioned from his *ébéniste* Charles Cressent in the late 1730s.

That Jean-Démosthène Dugourc (1749-1825) was well aware of his own talents is evident from the short autobiography he wrote in 1800, in which he arrogantly claimed that for the ten years preceding the revolution "everything fine and tasteful which has been created in Paris during this time was either his work or was submitted to him for approval." Among his first activities was the painting of trompe l'oeil cameos and bas-reliefs incorporated into stucco decoration for the château of Bagatelle under the supervision of his brother-in-law, the architect Belanger, in the late 1770s. He soon seems to have progressed to design rather than execution, being appointed Dessinateur du Garde-Meuble in 1784. For the Garde-Meuble he designed silks and furniture, while for other clients, such as the Comte de Provence, the Duc de Deux-Ponts, the banker Laborde and the Prince des Asturies (soon to become King Charles IV of Spain), he produced interiors in the "arabesque" or "Etruscan" style, which he was later to claim he had pioneered. At the same time, he made numerous drawings for gilt-bronze and furniture for craftsmen such as Georges Jacob. Dugourc described himself as an architect, but the twentieth-century term interior designer might be more accurate.

# ARTISTS AS DESIGNERS

Some draughtsmen were not trained as architects but as sculptors or painters. They would execute their designs themselves, or would entrust them to specialist craftsmen.

A number of important artists practised in the field of decorative arts. As well as executing overdoor, overmantel and wall painting, François Boucher made an important contribution to tapestry design and Sèvres porcelain. Jean-Baptiste Oudry was for many years director of both the Beauvais and Gobelins tapestry works, and Jean-Jacques Lagrenée decorated the ceiling of Marie Antoinette's theatre at the Petit Trianon, in addition to providing designs for the Sèvres factory in the 1780s. He was stated in an obituary by his nephew Vaudoyer to have painted on canvas, wood, glass and marble, in the most ingenious manner which showed the influence of his visit to Rome, and his contribution to the "Etruscan" style was considerable.

*D*esign for a tureen in the arabesque style by Jean-Jacques Lagrenée, mid-1780s. In the Sèvres factory archives, in a folder containing designs for objects intended for Marie Antoinette's dairy at Rambouillet.

*T*erracotta model for a clock by Felix Lecomte (1737-1817), signed and dated 1792. The two figures symbolize Faith and Charity, and could have been executed in gilt- or patinated bronze, marble or biscuit porcelain. The case of the movement could have been engraved as a terrestrial globe. Lecomte was a pupil of Falconet and Vassé, and became a member of the Académie Royale in 1771. He executed the life-size marble figures of Rollin and Fénélon for the *Grands Hommes* series ordered by d'Angiviller for the gallery at the Louvre. Lecomte supplied small terracotta versions of the figures to the Sèvres factory, which produced the series in biscuit porcelain.

# SPECIALIST DESIGNERS FOR DECORATIVE ARTS

Most designers specialized not in general decoration but in specific fields. Nicolas Pineau, who was trained as a sculptor, published designs for carved decoration for walls, ceilings, fireplaces, console tables and torchères. Jean-Claude Duplessis was chief designer of shapes at Vincennes and later at Sèvres, and his designs are close to those of contemporary silver. This should not surprise since he was also a sculptor-member of the Académie de Saint Luc (the guild of designers), as well as being a Fondeur du Roi, which enabled him to trade in goldsmith's work and decorative carving, including gilt-bronze. He later became a *maître-orfèvre*. It is probable that, like Meissonier, his chief activity was to provide designs, and that his guild memberships enabled him to sub-contract manufacture and act as a retailer. His identically-named son was more specialized, being only qualified to work in bronze.

## JUSTE-AURÈLE MEISSONIER

Juste-Aurèle Meissonier (b. Turin 1693-d. Paris 1750), justly famous for his extravagant rococo designs, was named Peintre, sculpteur, architecte et dessinateur de la chambre et du cabinet du Roi in 1726. He was qualified to practise as a goldsmith but it seems he rarely if ever applied his mark to any piece, and confined his activity to providing drawings, some of which were subsequently engraved. Unfortunately his personal

*E*laborate design by Duplessis for a Vincennes porcelain dish in the Louis XV *bleu céleste* service. Circa 1752, probably not used.

*Projet de Sculpture en argent d'un grand Surtout de Table... et les deux Terrines qui ont été exécutée pour le Millord Duc de Kinston en 1735.*
*A Paris chés Huquier rue S.<sup>t</sup> Jacque au coin de celle des Mathurins CPR.*

involvement with the actual execution of his designs is largely unknown. That he could practise as *marchand-orfèvre* explains his involvement in the Kingston tureens: he was commissioned to produce a design but it is likely that he had the tureens made by a subcontractor, before selling them himself to the Duke of Kingston.

His published volume of designs contains projects of a staggering variety: elevations for the exterior and interior of houses and churches, and ground plans of rooms; designs for candlesticks, picture frames, inkstands, scissors, cane handles, sledges, tables, chairs, snuffboxes, sword hilts, watches, *surtouts de table*, tureens, wine coolers, salt-cellars, *porte huiliers*, nefs, candle snuffers, candelabra, looking-glasses, monstrances, crucifixes, chalices, censers, lanterns, clocks, sofas, wind dials, funerary monuments and altars; and a project for a grand architectural setting for the firework display to celebrate the wedding of Louis XV's eldest daughter. The variety of his clientele is interesting. Apart from his work for the King and the church, he provided designs for Polish, English and Portuguese clients, as well as for French ones. It cannot be doubted that the designs were mostly specially commissioned, even though he did not always include the client's name with the engraving. He frequently did, however, describe the material from which an object was to be made, for example mentioning a porcelain inkstand for the Comte de Maurepas.

The nineteenth century coined the name *ornemaniste* to describe these designers, but during the eighteenth century they were usually known according to the art in which they had received their training,

*Projet de sculpture en argent d'un grand Surtout de Table et les deux Terrines qui ont été éxécutée pour le Millord Duc de Kinston* [sic] *en 1735*. Engraving by Huquier, plate 70 of Juste-Aurèle Meissonier's *Oeuvre*. Only the tureens were delivered to the Duke of Kingston, in 1740. Count Carl-Gustav Tessin, writing to his architect Hårleman in October 1741, complained about the expense of these pieces: "such virtuosi are so inhuman as to make the Duke of Kingston pay 32,000 *livres* for two tureens" (*les Virtuosi de cette espece poussent l'inhumanité jusqu'a faire payer au Duc de Kingston 32,000 Livres de façon pour deux Pots a Oglie* [sic]). These survive in the Cleveland Museum of Art, and in the Thyssen-Bornemisza Collection, Lugano. The Bibliothèque Nationale in Paris owns a preparatory drawing showing the centrepiece and tureens in reverse, without the extravagant rococo interior included here. The doors in this have *arc d'arbalète* tops, and wall lights emerge from the frame of the looking-glass above the fireplace. The engraving also shows that the functional aspect of the centrepiece itself was not neglected: it holds sugar-casters and oil and vinegar bottles.

even if they did not go on to practise it.

"May I suggest a young sculptor who can also design architecture; he is familiar with building and furniture, will model in terracotta or wax, and can carve stone or stucco if required." This letter of 1768 from an agent in Paris of the Court of Parma, offering the services of an unknown artist, shows that the role of designer and craftsman could be combined. This is confirmed by a number of craftsmen who were members not only of their own specialist guild, but also of the Académie de Saint Luc.

# THE GUILD SYSTEM

Under the *ancien régime*, all trade was subject to strict control through the specialist guilds (*corporations*). The object of this control was to ensure quality of work and protect guild members. The system had been developed gradually since the Middle Ages, and the guilds had individual sets of rules which were periodically updated by Royal edicts. Anyone could practise a craft for himself, but membership of the guild which controlled that craft was necessary to trade in the products or services concerned. The chief benefit of guild membership consisted of the right to offer goods for public sale. Thus Meissonier, who was not a practising goldsmith, was nonetheless a member of the goldsmiths' guild although his principal activity was design.

Guild membership was applicable to craftsmen practising a trade on their own, but similar protection was available to large enterprises which did not fit within the established guilds. There was no such thing as corporate membership, but it became customary for businesses to apply to the King for a Privilège, or exclusive right to manufacture a specific product. The aim was to ensure protection from competition, particularly in the early and difficult stages of production, and to protect any manufacturing secret. Such rights were obtained by the tapestry workshops, as well as by the young Vincennes porcelain factory and the Martin family of lacquerers.

Every trade had its own guild. The Académie de Saint Luc was the guild of decorative painters, designers and sculptors, but most of the others were called by the names *corporation* or *jurande*, in reference to the oath of adherence. There were frequent conflicts between them, relating to borderline objects, or those whose manufacture involved two or more specialities. The case of the *ébénistes* and the *bronziers* was typical. Fine furniture was mounted with gilt-bronze, but the cabinet-maker did not have the right to design, cast, chase or gild the mounts. He might, however, commission designs from a sculptor, and become the owner of the models. The sculptor in this case had to be a member of the Académie de Saint Luc.

Guild officers, known as *jurés*, were responsible for paying regular visits to their members to enforce the guild laws, particularly those concerning quality. They also carried out dawn raids on unlicensed premises, confiscating goods and equipment which were then auctioned, the proceeds being divided between the guild and the State. Some guild rules, while they were atrociously inconvenient, were rigidly enforced: all goldsmiths' work, for example, had to take place within six *pieds* (2 m) of the street, and in full view of passers-by; petty infringements were rigorously punished.

To become a member of a guild (a *maître*), it was necessary to complete a lengthy apprenticeship. In some guilds, this was divided into two parts, the *apprentissage* and the *compagnonnage*. For the furniture makers, this lasted six years. A *chef-d'oeuvre de maîtrise* or masterpiece was required before full qualification, as well as payment of a substantial sum. Sons, sons-in-law, and second husbands of widows of *maîtres* paid very much reduced entry fees. This had the effect of encouraging the continuation of family workshops, as well as excluding poor but competent craftsmen. These latter were known as *ouvriers libres*. They could obtain work, but only if they either sold directly to the public and the customer carried the object through the streets himself, or sold to a member of the guild of dealers. Members of the specialist guilds were not permitted to buy from them, even if they had shops selling directly to the public.

A number of areas in Paris were not subject to the jurisdiction of the courts. These were known as *enclos privilégiés* and many marginal activities flourished there. They were home to prostitutes and bankrupts, for example, and *ouvriers libres*, too, were safe from prosecution there. Part of the Faubourg Saint-Antoine, where most of the *ébénistes* worked, belonged to a monastery and was thus an *enclos*. Surviving records of court actions show how difficult it was to police the rules on this subject.

# THE ACADÉMIE DE SAINT LUC

This was the name given to the guild of decorative painters and sculptors. Originally called the "Communauté des maîtres peintres et sculpteurs", it formed a body distinct from the Académie Royale de Peinture et de Sculpture. The implication was that the latter were artists, while the former were craftsmen. In practice, there was a certain fluidity of

*G*iltwood bracket, oil sketch by François Desportes, early eighteenth century.

Console table, circa 1725. This table, a detail of which is shown on the right, is closely associated with the designs of Nicolas Pineau. Architectural woodwork was normally made and assembled by a *menuisier* who then handed the piece to a *sculpteur*. In the case of tables such as this, the *sculpteur* may have made the frame himself rather than explain the complex shape to a *menuisier*. This type of console was known as a *pied de table*, or table support. The word *table* signified the marble top.

membership, and no small amount of jealousy. The change in name at the beginning of the eighteenth century came in a Royal edict granting the Communauté the right to a life class, to be called the "Académie de Saint Luc". Thereafter that more distinguished name was used in preference to their old one.

Members of the Académie de Saint Luc had, in common with those of the Académie Royale, the exclusive right to trade in decorative painting and sculpture. This included easel painting, such as landscapes, copies of Old Masters and religious paintings and portraits, as well as wall decoration. In the field of sculpture, carvers of wall panelling, picture and mirror frames, torchères, chairs and tables were members, but in many cases they were obliged to employ a *maître-menuisier* to make the basic shape before they could decorate it. Exemptions existed in some cases, including for example very elaborate console tables, because it would have been impractical to explain the complexity of shape required to another craftsman. Some sculptor-members also made busts and other sculpture.

Many members of this guild were craftsmen as well as designers. Indeed, some probably became members so that they could design objects within their own specialities. Gilt-bronze workers were obliged to obtain the designs from which they worked from a member of the Académie de Saint Luc. It is therefore not surprising to find a number of prominent *bronziers*, including Jacques and Philippe Caffiéri, Etienne Martincourt and Quentin-Claude Pitoin listed among the membership.

Artists whose principal activity was the provision of designs for various elements of decoration were also members. Jean Hauré exhibited at the guild's Salon in 1774 a "Design for a clock case incorporating portraits of the King and Queen, presented to France by Fame". Hauré became a *maître-fondeur* only in 1782, and even then seems to have acted in a principally commercial capacity, supervising

*Profile medallion of Louis XVI in white marble, signed by Philippe-Laurent Roland and dated 1787, with a carved, marbled and gilt frame. This type of object was often intended to hang above an overmantel mirror in the *salon* or bedroom of an *appartement de parade*, as can be seen on the Choiseul snuff-box (see page 26). Among Roland's other work in interior decoration were the plaster Muses to act as overdoors in Marie Antoinette's boudoir at Fontainebleau.*

the delivery of furniture and gilt-bronze objects to the Garde-Meuble de la Couronne. Other members of the Académie de Saint Luc included the entire Martin family of *vernisseurs* (there was also a separate guild for *vernisseurs*); Neufmaison and Tramblin, the heads of the lacquer workshop at the Manufacture Royale of the Gobelins; Nicolas Heurtaut, who carved mainly chair-frames; the *ébéniste* Charles Cressent, whose furniture mounts are of an especially bold and sculptural nature; the enameller Antoine-Nicolas Martinière; and the painter of trompe-l'oeil grisailles, Piat-Joseph Sauvage.

The activities of members were varied: "decorative sculptor", "sculptor of wooden frames" (J. Bouillard, J. Chérin, E. L. Infrois), "fan-stick sculptors", some painters at the Sèvres porcelain factory who qualified either when they started there or when they left, so that they could practise on their own (J. J. Antheaume, F. Binet), the *entrepreneur de la manufacture de faience japonnée de Sceaux* (Chapelle) and Madame de Pompadour's gem engraver, Jacques Guay.

Jean-Baptiste Boiston was a decorative sculptor who worked in Paris in the second half of the eighteenth century. He became a member of the Académie de Saint Luc in 1762. Fourteen years later, he was named Sculpteur des Bâtiments de Son Altesse Sérénissime Monseigneur le Prince de Condé. He worked for the Prince at the Palais-Bourbon from 1768 to 1780, under the supervision of its architects, first Antoine-Michel Le Carpentier, and after his death Claude Billard de Bellisard (as a result, he netted a number of commissions in the neighbouring Place du Palais-Bourbon). As well as carving exterior stonework, he provided wax models for interior ornament, including columns and a frieze for a marble fireplace (the fireplace was by Dropsy and the gilt-bronze ornaments by Philippe Caffiéri), wall lights, candelabra, tables, armchairs and sofas, and for the bust of the Prince's illustrious ancestor, the Grand Condé, cast in bronze by Philippe Caffiéri. Boiston also made a plaster replica of a Bouchardon sculpture for the top of a stove, and capitals for pilasters. His versatility is shown by his work at the new Comédie Française, circa 1780; he executed the carved decoration which was not only in stone and wood, but also in plaster and *carton* (papier-maché).

# MARCHANDS-MERCIERS

*PIROTTE FERBLANTIER ordinaire de la Maison du Roi et Lustriée Ordinaire de Son Altesse Sérénissime Monseigneur le Prince de Condé . . . Décorateur, tient Magazin de bras, feux, lustres, lanternes, girandolles et caraffes, garnis en bronze doré et cristal de roche et de Bohême, en feuilles, fleurs de porcelaine, animaux, insectes et autres marchandises, de bijouteries* (Pirotte, supplier of metalwork by appointment to the Royal household, and chandelier supplier by appointment to his Serene Highness the Prince de Condé . . . Decorator, has in his shop wall lights, firedogs, chandeliers, lanterns, candelabra and storm shades, mounted in gilt-bronze, with rock crystal and Bohemian glass, porcelain leaves and flowers, animals, insects, and other goods, such as trinkets). This tradecard conveys an idea of some of the wares sold by dealers in decorative fittings for interiors in Paris in the eighteenth century. Jean-Lambert Pirotte worked for a number of important clients, notably the

Prince de Condé, the Marquis de Brunoy, and the actress Mademoiselle Guimard through the intermediary of the architect Claude-Nicolas Ledoux.

Dealers in furniture and decorative objects played a vital role. While they were not decorators, in the sense that they did not provide decorative schemes, they sold all that was necessary to furnish rooms. Their creative input was to employ artists to provide designs, and to have these executed by a variety of craftsmen. Craftsmen – guild members as well as *ouvriers libres* – did not on the whole sell directly to the public (except in the cases where they themselves set up as dealers) but worked directly on commissions from dealers. Some well-established furniture makers, such as Migeon, Boudin and Tuart became *marchands-ébénistes*, trading in the goods they had made as well as in the productions of colleagues, while *bronziers* usually relied on the dealers (or on clockmakers) to sell their wares for them. Like those of the *marchands-merciers*, the shops of the craftsmen dealers bore alluring names such as *"Au Goût du Jour"* (The Latest Fashion) owned by one Poix in the Rue Saint-Denis.

The Garde-Meuble de la Couronne and other large households did

*L*ouis XV's bidet, made by Bernard van Risamburgh (stamped BVRB) and delivered by the *marchand-mercier* Thomas-Joachim Hébert to Versailles in 1743, for the King's *garderobe*. It contained a faience bowl.

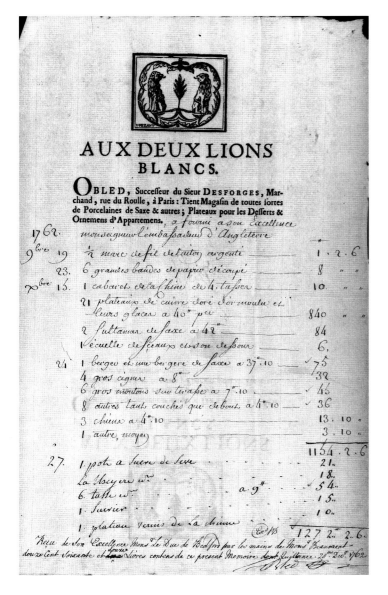

*I*nvoice from the dealer Claude-Jean Obled to John, 4th Duke of Bedford, during the latter's visit to Paris in 1762 to sign the preliminary treaty of peace at the end of the Seven Years War. Silvered copper wire (*fil de laiton argenté*) could have been used to hang crystal drops from chandeliers or *girandoles*. The paper may have been to hang on the wall. The Meissen figures were probably intended to stand on the trays, forming a splendid *surtout*.

however often bypass the dealers. Claude Bonnet was the Paris agent for the ducal Court of Parma and his report shows the possible financial gain: "I have saved the Infant [the Duke of Parma] more than 3000 francs on the work with which I have been entrusted, through the considerable trouble I have taken to go and seek out myself, in the furthest suburbs . . . the finest craftsmen because these people, delighted to be paid immediately (unlike the dealers, who usually make them wait a long time) sold me at very reasonable prices things for which I have often paid double at the fashionable dealers such as Lebrun, Migeon and others. These dealers owe their reputation to the very craftsmen I have been able to employ cheaply."

Dealers were prevented by guild rules from manufacturing anything themselves, and this may have contributed to the variety of what they sold. They could choose to employ any specialized craftsmen, a

freedom which undoubtedly contributed to their enormous success, and in some cases (the *ouvriers libres*), these did not even have to be a member of the guild which controlled their craft. The *ouvriers libres*, however, although skilled, did not usually have access to designers or exotic materials. If this were the case the dealers acted both as organizers and as middlemen.

The dealers' common title, *marchands-merciers* derives from the fact that dealers in works of art were originally also dealers in textiles and upholstery materials (*merciers*, or "mercers" in English), but by the eighteenth century it was uncommon for a dealer to combine the two specialities. Nevertheless they remained members of the same guild, and the name *mercier* was occasionally applied to them, as in Diderot's *Encyclopédie,* where they are described as *marchands de tout, faiseurs de rien* (they deal in everything, but they make nothing). The dealers who sold works of art used in interior decoration usually called themselves simply *marchand* on their trade labels and invoices (see left), but clients referred to them by names which reflected their main specialities. Thus the Baronne d'Oberkirch, writing about her visit to Paris in 1782, refers to Granchez as a *bijoutier* and to Daguerre as a *marchand-ébéniste*. Associated specialists include *ferblantiers*, who sold mostly gilt-bronze objects ornamented with glass or crystal drops, *miroitiers*, who sold mirrors, and *tabletiers* who sold small furniture, especially games tables with all their fittings.

The shops of the *marchands-merciers*, mostly situated in the fashionable quarter of the Rue Saint-Honoré, attracted a wealthy clientele through the display of a splendid selection of furniture, gilt-bronze and other works of art. These might have been bought ready-made from craftsmen, but the great skill of the dealers lay in arranging for different materials and techniques to be combined to create interesting, beautiful and exotic objects. Rare or expensive materials, such as Japanese lacquer, Oriental porcelain, hardstone vessels or panels, were bought by them and entrusted to the craftsmen who would then adapt them, transforming them into appealing and usable works of art. Clients had little use for Japanese lacquer cabinets, since their shape (derived from seventeenth-century European cabinets on stands) did not fit into modern decorative schemes, so the cabinets were cut up and their panels used to veneer onto furniture of fashionable shape. Similarly panels from Florentine and Gobelins hardstone cabinets, as well as from Boulle furniture, were reused. Oriental porcelain was mounted with silver or gilt-bronze, transforming vases into ewers, perfume fountains or pot-pourris.

Bringing porcelain and gilt-bronze together was one of the dealers' main activities. In 1752, Lazare Duvaux supplied to the Marquise de Pompadour "A small square glazed lantern, with trelliswork and four small porcelain busts in the corners, decorated with gilt-bronze branches with Vincennes flowers, with a white and blue silk cord with tassels".

The dealer Simon-Philippe Poirier pioneered the use of Sèvres plaques in furniture and decoration. While he was not the first to use them, he became by the 1760s by far the biggest buyer of plaques from Sèvres. These were mounted into furniture of all types, as well as objects such as inkstands. His partner and successor, Dominique Daguerre, continued the practice into the 1790s. The creation of a writing table mounted with Sèvres porcelain plaques was a highly

BELOW LEFT

*D*rawing of a gilt-bronze and Sèvres porcelain ewer, signed *Kirn cad. d'Artill: delin:*, from Daguerre's group of drawings (see below). Similar ewers are in the Royal Collection and the Wallace Collection. These differ only in that their handles are in the shape of a naked woman standing on a cushion, clutching the shell at the back of the neck of the vase. The signature appears to be that of Georg Heinrich von Kirn, a fountain designer in Coblenz and Trier. He may have worked for the Sachsen-Teschens, which reinforces one theory about these drawings, namely that they constitute a pictorial inventory of the contents of the Palace of Laeken, near Brussels, where the Sachsen-Teschens were based as Governors of the Austrian Netherlands.

*D*rawing of a *bonheur-du-jour* with Sèvres porcelain plaques, from a group of designs which may have been shown by the *marchand-mercier* Daguerre to the Duke and Duchess of Sachsen-Teschen (Marie Antoinette's sister and brother-in-law) in 1782. It shows a later variation on the more familiar model by Martin Carlin, having straight instead of curved legs. Two such pieces by Carlin are in the Philadelphia Museum of Art (see right).

*T*rade label of the *marchand-mercier* Dominique Daguerre, from the underside of a writing table mounted with Sèvres plaques by Martin Carlin. The table was made circa 1778, and was bought from Daguerre by the Comte and Comtesse du Nord in 1784.

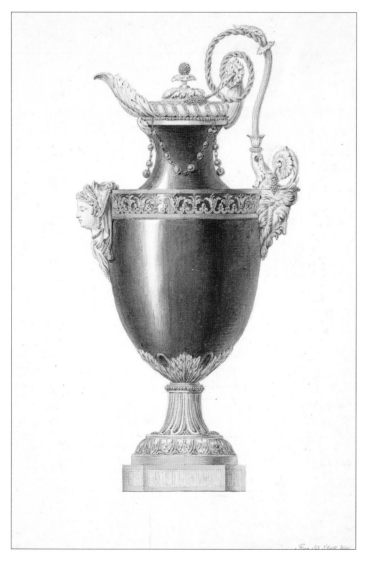

complicated activity. First, a design had to be commissioned. The plaques, of specific shapes and sizes with matching decoration, were then ordered from Sèvres. The *ébéniste* was instructed to make and veneer the carcass of the table, with spaces for the plaques; gilt-bronze mounts were ordered, involving several specialist craftsmen. The role of assembling the parts was probably fulfilled by the *ébéniste*. The drawer which was to contain the ink-pot and sand-box was sent to a silversmith to have these fitted. If there was to be a leather top, this was applied by the *gainier*. Lining the drawers with silk was yet another specialist job. It is small wonder that such pieces were very much admired and highly sought after. The Baronne d'Oberkirch accompanied the future Russian empress, Maria Feodorovna, to Daguerre's shop in the Rue Saint-Honoré in 1782 to buy such a piece, and she described the scene: "it was impossible to get near his shop on account of the crowd."

*Dulac Md Rue St. Honnore Inveniste*: this proud engraved inscription on a gilt-bronze mounted Sèvres vase in the Wadsworth Atheneum, Hartford, Connecticut, could imply that the dealer Dulac had designed it himself. Antoine Dulac had been a major client of Sèvres from

1759; in 1765, when his widow was running his shop, the Reverend William Cole accompanied Horace Walpole there to buy a set of three Sèvres blue vases (Cole thought they were enamel) with gilt-bronze mounts for John Chute of the Vyne in Hampshire. Cole was clearly intimidated by Madame Dulac, calling her shop "dangerous". Her son Antoine-Charles appears to have become a member of the Académie de Saint Luc in 1758, but did not qualify as a *marchand-mercier* until 1770. As well as helping his mother it is likely that, in view of the word "*Inveniste*", he designed these mounted vases himself, and commissioned Sèvres to produce the bell-shaped bowls (called *vases en cloche*) and

*Bonheur-du-jour* with Sèvres plaques, stamped by Martin Carlin, who became a *maitre-ébéniste* in 1766. The Sèvres plaques bear the date-letter *Y* for 1776, and painters' marks for Taillandier and Tandart. Some of the plaques still have their original labels, with printed interlaced *L*s and manuscript prices. It differs from the drawing in having rounded ends to the superstructure, and in the decoration of the plaques, which consists of scattered roses within a *bleu céleste* border.

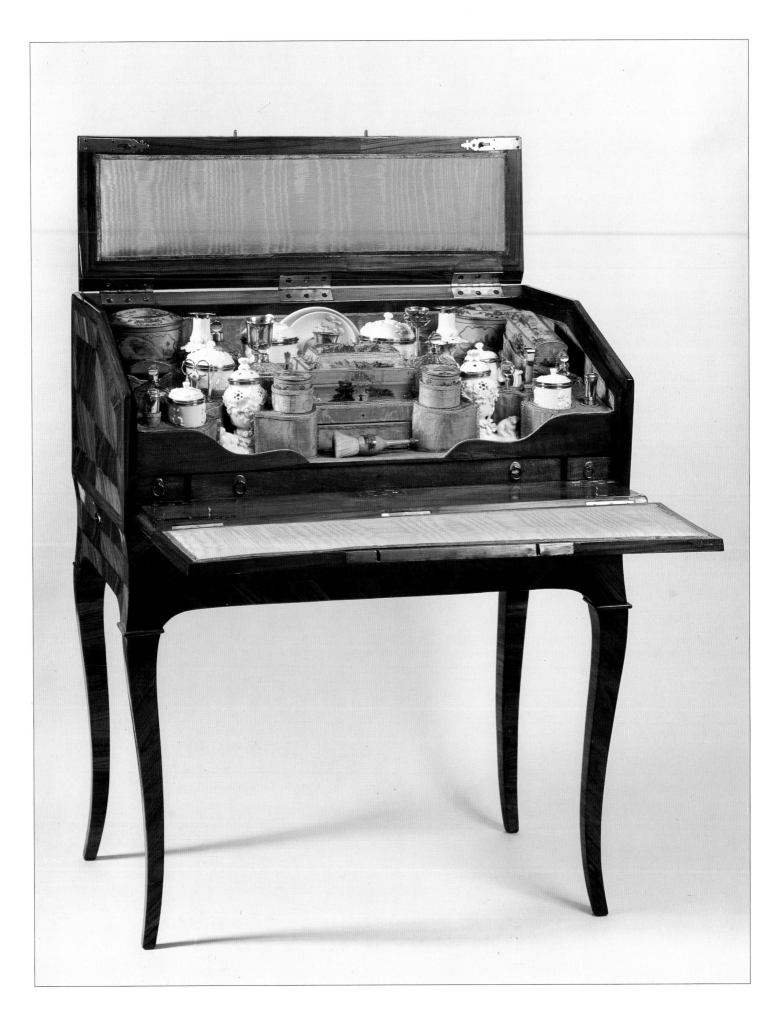

the lids. In theory, he could not have provided such designs without belonging to the Académie de Saint Luc. As well as being made with pierced rims for pot-pourri, some of these vases have surprises, the Wadsworth one (which originally belonged to Madame de Pompadour) being fitted with a miniature model in gold and silver of Bouchardon's equestrian monument to Louis XV in the Place Louis XV, now the Place de la Concorde in Paris. The monument springs up at the press of a button. Less kitsch versions are equipped with spring-loaded candelabra arms.

One of the best-known of the dealers of the eighteenth century was Lazare Duvaux, who called himself Marchand-Bijoutier ordinaire du Roi and whose shop, "*Au Chagrin de Turquie*", was situated with the others in the Rue Saint-Honoré. His widow went bankrupt in 1759, obliging the firm's day-book (*livre-journal*) to be deposited with a *notaire*. This survived in the archives of the City of Paris until the fire of 1873, by which time it had fortunately just been published in full. Covering credit sales from 1748 to 1759, it described in detail the names of the firm's clients and their purchases. Duvaux's client list was extensive. Headed by Louis XV and Madame de Pompadour, it included the names of some of the great nobles of the period, such as the Ducs de Rohan, Villeroy, Richelieu and La Vallière, as well as a large number of financiers, *fermiers-généraux*, artists such as François Boucher, and other dealers and craftsmen.

The variety of Duvaux's stock is impressive. Among the furniture he sold were commodes, bureaux, folio cabinets, corner cupboards with openwork shelves above and bedside tables, of plain wood, marquetry or lacquer, both European and Oriental, and folding screens or firescreens covered in Chinese painted wallpaper. He also sold Oriental, German and French porcelain, some mounted with silver or gilt-bronze. Gilt-bronze objects abound, including firedogs, tongs, shovels, pincers and fireguards, wall lights and lanterns (some mounted with porcelain flowers), and chandeliers, some hung with crystal drops, and his stock included lacquer boxes and trays, gold boxes and leather purses.

Duvaux did not merely buy and sell. Although it is not possible to document the creation of much of what he sold, nevertheless accounts for repair and alterations of objects show that he could call upon a wide variety of craftsmen, including cabinet-makers, lacquerers, gilt-bronze workers, goldsmiths, polishers and assemblers of mounted objects. Some of these he sent out to fit, clean or repair pieces in houses. It is clear that he could and did have items made up, but the majority of these would have been for stock. In some cases, however, he arranged to have pieces made to order, as the following entry for June 1754 under Madame de Pompadour's name testifies: "To mounting in gilt-bronze two urns of celadon porcelain, models executed especially by

*L*ouis XV dressing table with Mennecy porcelain, *Vernis Martin*, glass and silver fittings, mid-eighteenth century. The table is stamped by Brice Peridiez, who became a *maître-ébéniste* before 1737, and some of the silver bears the *décharge* mark for 1744-50. The piece was evidently put together by a *marchand-mercier*, who bought the porcelain from the Mennecy factory, had the silver fittings applied by a silversmith, and ordered lacquer boxes, brushes and a mirror. Peridiez was employed to make the table and fit the contents, which are extremely varied, including containers for pot-pourri, candlesticks, cups and saucers and embroidery equipment as well as *toilette* requisites.

Duplessis". The price of specially ordered objects tended to be high, but this may have been because they were more elaborate than ordinary stock items. In this particular case, Duplessis acted as designer, and also probably made the mounts. In October 1754, Duvaux sold a wall clock and matching barometer to S. A. R. l'Infant don Philippe (the Duke of Parma). These had to be designed especially, and were made of silvered bronze, with lacquered trelliswork decorated with "the finest Vincennes flowers".

The Garde-Meuble employed the services of dealers in a variety of ways, and could furnish them with raw materials if required. In 1784, Dominique Daguerre was entrusted with a close-stool of Japanese lacquer which had belonged to Louis XIV, and instructed to cut it up to veneer the panels onto a secretaire for Louis XVI's *cabinet intérieur* at Versailles and a writing table for Marie Antoinette. He used Adam Weisweiler to make the pieces, but there was not enough lacquer on the *chaise d'affaire*, and he was able to supply from his own stock panels of Japanese lacquer of very nearly the same exceptional quality. When the dealer Michel-Alexis Delaroue delivered a chandelier for the Cabinet du Conseil at Versailles in 1738, one of the Slodtz brothers was associated with the order, as well as having probably designed the chandelier himself in his capacity as Dessinateur de la chambre et du cabinet du Roi. Since the Garde-Meuble supplied some of the crystal drops, Slodtz may have designed it around them.

Delaroue was a regular supplier to various members of the Royal family, both of decorative bronzes and of other objects, such as stands and glass cases for the gold sugar-bowls produced for Louis XV by François-Thomas Germain in 1765, and a carved wood mirror frame and mirror for the Comtesse de Provence at Montreuil in 1781.

Simon-Philippe Poirier, and his partner from 1772, Dominique Daguerre, counted the Comtesse du Barry among their best clients. As well as Sèvres and furniture she bought more exotic curiosities: "An extremely large, nearly life-size figure, from China, dressed in material". This was equipped with "A Chinese instrument, a sort of organ, to fix to the arm of the figure".

Other dealers also acted as importers. Count Tessin noted of the dealer Gersaint that "During the summer he travelled and searched in foreign countries, and, back in Paris for the winter, he turned his trinkets into hard cash." When chandeliers were ordered from Jean-Claude Julliot for the wedding of the Dauphin in 1770, he not only had to obtain parts from Paris colleagues, but also had to execute models to send to England for manufacture.

Charles-Raymond Granchez's shop on the Quai de Conti was another fashionable resource for Parisians. The Baronne d'Oberkirch, writing in 1782, enthused that "nothing is as beautiful and shining as this shop." The name of Granchez's shop, "*Au Petit Dunkerque*", derived from his town of origin, and it seems that he had used his proximity to England to commercial advantage, since he advertised English saddlery and polished iron objects (possibly from Birmingham), in addition to French-made luxuries. He sold objects with lacquered tin ("tôle") imitations of Sèvres porcelain plaques, including inkstands and jardinières, as well as products of some of the Paris porcelain factories. Baronne d'Oberkirch summed up neatly (and untranslatably) the selection of objects available there: "*de ravissants bibelots et de petits riens élégants*".

*La Toilette*, signed and dated F. Boucher 1742. Painted for the Swedish ambassador Count Carl-Gustav Tessin, a friend and regular patron of Boucher.

The wall is hung with a yellow damask material, and the woodwork is painted a shiny dark green and gilded. The two chairs in the room are painted and upholstered *en suite* with the wall painting and covering. They are of the typically Louis XV type with scroll legs and flat backs (*chaises à la Reine*) and the upholstery is held on with round-headed, gilt-iron nails. The chest-height shelf of the chimneypiece is deep enough to accommodate vases and candlesticks. The overmantel mirror is held in a plain frame of giltwood which is incorporated into the panelling. On either side of it is a pair of gilt-bronze wall lights, as usual set as close as possible to the edge of the glass in order to reflect the light. The candlestick on the shelf is of silver or silvered brass, with a drip-pan of the same material or possibly of glass. The vase next to it is of Oriental celadon porcelain, mounted with foliate gilt-bronze feet and knop, and a gilt-bronze pierced collar, enabling it to be used for pot-pourri. The fire-tongs have a gilt-bronze finial, as does the iron hook upon which they rest. This is fixed to the inside of the fireplace.

The burning fire rests on iron supports (*grille*), which have two horizontal bars going from front to back, and projecting uprights to prevent the logs from hitting the foliate gilt-bronze firedog (*feu*), which sits in front and which would normally hide the iron structure. Indeed, the *feu* appears to be leaning against the chimneypiece. This is probably because it has no support at the back and would have slotted on to the front of the *grille* when the fire was not lit. It may have been feared that the mercury gilding would suffer if it was close to the flames. The brush with a turned wood handle on the floor is to sweep ashes or embers back into the fireplace. It has a loop of cord attached to the end to hang it up when not in use. The bellows are of wood, either painted or lacquered black, and red leather, with a brass spout. The small fan on the floor has a turned wooden handle and a paper or card panel painted white and blue.

The screen before the fire is in natural wood, with a footrest and a textile panel that can be raised to shield one's face from the fire. There is usually a clip at the side of such screens to hold the panel at one of a number of height settings. Two-thirds of the way up the panel is a writing or reading slide, shown lowered out of use. It can be raised to the horizontal and is then held up by two S-shaped iron supports. Its back and sides have raised borders to prevent objects from falling off. In order to make it easier to read or write using the slide, adjustable silvered light brackets are fixed to probably each side of the screen. The larger eight-fold screen behind the figures is protecting them from the draught, and would have been in quasi-everyday use. This example is also visible in a portrait of Boucher's wife in the Frick Collection, New York, suggesting that this room could have been in Boucher's own house. The screen is covered with a Chinese painted wallpaper. Madame de Pompadour owned many panels covered in the same way, some mounted as screens, and some fitted to the sliding doors of wardrobes.

A *toilette* in red lacquer, which probably has gilt foliate decoration is on the dressing table. The mirror is of a shape characteristic of Boulle mirrors of slightly earlier date, as is the box with the pincushion lid. The white porcelain pot is most likely Mennecy or Saint-Cloud, with a silver rim enabling the lid to be hermetically closed to protect the cream it contained. The dressing table itself is not visible, but hidden under a cloth called a *toilette*, giving the entire set its name. The table to the right of the chimneypiece is of ebonised fruitwood with turned legs, and probably an X-shaped stretcher, and dates from the very beginning of the eighteenth century. The porcelain on it is perhaps Chantilly, with a Kakiemon decoration in blue and red of a wheatsheaf pattern (see page 167). The cups are upside-down in the saucers in the eighteenth-century manner.

# 3
# STYLES AND INFLUENCES

The two parallel aims of the French baroque style, developed by Louis XIV's team of architects and designers, were measured grandeur and dazzling magnificence. The "classical orders" of architecture helped to create ponderous interiors in which spare space was made into ordered panels by the use of bold mouldings, sometimes enclosing heavy painted and gilded arabesques. The great tapestries which, with cabinets and other traditional furniture, formed the principal furnishings of rooms were used by their owners to impress rather than to charm. Ceiling painting, often of mythological subjects, contributed to the generally awesome character.

By the end of the seventeenth century a reaction was already underway. When Louis XIV gave Jules Hardouin Mansart in 1698 his famous instructions to lighten his designs for the Ménagerie at Versailles ("the subjects are too serious ... there should be youth mixed into these designs"), he was expressing a concern for change which was ratified the following year with the appointment of Pierre Lepautre as Dessinateur des Bâtiments. Lepautre, whose activity prior to his appointment had been mainly in the field of engraving, was among those who were to place more emphasis upon the decoration which was within the architectural framework than upon that framework itself, and, by so doing, was to sow the seeds of the rococo style.

## EXOTIC INFLUENCES

In the late seventeenth century, there was growing interest in anything exotic. The Siamese embassies to Louis XIV were the direct cause of what Félibien called "the Chinese craze", but other parts of the world

provided inspiration too. Accounts of the extravagance of the Turkish embassy to Paris in 1742 more than echo Monsieur Jourdain and the *fils du Grand Turc (Le Bourgeois Gentilhomme, 1671)*, while in 1699, the Duchesse d'Orléans (the Princess Palatine), writing about the Duchesse de Retz, cited an extreme example which Molière himself could not have bettered: "when she drinks coffee her ladies are obliged to dress as Turks, and she does likewise; when she drinks tea, Indian dress is worn." The famous paintings by Carle Van Loo of Madame de Pompadour as a *sultane*, intended for her bedroom at Bellevue, are further examples of how the exotic could create a link between interior decoration, dress and mode of life.

Objects from unusual and romantic places formed a major and necessary part of interior decoration. These were usually from the Far East, such as porcelain, lacquer or wallpaper, but the exotic was also employed as a source of inspiration parallel to the rococo or the neo-classical for French-made textiles, furniture and objects, partly at least because of the variable availability of genuine Oriental objects. French interpretations of the life and art of faraway places could at best be outlandish, and at worst completely ridiculous, an idealized view of the way of life of a mythical "noble savage". The Gobelins ordered tapestry cartoons from Alexandre-François Desportes in 1735 for a *tenture* (set of hangings) to be called *Les Nouvelles Indes*. One tapestry from this suite, "Le Chameau", features animals from all over the world in the same landscape: a llama is placed in front of a monkey riding a camel next to a tree in which parrots perch, while in the background ostriches stride beneath palm trees. Nearly fifty years later, French perception of the exotic had changed little: the clock made by François Rémond for the Comte d'Artois's Cabinet Turc at Versailles in 1781 stands on caparisoned camels, has two turbanned female figures flanking the dial, and is surmounted by negro boys watching winged putti play with garlands of flowers.

Turkey, America and Egypt were among the places that inspired craftsmen in their creation of charming and luxurious interiors. When Dufort de Cheverny went to dine at the house of Du Jonquoy de

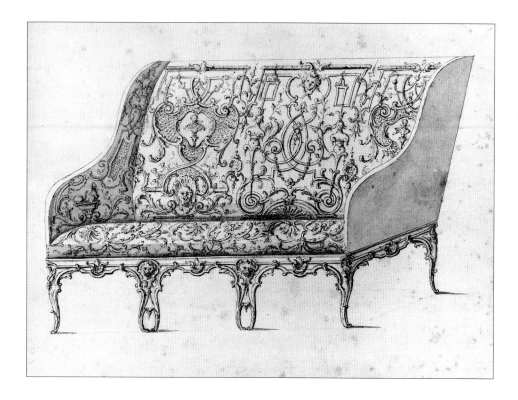

*D*esign for a *canapé* (sofa) by Thomas Lainé, circa 1720. As well as showing the frame, the drawing includes a project for upholstery, either in tapestry or embroidery, which is related to the grotesques of Bérain.

*R*ouge Royale marble and gilt-lead fountain, beginning of the eighteenth century. Such fountains served as wine coolers, with servants retrieving the bottles.

Monville (the creator of the Désert de Retz) in the Rue de la Bonne-Morue in Paris, he was amazed by what he saw. After crossing two sumptuously furnished *antichambres*, a columned *salon* and a bedroom in crimson velvet with gold braid, he came upon his host, who was dressed as Suleiman the Magnificent, leaning against a *bureau de porcelaine*. Suleiman then led him into a *salon turc*, panelled entirely in mirror glass. The sliding doors, which were operated by a secret mechanism, were also in mirror glass, and natural light came from above, while musicians played from a hidden gallery. On the floor lay a thick Turkish carpet (certainly the only authentic Turkish object there), and an *ottomane* covered in crimson velvet with gold braid encircled the room. Italian taffeta cushions were generously heaped upon it. The room gave entrance to a stuccoed dining room with bronze caryatids holding candelabra. Despite Dufort's understandable verdict ("Never in my life have I attended such a jolly and pleasant party") no Turk would have felt at home here, and the intention was never to accurately recreate a Turkish interior, but to impart a feeling of "Oriental" opulence.

# STYLES AND REFERENCES

Many of the terms used today to describe the various styles of the eighteenth century were coined in the nineteenth. In the case of Régence, Louis XV and Louis XVI, the reigns and the styles do not correspond accurately, but these are nevertheless in general use. What is now called rococo was known to contemporaries as *rocaille*, *goût pittoresque* or *style moderne* (until it went out of fashion), in contrast with the neoclassical, the various manifestations of which were described as *goût antique*, *goût grec*, *goût étrusque* or *goût arabesque*. The word *Gothique* was frequently and disparagingly employed to designate something which was old-fashioned, but care should be exercised here too. The gothic style crept back into fashion as a result of the growing *anglomanie* of the 1780s, and Mesdames Victoire and Adélaïde (daughters of Louis XV) had a gothic tower built as part of their *hameau* at Bellevue in 1783.

## RÉGENCE, CIRCA 1710-35. THE GENESIS OF THE ROCOCO

Jean Bérain the younger (1674-1726), who, like his father, held the post of Dessinateur ordinaire du cabinet et de la chambre du Roi, was among the artists who perfected elaborate and elegant arabesque designs in which foliage, strapwork and other fanciful motifs were used symmetrically to create panels for the decoration of walls, ceilings, furniture and tapestries. Lepautre engraved many of these designs and was to use them in his work for the Grand Dauphin at Meudon, for example. They are of extreme importance in French decorative arts, for they ultimately derive from the grotesques found in Rome during the Renaissance and used on French sixteenth-century furniture. They were therefore already part of the French artistic tradition, and engravers were to publish arabesque or grotesque designs continuously until the very end of the eighteenth century. The paradox here is that they should form one of the mainstays of French interest in ancient art and yet also be at the root of the reaction to it which is now called the rococo.

Artistic inspiration, which had traditionally come almost exclusively from classical Antiquity, albeit much distorted, began to be sought

formal room of a house, the *salon*, in the form of pilasters. Walls were decorated with trophies or panels of foliage and scrolls arranged symmetrically into curves that gradually became more sinuous, with correspondingly less abrupt interruptions of line. This decoration could be carried out in carved wood and then painted, with gilding used to outline the carving. The panels were framed with mouldings. At the beginning of the century these still followed the rectilinear construction of the panels themselves, sometimes with arched tops, but gradually the mouldings adapted to the fanciful shapes inside them. By the 1720s, there was enormous variety in the shapes of panels, and the carved decoration was often concentrated in one part of a panel, either the centre or the top.

## LOUIS XV: ROCAILLE, STYLE MODERNE OR ROCOCO, 1735-65

The *rocaille* style was the eventual outcome of the increased role played by decorative motifs such as the grotesques of Bérain, mixed with natural motifs such as rockwork, and countless exotic features. By the mid-1730s, all surviving architectural framework had disappeared, soon to be followed by many of the details which had given the Régence style its special characteristics, such as the dragons, monkeys, masks and loosely laced female torsos of the gilt-bronze mounts fixed on to furniture by the Régent's *ébéniste*, Cressent.

Jacques-François Blondel, the great theoretician of French eighteenth-century architecture, credited Nicolas Pineau with a major role in the development of the *rocaille* style: "it was he who invented variety in ornament". Pineau published a large number of influential engravings of wall decoration and furniture, as well as carrying out decorative sculpture himself. Blondel continued by deploring the part played by other designers: "His taste was unfortunately imitated by a multitude of artists, who, lacking his imagination and his skill, have produced an infinity of wild dreams and extravagances." Charles-Nicholas Cochin, a violently outspoken critic of the rococo, disagreed with Blondel only insofar as he happily included Pineau among the culprits, along with Lajoue and others, whom he accused of producing "practically worthless ornamental designs".

In the rococo *style moderne*, flowing curves became obligatory. The "orders" of architecture were abandoned or misused completely, by being twisted or made to hang in mid-air. Sinuous scrolls incorporated many sorts of fantastic detail, such as shells, masks, flowers and plant-life of all kinds, although they generally remained subordinate to the flowing, uninterrupted movement. Even structural features deliberately avoided straight lines, preferring to use successions of curves. The result is a very elegant and insubstantial style, human rather than architectural in scale. This was of course to be its downfall, since it implied a lack of reverence for classical architecture, which became unacceptable to the new generation of French Rome-trained architects.

*Cadran à vent de M<sup>r</sup>. le Duc de Mortemart en 1724*. Engraving by Huquier, plate 54 of the *Oeuvre* of Juste-Aurèle Meissonier. This rococo design (advanced for 1724) shows the concave corner of a room, with a wind dial asymmetrically supported by allegorical figures of the winds and a river god pouring water into a shell. It is closely related to Cressent's cartel clocks, and it is conceivable that Meissonier provided designs for Cressent.

from nature. Strange "natural" and exotic motifs such as shells, rockwork, pouring water, monkeys in Chinese costume and dragons combined with Bérain-style arabesques to produce a repertory of ornament which began to be used in a three-dimensional manner on wall decoration, furniture, silver and other materials. A residual sense of majesty ensured that proportions remained noble, and baroque notes are still to be found, such as the use of articulated strapwork and masks, although by now these sported smiling faces and pointed ears.

During this period, the "orders" of architecture were employed with less frequency in decoration, being usually confined to the most

*M*id-eighteenth-century bracket clock with case by Jean-Pierre Latz, and movement by Francis Bayley, Ghent. It may have been intended for export, since the squared, arched shape of the dial was more common in the Netherlands or England at this period.

Pl. VI.

Echelle de ⊢————┼————┼————┤ 5  10  15. Toises

*Profil de l'Edifice sur la longueur.*

Perhaps the most typical and enduring success of the French *rocaille* style is the Louis XV armchair. Louis XIV armchairs had conveyed an impression of static strength and architectural massiveness, while Louis XV examples are light and graceful, with long continuous curves avoiding sharp breaks, outlined by mouldings and punctuated by the occasional carved flower or cartilaginous cartouche. The proportions remain balanced through a complete symmetry, and an advanced sense of comfort and voluptuousness prevails.

Juste-Aurèle Meissonier's designs, whether for chairs, picture frames or soup tureens, consist entirely of harmoniously flowing scrolls, from which emerge foliage and the occasional putto or falling-water motif. Asymmetry reigns supreme, and those of Meissonier's designs known to have been executed are mostly for objects in which symmetry is not a structural or occupational requirement, such as tureens and candlesticks. Gilt-bronze cartel clocks shaped as asymmetrical cartouches provide another example of this trend, which in the end lost out to the symmetrical rococo, a more sober and restrained style with a consequently wider appeal. Cochin, one of Marigny's companions on his Italian visit, castigated Meissonier in his memoirs for being "an unruly genius, and, what's more, spoilt by Italy".

*Design for a monument at the top of the Champs-Elysées (the site of the present Arc de Triomphe) by the engineer Ribart de Chamoust, 1758. The ultimate in rococo extravagance. Note the dining room with centrepieces on the table, and, above it, a room decorated with palm trees.*

*Silver-gilt tureen and stand by François-Thomas Germain, Paris, 1759. One of eight in a service ordered from Germain by the Czarina Elizabeth. This version of the rococo exhibits the largely symmetrical exuberance that prefigured the goût grec.*

One of the main driving forces of the rococo style may have been the abundance of highly gifted craftsmen who were also competent designers, but were not trained as painters or architects in the classical tradition, and therefore not bound by classical proportions or restraint. Meissonier described himself as an architect, but the word could be synonymous with designer, and he used it in this context, although his collected engravings include designs for interiors in which the rococo elements merge with elaborate baroque features.

Writing in 1738, Blondel showed himself to be an active partisan of the restrained version of the rococo style: "We have been freed from the slavery of squares and circles to which tradition had formerly bonded us . . . in the last few years more life and less dryness has been introduced in ornament: I am not referring to those which result from a disordered imagination, but to those which chart a balanced course between the barrenness of former times and the fecundity of the present". This was in fact a specific comment about the frames of overdoor paintings, and Blondel continued by criticizing the use of palm trees as uprights for looking-glass frames because of the difficulty of designing a plausible cross-piece, preferring mouldings and scrolls instead. This was of course not a criticism of the rococo, but of its abuse.

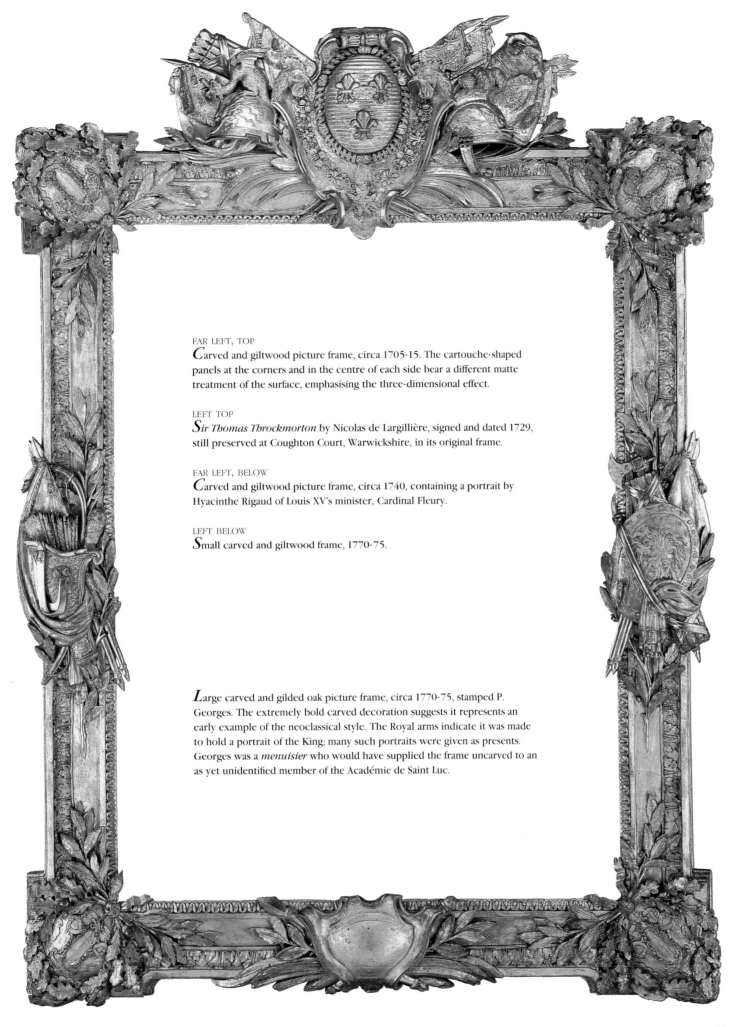

FAR LEFT, TOP
*C*arved and giltwood picture frame, circa 1705-15. The cartouche-shaped panels at the corners and in the centre of each side bear a different matte treatment of the surface, emphasising the three-dimensional effect.

LEFT TOP
*Sir Thomas Throckmorton* by Nicolas de Largillière, signed and dated 1729, still preserved at Coughton Court, Warwickshire, in its original frame.

FAR LEFT, BELOW
*C*arved and giltwood picture frame, circa 1740, containing a portrait by Hyacinthe Rigaud of Louis XV's minister, Cardinal Fleury.

LEFT BELOW
*S*mall carved and giltwood frame, 1770-75.

*L*arge carved and gilded oak picture frame, circa 1770-75, stamped P. Georges. The extremely bold carved decoration suggests it represents an early example of the neoclassical style. The Royal arms indicate it was made to hold a portrait of the King; many such portraits were given as presents. Georges was a *menuisier* who would have supplied the frame uncarved to an as yet unidentified member of the Académie de Saint Luc.

# THE NEOCLASSICAL REVIVAL OR GOÛT GREC, 1755-65

The artists and architects who frequented the French Academy in Rome in the 1740s had ample opportunity to study and appreciate the classical style, through examples of late Italian baroque as well as by admiring the ruins of Ancient Rome, still tantalizingly clad in romantic vegetation. By the time the Marquis de Marigny arrived in Rome on his Grand Tour in 1750 in the company of the engraver Charles-Nicolas Cochin, the Abbé Le Blanc and the architect Jacques-Germain Soufflot, there were many young artists who were extremely familiar with classical architecture and who had proven competence in providing designs in this style. It was when they returned to France and started to do the same there that the neoclassical revival took recognizable shape. Cochin was later to claim that the turning point had been Marigny's journey, but this hardly seems likely since the first neoclassical interiors did not appear until the mid-1750s at the earliest. The reaction against the rococo took root among intellectuals and architects for whom noble classical proportions symbolized the supposed philosophical and political purity of the ancient world, contrasting with the obvious association of the unruly rococo with modern depravity.

Classical architecture had never been totally abandoned, but had continued to be employed even at the height of the rococo because of the grandeur and magnificence it could provide so well, for the porticoes of churches or the decoration of a ceremonial room such as a *salon*, for example. This formed part of the continuing tradition of the baroque, a tradition also visible internally in the Boulle furniture and

*S*èvres hard paste *seau à verre à draperie*, circa 1780. The drapery recalls that on a type of bottle-shaped vase, called a *vase bouteille en écharpes*, introduced at Sèvres in the mid-1760s. It probably reflects the manner in which damask napkins were draped around silver bottle coolers on buffets. The Prince de Nassau purchased two of these *seaux* in 1782.

*C*abinet stamped JOSEPH for Joseph Baumhauer, circa 1765. Baumhauer, who always signed with his first name, made *goût grec* furniture in the 1760s without having passed through the transitional style. Unusual Japanese lacquer panels are framed by heavy Ionic pilasters in ebony and gilt-bronze, while the apron mount combines the Greek key pattern with a hint of Chinese fretwork. Later neoclassical furniture, by Riesener and others, is less massive and more graceful.

RIGHT
*S*ecretaire stamped by Nicolas Petit, circa 1770-75. The shape of the piece is outlined with powerful *goût grec* motifs such as the fluted frieze, and the marquetry of ruins was probably copied from engravings.

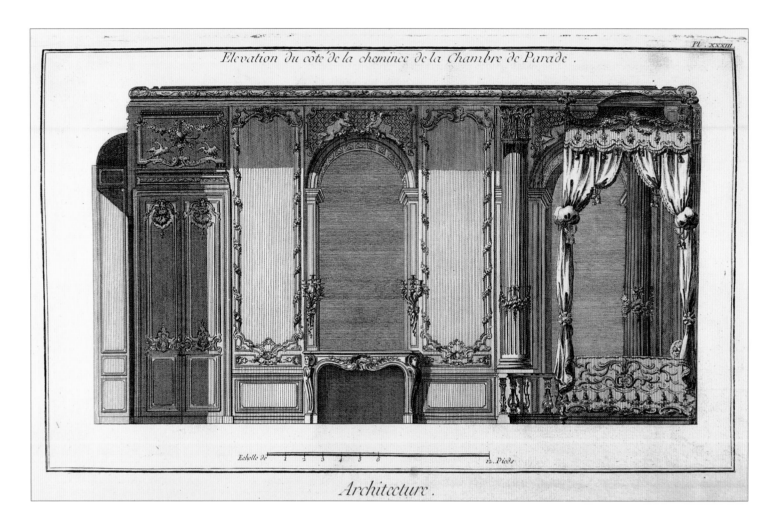

*Elévation du côté de la cheminée de la Chambre de Parade* in the Duchesse d'Orléans's apartment at the Palais-Royal, from the *Architecture* section of Diderot's *Encyclopédie*, 1762. These rooms were decorated by Pierre Contant d'Ivry in 1755-7. Blondel, who wrote the captions for this section, stated that *Cette décoration est du meilleur genre. De belles parties, des détails heureux, des matières précieuses, des étoffes de prix, tout concourt à procurer à cette pièce une très-grande magnificence.* (This decoration is in the best possible taste. A fine composition, judiciously chosen details, materials of quality, expensive fabrics, all contribute to the great magnificence of the whole).

seventeenth-century sculpture which had remained in the grand reception rooms of many houses.

Writing in Diderot's *Encyclopédie*, Blondel ascribed to Pierre Contant d'Ivry, an architect who had never even visited Italy, a crucial role in the genesis of the neoclassical style, on account of the redecoration undertaken by Contant at the Palais-Royal in the second half of the 1750s (see above). The classical elements (columns, pilasters, arches) employed here owe a great deal to the baroque, and Contant used them in a context which did not need to reject the rococo. He could therefore feel justified in including furniture, such as console tables and sofas, as well as gilt-bronze wall lights, in a balanced version of the now-traditional *rocaille* style. The result was praised by Blondel

because while it appeared logical to employ noble classical features and proportions for the walls of ceremonial rooms, it made no sense to inflict an architectural style upon theoretically mobile furniture and gilt-bronze lights.

The next major step in the neoclassical revival was taken by Le Lorrain, with the Lalive de Jully suite of furniture. Louis-Joseph Le Lorrain, an architect who had lived in Rome from 1740 to 1748, had become familiar with the language of Ancient Greek architecture, probably through his correcting of some of the drawings for Julien-David Le Roy's *Les ruines des plus beaux monuments de la Grèce*, which appeared in 1758. At about the same time Le Lorrain was responsible for the design of a suite of neoclassical furniture for Ange-Laurent de Lalive de Jully. This large set, comprising a massive writing table with its *cartonnier* (filing cabinet) surmounted by a clock, as well as a series of display cabinets for a shell collection, is of ebony with bold gilt-bronze mounts that feature Vitruvian scrolls, Greek keys and lion pelts, clearly inspired by Ancient Greek architectural motifs. All the elements are rectilinear, the only curves being the laurel garlands hanging from heavy gilt nails (see page 97). It owes a great deal not only to the ancient world but also to the splendid Boulle furniture of the reign of Louis XIV. Indeed, Lalive's interest in Louis XIV may have been his inspiration, for Dufort de Cheverny, who shared with Lalive the post of Introducteur

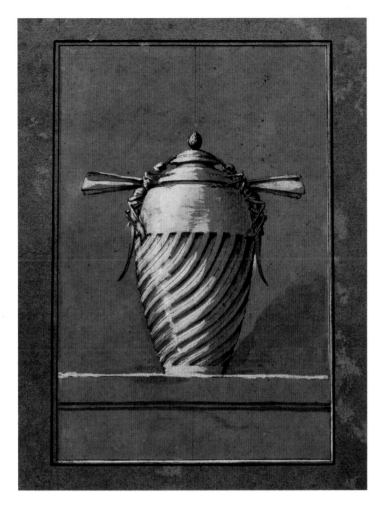

des Ambassadeurs, states in his memoirs that his friend and colleague began to appear at parties wearing costumes in the Louis XIV style. Unfortunately for Lalive, this behaviour was diagnosed as nascent insanity in the early 1760s, and his family was later to have him declared legally incompetent.

Whatever Lalive's state of mind, his furniture proved that a French architect trained in Rome was able to design in a pure classical style, influenced by the baroque but also for the first time by Ancient Greece. It heralded a movement which became known as the *goût grec*, the outcome of an exaggerated passion for Ancient Greece, seen not only in architecture and decoration, but also in clothes and literature. Bold Greek key friezes competed with heavy swags of laurel and countless

*D*esign for a decorative vase, by Ennemond-Alexandre Petitot, 1764. After studying architecture in Rome from 1746 to 1750, Petitot went to Parma in 1753 as architect to the ducal Court. His version of the *goût grec* is often heavily spiced with applied decoration such as foliage, or, in this case, grasshoppers. In 1764 he published a series of engravings of vases, for which this is one of the preliminary sketches. Some of the designs were translated into objects, such as porphyry vases with gilt-bronze mounts. Duplessis's probate inventory in 1774 records that he owned engravings by Petitot.

*L*it à la turque. A vigorous example of the *goût grec* in carved furniture, about 1765-70.

other details drawn from Ancient Greek architecture. All branches of the arts succumbed to this trend; Vien painted pictures of Ancient Greek priestesses sprinkling incense over classical tripods; Boucher designed gilt-bronze mounts for vases with rams heads and laurel garlands, and Sèvres started to employ vigorous classical details such as Vitruvian scrolls in the modelling of porcelain trays and vases. In furniture, Joseph Baumhauer, the *ébéniste* probably responsible for the execution of the Lalive suite, henceforth showed himself capable of making pieces entirely in the new style.

## TRANSITIONAL STYLE, CIRCA 1760-70

Many craftsmen were slow to adapt, and the *rocaille* style continued to be employed while the *goût grec* gradually encroached. Craftsmen continued to work to established models and templates, many of which can be seen, from inventories, to have represented a substantial part of their wealth. A hybrid style emerged employing a mixture of rococo and neoclassical elements, and now known as "transitional".

The practical application of this style is most visible in furniture. Individual pieces of rococo shape and marquetry were produced, with possibly at first an inlaid frame to the marquetry incorporating Greek keys at the corners, and later whole panels of marquetry depicting ancient ruins. The gilt-bronze mounts might be of a wholly neoclassical nature since many of the *bronziers* appear to have been seduced early by the attraction of the *goût grec*. The sculptors who carved ornaments on *menuiserie*, and provided models for the *bronziers* who supplied mounts for case furniture, were artists who were more likely to have easy access to neoclassicism than the humble *menuisier* whose life was spent making chairs. The most avant-garde craftsmen, such as Baumhauer and Pierre Garnier, bypassed this hybrid style, probably because of their involvement with the *marchands-merciers*, for whom the constant need for novelty was a necessary commercial driving force, although it would appear that Baumhauer also continued to produce work in the traditional style.

The adoption of the new style could be as sudden in one case as it could be slow in another: no objects made entirely of gilt-bronze appear to combine elements of the two styles, indicating that once a *bronzier* had been smitten by the new craze he did not allow it to mingle with the old (although some made rococo and neoclassical pieces at the same time). In the case of furniture, rectilinear shapes were gradually adopted during the 1760s, for example in the body of a commode, although the legs remained curved. The *bureau du Roi*, ordered by Louis XV from Oeben in 1760, but not completed until 1769 by his successor Riesener, is a fine example of these paradoxes. On a basically Louis XV shape, fairly traditional marquetry of trophies and flowers has been applied, as well as more avant-garde marquetry, both of realistic attributes and of a formal trelliswork pattern. The gilt-bronze mounts, modelled probably by the elder Duplessis, incorporate neoclassical

*O*ne of a set of eight wall lights delivered by the *marchand-mercier* Darnault for the *grand salon* of Mesdames Adélaïde and Victoire at Bellevue in 1784. Two lanterns in the same style were delivered with them.

details such as lion pelts, cornucopiae, terms and vases, as well as lush foliage, whose sense of movement recalls Contant d'Ivry's furniture for the Palais-Royal. Perched incongruously on either side of the clock on the top of the piece are small gilt-bronze replicas of the porcelain tureens designed by Duplessis ten years previously for Louis XV's *bleu céleste* Vincennes service.

# LOUIS XVI AND GOÛT ÉTRUSQUE OR GOÛT ARABESQUE, 1765-90

While a number of designers were eagerly inflicting the wilder extravagances of the *goût grec* upon a public happy to find an alternative to the *rocaille*, however absurd, a parallel trend was under way, resulting in the complete adoption of a more restrained neoclassicism, in some fields via the hybrid transitional style. Certain architects began to work in a dignified and elegantly proportioned version of the classical style, which was to be more long-lasting and which is now described as "Louis XVI", although it was firmly established by the time of that monarch's accession to the throne in 1774. This style gradually brought together the conflicting strands of the other styles, but in an unexaggerated form. Interior decoration took the lead, and by the late 1760s the Petit Trianon and the Pavillon de Louveciennes proved that the elegance of classical proportion, often without features such as columns, pilasters, or other architectural details indispensable to the *goût grec*, could be combined with a variety of motifs, some traditional and some innovatory, to create a style which could be as successful as the *rocaille*. The sculptural detailing, whether on wood, gilt-bronze, porcelain or silver, was of an unprecedently exquisite fineness, best seen in the carving of leaves and garlands of flowers on the delicate mouldings of gilt-bronze or wood.

From the rococo style, the exuberance of nature was taken and

*L*ouis XVI giltwood *Athénienne*. A notice in the newspaper *L'Avant-Coureur* in 1773 spoke of this curious new piece of furniture, claiming it had as many as eight uses:

1. It is a useful ornament in a room.
2. By replacing the pierced lid with a marble slab, it may be used as a console table, to stand in front of a mirror or in the corner of a room, to support a candelabrum, a bust or other sculpture.
3. It will turn into a *cassolette*, by removing the marble top, filling the tub with pot-pourri and heating it with a spirit lamp to perfume rooms.
4. With the spirit lamp you can make coffee, tea or chocolate.
5. If you unscrew the spirit lamp, the bowl may be used as a tank for little Chinese goldfish.
6. A pot filled with earth can be lowered into the bowl and filled with bulbs.
7. The tank filled with water can become a flower vase.
8. A pierced gilt-copper plaque, put in place of the marble, can be used with the spirit lamp to keep dishes warm.

FOLLOWING SPREAD

*G*rand salon of the Hôtel Baudard de Saint-James, Place Vendôme, Paris, circa 1775-80. Designed by François-Joseph Belanger, and with overdoors painted with mythological scenes by Jean-Jacques Lagrenée. Now the headquarters of Chaumet.

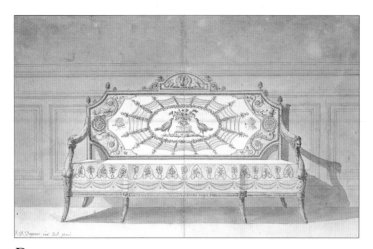

*D*esign for a *canapé arabesque*, signed by Dugourc, late eighteenth century. The upholstery was probably to be of woven and embroidered silk.

tamed, with flowers now tied in elegant bunches by multicoloured ribbons, or placed in classical vases. Martial trophies became so graceful as to be almost feminine, and garlands of fruit and flowers hung rhythmically from gilt nails, tied by ropes with tassels, as did friezes of fringed drapery.

Naturally, a style which owed its framework and proportions to classical architecture happily incorporated numerous classical features, but not in such an extravagant manner as the *goût grec*. A Louis XVI commode, console table or chair will be supported upon straight, often turned, tapering and fluted legs, sometimes topped by an Ionic capital, but the eye is drawn rather to the perfect proportions, often outlined by a gilt-bronze moulding, an arabesque frieze, and the contrast of well-chosen materials, such as mahogany and gilt-bronze, or sky-blue silk and giltwood. The impressionist nature of the *rocaille* style had allowed details to be sketched in, but here their precision is the hallmark of perfection.

The revival in the popularity of arabesques owed as much to the Renaissance and the early eighteenth-century versions of artists such as Gillot as it did to the rediscovery of Pompeii and Herculaneum. This was partly because of the wide availability of arabesque engravings of the seventeenth and early eighteenth centuries. Jean-Démosthène Dugourc claimed in his autobiography, written in 1800, that "he was the first to give the example of the use of the Arabesque and Etruscan styles." That this is exaggerated is amply demonstrated by the arabesque panels of Madame Sophie's library at Versailles (1769), executed long before Dugourc rose to prominence. Nevertheless, in the 1780s he may have been the principal designer to use this variation of the Louis XVI style, influencing the *menuisier* Georges Jacob and other craftsmen who worked for Marie Antoinette and her circle as the principal clients of the *marchand-mercier* Daguerre. Daguerre employed the services of skilled craftsmen such as the *ébéniste* Weisweiler and the *bronzier* Rémond, who created objects which combined an unparalleled exotic inventiveness with a hitherto unknown attention to detail. The château of Bagatelle, created for the Comte d'Artois in the late 1770s, marked a new, refined departure from the ordinary "flowery" Louis XVI style, with its painted relief arabesques, frequent allusions to antiquity or to the exotic, and with the *maître de maison*'s bedroom, which was draped with blue silk and decorated with martial trophies, symbolizing a victorious Roman general's rest after battle. This theatrical tendency was one of the signals of the new movement. The famous actress Mademoiselle Dervieux, who was to marry Dugourc's brother-in-law Belanger during the Revolution, had a bedroom hung with "elaborate banners covering the walls in the Arabian manner".

The gradual growth in popularity of this style, together with a renewal of interest in archaeology and the temporary decline in standards of craftsmanship during the period of the revolution, was to lay the foundations for the *Directoire* and Empire styles.

*La Conversation Galante* by Jean-Baptiste Mallet. Gouache, circa 1790. Note the frieze inspired by Greek vase painting.

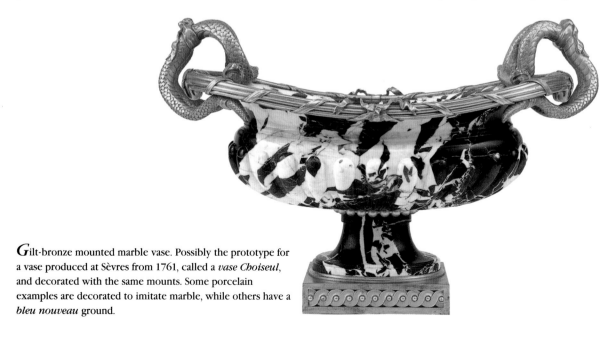

*G*ilt-bronze mounted marble vase. Possibly the prototype for a vase produced at Sèvres from 1761, called a *vase Choiseul*, and decorated with the same mounts. Some porcelain examples are decorated to imitate marble, while others have a **bleu nouveau** ground.

# 4

# THE DISTRIBUTION, USE AND CONTENT OF ROOMS

"The character of the master of a house, ... can be judged by the manner in which it is arranged, decorated, and furnished." Thus the architect Germain Boffrand, writing in 1745, affirmed the importance of personal taste in decoration, as well as suggesting that the social status or aspirations of the occupant are easily discernible.

Jean-François Bastide's novel *La Petite Maison*, written in 1752, relates the attempted seduction of the courtesan Mélite by the Marquis de Trémicourt. What makes the story of compelling interest to students of interior decoration is that the method chosen by Trémicourt is to expose Mélite to the delights of his *petite maison*, a love-nest on the banks of the Seine which is therefore meticulously described by Bastide, with an accuracy which leaves no doubt that the author was describing one or several houses he knew well; he warned that "nowhere in Paris or in the rest of Europe is as romantic or finely arranged."

The first room approached by Mélite and Trémicourt is the *vestibule*, which leads into a *salon* looking out on to the garden. "It is of circular shape, with a domed ceiling painted by Hallé; the panelling is lilac coloured, with fine looking-glasses; overdoors by the same painter contain scenes of lovers. Carving is used here with taste, and its beauty is heightened by the shine of the gilding. The colour of the upholstery matches the panelling ... Night was falling; a negro came to light thirty

*Salon* in the Hôtel de Villette, Paris, late 1760s. The architect was Bernard Poyet, who employed Jean-Baptiste Boiston for the decorative sculpture, and Pierre-Nicolas Belleville for the wall and ceiling painting. The Marquis de Villette invited Voltaire to stay in the house at the time of his triumphant return to Paris in 1778.

candles, which were arranged in a chandelier and candelabra of Sèvres porcelain [flowers], artistically disposed, and held in gilt-bronze supports."

Next came the bedroom. "This room is of square shape, with diagonal corners; a bed covered in yellow Chinese silk, brocaded with brilliant colours, is enclosed in an alcove opposite one of the windows, which look out on to the garden: looking-glasses have been placed in each of the four angles. This room has an arched ceiling containing in a round frame a painting in which Pierre, with his customary artistry, has painted Hercules in the arms of Morpheus, awakened by Love. All the panelling is a soft tone of sulphur. The parquet floor is marquetry of purplewood and cedar; all the marble is blue-grey. Fine bronzes and porcelains have been tastefully and sparingly positioned on marble-topped console tables placed below each of the four looking-glasses."

After the bedroom came the boudoir. "The walls are entirely lined with looking-glass, and the joins between them have been hidden by false tree trunks, with carefully arranged branches and leaves. These trees are spaced in the manner of a formal garden; they are covered in flowers, and candles on branches reflect their gently graduated light in the looking-glasses ... the effect is that of a natural arbour, lit without the help of art. The alcove containing the *ottomane*, a sort of daybed which stands on a floor of patterned rosewood marquetry, is decorated with green and gold trimmings and cushions of different sizes ... the woodwork and carving are painted to accord with the objects they represent, and this colour has been applied by Dandrillon in such a way as to exhale the perfume of violets, jasmine and roses." Dandrillon (a member of the Académie de Saint Luc) was a decorative painter and sculptor who was said to have invented a method for incorporating durable scent into paint.

PLAN ELEVATION ET COUPE DU PAVILLON DE VENUS DANS L'ISLE D'AMOUR

Section of the Pavillon de Vénus in the Ile d'Amour at Chantilly, built for the Prince de Condé in 1765. From an album of watercolours painted by Chambé as a result of the visit of the Comte and Comtesse du Nord in 1782.

PLANS, ÉLÉVATIONS, ET COUPES, DU SALLON ET DE LA SALLE
A MANGER DU HAMEAU

Coupe prise sur la ligne C.D.

Coupe prise sur la ligne C.D.

Coupe prise sur la ligne A.B.

Coupe prise sur la ligne A.B.

Exterieur du Sallon

Exterieur de la Salle a Manger

Plan du Sallon

Plan de la Salle a Manger

Cabinet de Trictrac

Garderobe

office

Garde robe

Section of the *salon* and the dining room of the *hameau* at Chantilly, from the same album.

The *appartement des bains* followed: "Marble, porcelain and muslin abound. The panelling is painted with arabesques by Perrot to the designs of Gillot, tastefully arranged in panels: marine plants [coral?] mounted in bronze by Caffiéri; pagodas, crystals and seashells, artistically mingled, decorate this room, in which are two niches, containing a bath and a bed upholstered in Indian muslin, embroidered and decorated with tassels. Next door is a *cabinet de toilette* with panelling painted by Huet with fruit, flowers and exotic birds among garlands and medallions, in which Boucher has painted monochrome scenes of lovers, as in the overdoors. A silver *toilette* by Germain has not been forgotten; natural flowers spill from dark blue and gold vases, chairs upholstered with material of the same colours, with their frames of aventurine applied by Martin, complete the enchanting effect of this suite . . . the upper part of the room is fitted with a cornice of an elegant profile, above which are motifs of carved and gilt lambrequins, which act as a border for a shallow dome containing a golden mosaic with flowers painted by Bachelier."

Serving the *appartement des bains* as well as the remainder of the house was a *cabinet d'aisance* "with a marble bowl fitted with a valve, with a cover of marquetry of scented woods, encased in an alcove simulating an arbour of clipped hornbeams, this effect continues over the walls and domed ceiling, with a space at the top painted to resemble a sky with birds. Vases and porcelains filled with scent are artistically arranged on brackets: cupboards hidden in the walls contain crystals, vases, and all the necessary fittings for the use of this room."

Another room which gave into the *salon* was a *cabinet des jeux*: "This *cabinet* is panelled in the finest Chinese lacquer; the furniture is of the same, covered in embroidered Indian material; the candelabra are of rock crystal, and contrast with pieces of the finest Meissen and Japanese porcelain, artistically disposed on gilt brackets."

Trémicourt's *pièce de résistance* was the dining room, which had "walls with stucco of an infinite variety of colours, applied by the famous Clerici. The panels contain bas-reliefs of the same material, carved by the renowned Falconet, with the Feasts of Comus and Bacchus. The trophies decorating the pilasters are the work of Vassé. These trophies symbolize hunting, fishing, the pleasures of the table and those of love. From each of the twelve trophies springs a support for a six-light candelabrum." Mélite, who had been wondering why there were no servants, was amazed when "the table plunged into the kitchens which were in the basement, and from above came another one which fitted neatly into the opening left in the floor, which was nevertheless protected by a gilt-iron balustrade."

Weakened by this extraordinary progression of luxury, Mélite finally succumbed in the second boudoir, which "was covered with heavy dark green silk, on which were arranged symmetrically the finest engravings of the illustrious Cochin, of Lebas and of Cars. There was just enough light to be able to glimpse these masterpieces. The room was filled with sofas, daybeds and chaise-longues."

*R*ound dining room in the Comtesse de Provence's garden pavilion at Montreuil. The doors are hidden in the trompe-l'oeil decoration. The twenty-four chairs supplied by Jacob were of a simpler model than the ones for the *salon* (see page 86).

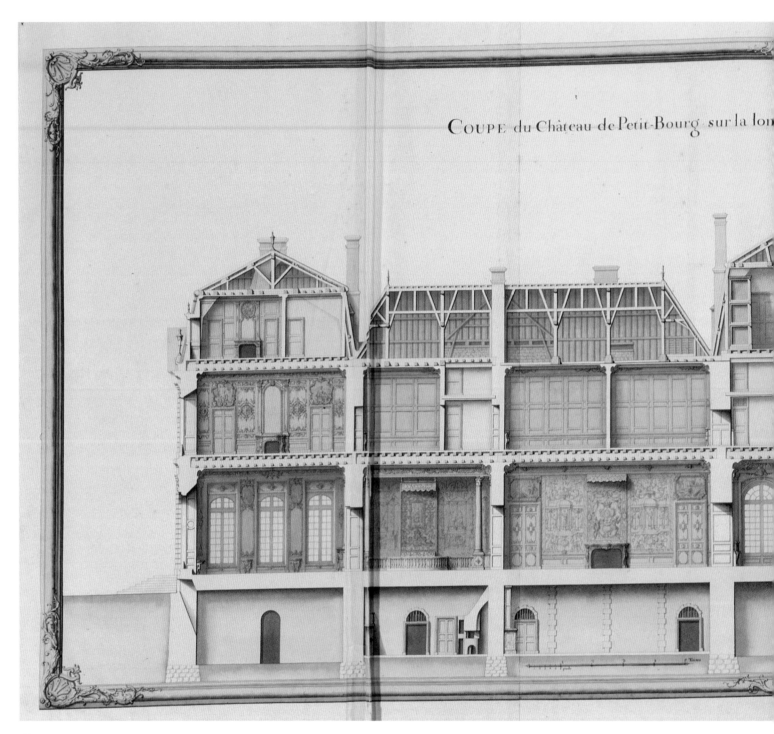

COUPE du Château de Petit-Bourg sur la lon

*Coupe du Château de Petit-Bourg sur la longueur par l'Enfilade des Appartements du Roy et de la Reine* (Lengthways section of the Château de Petit-Bourg, showing the King and Queen's suite of rooms). Petit-Bourg was rebuilt by the Duc d'Antin in the early 1720s. His important position as Directeur des Bâtiments required him to possess a house in which he could receive the King, equipped with *appartements de parade*. The central *salon* separated two of these on the ground floor. The King's, on the left, started with a *chambre du dais*, with a canopy of state placed above the chimneypiece. Gobelins tapestries were hung on the walls, and the doors were of carved and painted wood, as were the frames of the overdoor paintings. This was followed by a *chambre de parade* with a balustrade, also hung with tapestries, and a *grand cabinet ou galerie* which occupied the whole of the end of the house. It was decorated with console tables and huge looking-glasses above which were oval paintings. The apartment on the right begins with an *antichambre*, known as the Salle du Czar because of the portrait of Peter the Great placed there in commemoration of his visit to the previous château on the site in 1717, and continues with a bedroom and a *cabinet*. The *cabinet* at the end is decorated with elaborate panelling and overdoors by Oudry. From an album of 1730 containing 25 views of Petit-Bourg.

ar l'Enfilade des Appartemens du Roy et de la Reine.

# DISTRIBUTION OF ROOMS

By the end of the seventeenth century, the art of the distribution of rooms had become a separate discipline in architectural treatises. For Jacques-François Blondel, who published several, it was his leading pre-occupation. The problem was to reconcile two conflicting principles, namely the maintaining of noble classical proportions in exteriors, while arranging the rooms inside in a practical and comfortable manner. That this was no easy task was confirmed by Pierre Patte who complained in 1769 that excessive concern for room arrangement was incompatible with architectural integrity. Blondel conceded that the relative importance of comfort to proportions varied according to the grandeur of the house, and noted that variations in taste and fashion could alter distribution and decoration. Mid-eighteenth-century archi-tectural treatises sometimes reused older ground plans, changing nothing except the names of the rooms, making them more varied and more specific. By the end of the century, distribution had become more

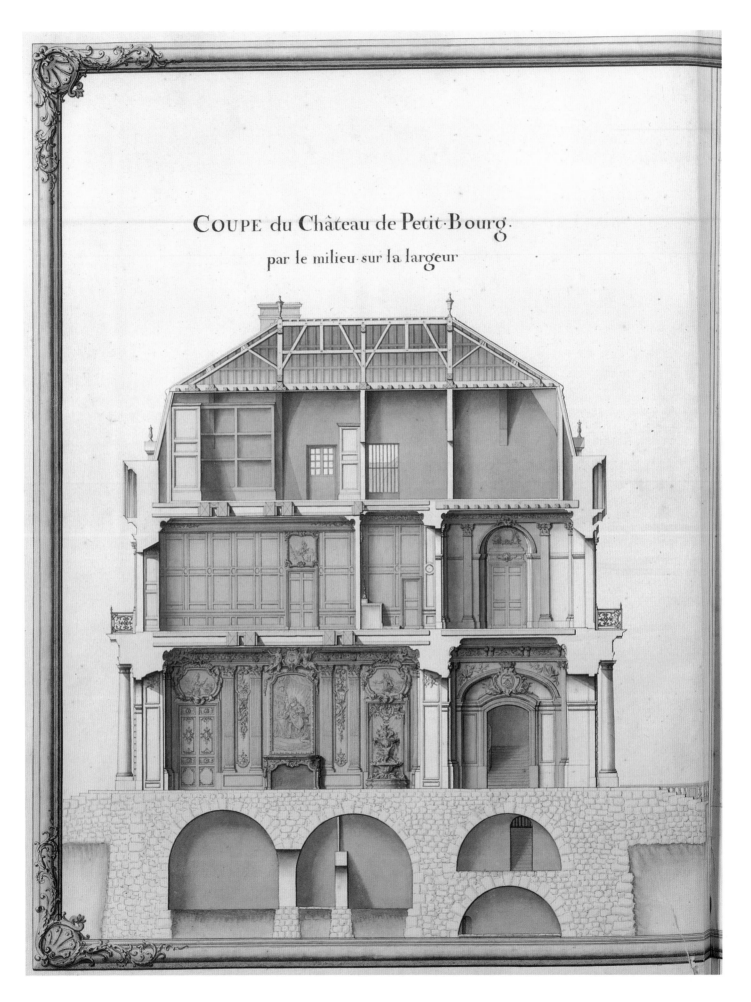

COUPE du Château de Petit-Bourg.
par le milieu sur la largeur

important still; Nicolas Le Camus de Mézières stated that by looking at the exterior of a building, one should be able to see how it is distributed inside.

Rooms were used for particular purposes, and different rooms varied in importance as the century progressed. The way a room was furnished indicated its use and the intended user. Large rooms used for receiving many people at a time remained sparsely furnished, contrasting with smaller, more intimate and highly cluttered rooms.

A gradual but complete change in the distribution of rooms within houses reflected an evolution in lifestyle. During the seventeenth century, houses contained two sets of *appartements*, or suites of rooms, one formal and one private. By the early 1700s there could be three types of suite, a formal one, an intimate one, and several private ones, but they gradually became absorbed into each other until, by the end of the eighteenth century, multiple suites were a rarity in all except the grandest houses. For this reason, names of rooms can be confusing. The name *salon*, for example, does not describe the same room at the beginning of the century as it does at the end. The *cabinet*, which during the reign of Louis XIV was the principal private room, became the *salon de compagnie* or *salon* for short, and the early eighteenth-century *salon* gradually became known as the *salle à manger*. Smaller *cabinets* became boudoirs.

By the late seventeenth century houses were built with a double thickness of rooms, necessary to accommodate the secondary apartments and the corridors which serviced them. The *enfilade* of principal reception rooms was placed on the garden side, while the secondary rooms were on the entrance side. Flues did not need to project into rooms, so the traditional arrangement of fireplaces, in the centre of the wall opposite the entrance into the room, could be respected even with a more complicated distribution. Partitions were erected in existing houses, to create smaller and more specialist rooms as well as passages. Traditional arrangements subsisted longer in châteaux in the country than in Paris houses and apartments; indeed, the need for multiplying the functions of rooms in town houses contributed to long-term change in room distribution. Some eighteenth-century châteaux have a curious arrangement of rooms which is a direct result of the transition experienced at this epoch; there are one or two main reception rooms but the bulk of the space is taken up by individual suites consisting of bedroom, *cabinet* or boudoir and one or more *garderobes*.

There were, of course, endless variations in room distribution. The first Palais-Bourbon, built in the 1720s, was considered a model in its time and offered the following progression: oval *vestibule* (entered not in the centre of the façade, but at one end), first *antichambre*, second *antichambre* also called *salle à manger*, oval *salon*, *chambre de parade*,

*grand cabinet, galerie*, and finally an *appartement des bains*. A further two rooms completed the formal ensemble, a *salle d'assemblée* and a bedroom with the bed area protected by a balustrade. Parallel were many small rooms comprising several private apartments. Three different purposes are served here: *parade* or receiving on a grand scale, *société* or everyday living with friends and relatives, and *commodité*, or living in practical comfort.

## THE VESTIBULE

According to the *Dictionnaire de l'Académie Française* of 1776, the *vestibule* was "The first room upon entering a building; from there one goes into other rooms." While it was often elaborately decorated, it was generally sparsely furnished, usually only with benches. Floors were laid with octagonal pieces of white stone alternating with small black marble squares (*cabochons*) laid diagonally, a type of paving that was often carried on into the next room, the dining room or *salon*.

Blondel, in his *Traité de l'architecture dans le goût moderne* of 1737-8, states of this room that it "is used to convey an idea of the grandeur of the rooms which follow it." The *vestibule* at the Château de Bellevue, built for Madame de Pompadour in 1749, was a large room paved with marble, with walls of visible masonry. The architectural ornament of the exterior was continued here (it was common practice to use this room as a transition between the outside and the inside), in this case with simple horizontal mouldings. Niches on either side contained life-size, allegorical, marble female figures, one of Music by Falconet (said to be Madame de Pompadour herself), and one of Poetry by Adam. It was furnished with marble-topped buffets, and therefore acted as a *salle des buffets*, the room found before the dining room.

The *vestibule* in the Comtesse de Provence's tiny pavilion at Montreuil (1784) was open to the elements on one side, but nevertheless had a ceiling painted in trompe l'oeil to look like the sky, and contained four benches supplied by Jacob.

As *vestibules* served as waiting rooms for servants, they were often known as *antichambres de la livrée*, as at the Hôtel de Lassay, bought by the Prince de Condé as an annexe to the Palais-Bourbon in 1768. It was also sometimes called the first *antichambre*, and was followed by a second, which Blondel states should be decorated as follows: "tapestries should be hung here, above panelling of chest height ... The overdoors should contain paintings with subjects appropriate to the pastimes or Offices of the Master of the house. Giltwood tables with marble tops may be placed between the windows."

In a letter to the Countess of Suffolk in 1765, Horace Walpole described the Paris house of the enormously wealthy banker Laborde: "You must have a first and second antechamber and they must have nothing in them but dirty servants." The sentiment was echoed by Blondel who states that looking-glasses should not be placed above fireplaces in *antichambres*. Instead there should be edifying pictures which must be out of reach so that the servants should be unable to dirty them by touching them.

The staircase often gave directly on to the *vestibule* or the *salon*. Blondel pronounced that noble staircases should be of stone, with pilasters, niches, and decorative sculpture in panels. Wood staircases were only suitable for servants.

*Coupe du Château de Petit-Bourg par le milieu sur la largeur* (Sideways section through the centre of the Château de Petit-Bourg). View of the *salon*, showing one of the fountains and one of the chimneypieces.

*S*taircase in a house in the Faubourg Saint-Germain, remodelled by the architect P. M. Mouret in 1751. The stark decoration is intended to act as a transition between exterior architecture and the interior.

*D*etail of the stair balustrade. About 1751.

# THE SALON AND SALLE À MANGER

The next room was usually referred to as the *salon* or *salle à manger*. Its purpose altered according to the size and importance of the building. Generally, it was used as a ceremonial reception room and for banquets (which took place not in the evening but in the afternoon), while the conditions for more intimate dining gradually came to be met by a separate room. The *Dictionnaire de l'Académie Française* describes the *salon* as "normally larger and more elaborately decorated than the others . . . The word *salon* is also used to describe a room which is not used as a *cabinet*, or as a bedroom, and in which one may assemble." Its importance was registered by Philippe Marnet, a Paris agent of the Court of Parma, who wrote in 1768 that "it is for these rooms that one

*Salle à manger* in the Château de Villette, near Pontoise, with wall fountains (shown in detail on the left) and buffets in stone. While the buffet dates from the end of the seventeenth century, the niches were added in 1748, at the same time as the panelling, which was invoiced in that year by Bouquelet and Duteille. The paintings inset in the panelling are by Descloches, a member of the Académie de Saint Luc, and are taken from engravings by Huquier after Boucher of *Scènes de la vie chinoise*.

*D*rawing of the *salon* of the Château de Brunoy, signed by Jean-Démosthène Dugourc and dated 1781. The Comte de Provence employed Dugourc at Brunoy, and the *salon*, though already finished in 1780, may have been his work; certainly the arabesques are typical. The torchères support crystal-hung candelabra.

tries to provide the richest decoration." It was often only in the *salon* that the "orders" of architecture were used, frequently as pilasters rather than as columns. The room was usually panelled in wood or stone, and not hung with tapestries or silk. It was heated by a fireplace or a stove, often a monumental one in an alcove, and could be fitted with marble basins with gilt-lead ornaments spouting water, and marble-topped tables set into the walls to act as sideboards. The floor was likely to be of stone or marble, and the lighting was provided by lanterns hanging from the ceiling, as well as by candelabra supported on torchères. In some cases, the candelabra supports were incorporated into the panelling. Permanent furniture was scarce, but tables and chairs were brought in for banqueting. André-Jacob Roubo states in his *L'art du menuisier* (1769-70) that caned chairs were often used for this purpose.

The name *salon à l'Italienne* was given to large rooms two storeys high, often domed and lit from above, and with elaborate decoration such as painted walls, as well as columns or pilasters.

The *salon* at Petit-Bourg, decorated by Vassé for the Duc d'Antin (the work was finished in 1724), was a large rectangular room. Its walls were decorated with fluted composite pilasters and allegorical trophies. There were portraits of Louis XIV and Louis XV above each of the two marble fireplaces, and marble fountains supporting putti holding shells of gilt-lead. The floor was paved with marble squares divided by bands of the same *vert campan* marble as the fireplaces and the fountains. The only permanent furniture was a set of benches. The once-popular practice of placing fountains in dining rooms (see page 55) was gradually abandoned, firstly because they encouraged damp, and

secondly because it became the habit to dine in smaller rooms without servants, and fountains therefore became impractical.

At Bellevue, built in 1749, the equivalent room is described both as the *salle à manger* and as the *grand salon*. The panelling was carved by Verbeckt with attributes of hunting and fishing, and painted white. Again there were two fireplaces, containing identical firedogs in the shape of putti holding arrows, glasses and bottles, and very large firetongs. These and all the other gilt-bronze objects were supplied by Lazare Duvaux. There were looking-glasses above the fireplaces, as well as above console tables facing the windows, and on either side of each were wall lights. The overdoors were painted by Oudry with hounds and game. Gilt-bronze mounted porcelain vases sat on the console

*O*ctagonal *salon* in the Comtesse de Provence's garden pavilion at Montreuil, near Versailles, built by her architect Jean-François Chalgrin in 1784. The garlands of flowers are executed in stucco. Georges Jacob provided for this room a set of eight lavishly carved armchairs with angled backs to fit into each of the eight angles. He also supplied a matching firescreen, two *fauteuils en cabriolet*, three *ottomanes* without backs and six chairs. None of this furniture survives *in situ*.

*F*auteuil d'angle* by Georges Jacob, circa 1784. Probably one of the eight delivered for the octagonal *salon* in the Comtesse de Provence's garden pavilion at Montreuil, near Versailles. Jacob's *Mémoire* describes the carving in great detail, including that of the supports of the armrests, which were originally painted: *tournées en balustre et enrichies de feuilles de laurier, cannelures, perles enfilées et tores de cordes* (baluster-turned and decorated with laurel leaves, fluting, strings of beads and rope-twist).

tables and on the fireplaces. Of the several gilt-bronze lanterns, one was mounted with Meissen birds and Vincennes flowers. This room was on the central axis of the house, with Madame de Pompadour's bedroom on one side, and a *salon de compagnie* or *cabinet des jeux* on the other.

It became the growing practice to exclude servants from dining rooms, both because of the need for intimacy and because space was too restricted. The Duchesse d'Orléans (Princess Palatine) complained of "twenty footmen who watch you eat every mouthful", while the lawyer Barbier considered it unusual enough to consign to his *Journal* in 1760 that the King had actually poured wine himself to the Archbishop of Paris, because the bottles were on the table: "this happens either in the country, or in the King's intimate supper parties at Versailles, because of the lack of space for servants."

The Princess Kinsky, an Austrian naturalized French in 1766, set up house in the Rue Saint-Dominique in 1774, and from 1777 proceeded to

*R*afraichissoir stamped by Nicolas Petit, 1765-70. The top is removable and reveals a white marble shelf and spaces for cutlery and a bottle, thus pointing to its use for meals such as the *soupers des petits cabinets* at Versailles.

redecorate the principal suite of rooms. This consisted of an *antichambre* followed by a *salle à manger*, leading to three rooms on the garden front, first the room known under the previous occupant, Madame de Gourgues, as the *antichambre des valets de chambre*, then a *salon de compagnie* and finally a bedroom. In the *salle à manger* the Princess placed a new variation on the usual fountain, situated in the centre of the room and with the dining table fitted around it.

When Blondel stated as early as 1737 that the *salle à manger* "should have a parquet floor, and walls with panelling painted white on which is carving picked out in gilding", he was referring to a specialist room which was no longer used as a *salon* in the traditional sense. As the century progressed, so did the use of the *salon*. At Montreuil, a tiny building of 1784, there was both a *salle à manger* and a *salon*. After the vestibule came the dining room, painted in trompe l'oeil to resemble a trellis pavilion in a garden, and then the octagonal *salon*, with arched mirrored panels (see previous page).

Writing about *salles de compagnie*, Blondel stated that "one should be careful to arrange chairs in a room according to the number of people who are going to use it, in order to avoid bringing in additional chairs, which would upset the arrangement of the remainder of the furniture, such as marble tables, torchères and benches." The *salon de compagnie* or *cabinet des jeux* at Bellevue had carved panelling, and six allegorical paintings by Van Loo, two above the doors (*Tragedy* and *Comedy*) and four above the windows (*Architecture, Painting, Sculpture* and *Music*). The chandelier and wall lights were hung with crystal drops. In 1751 Lazare Duveaux delivered for this room a pair of Meissen vases, painted with scenes after Watteau, and mounted with gilt-bronze and Vincennes flowers, for pot-pourri. He supplied a tric-trac games table in 1754. The main set of chairs consisted of four *bergères* with bolsters, four *fauteuils* and two chairs, all with loose cushions, while a further six chairs were upholstered normally, indicating that this room would have been used as a *salon* in the modern French sense of a drawing room.

The Princess Kinsky was an ardent musician and her *antichambre des valets de chambre* became a *salon de musique*. The ceiling was painted with a scene of Olympian gods listening to Anacréon, while the walls were decorated with carved and gilded pilasters and mirrors in niches. A white marble chimneypiece was placed between the two windows on the garden side. The models for the gilt-bronze ornaments were provided by Gilles-Paul Cauvet, who also carved the pilasters and the case of the harpsichord.

## THE LIBRARY

Libraries were normally equipped with built-in bookcases, carved, painted and gilded to match the remainder of the panelling. The Bellevue library was lacquered by Martin, and the inside of the bookcases lined with *papier de Paris* by Duvaux. The doors could be disguised as false bookcases; bookbacks were supplied by the Royal binder for such doors for the libraries of both Louis XVI and Marie Antoinette at Versailles.

*L*ibrary in an Hôtel in the Faubourg Saint-Germain, mid-eighteenth century. The incorporated bookcases are surmounted by plain panelling.

## THE GALLERY

"A room of much greater length than width, in which one can walk without getting wet". This bland description in the *Dictionnaire* hides the *galerie*, one of the great decorative achievements of the seventeenth century, the apotheosis of which was the Galerie des Glaces at Versailles. The importance of the gallery waned gradually during the eighteenth century, and it is only found in the very grandest houses. The *galerie* at the Hôtel de Toulouse in Paris, decorated by Robert de Cotte and François-Antoine Vassé between 1717 and 1720, represents one of the last major examples of the type. With rounded ends, and shaped panels separated by pilasters, it was designed to contain a collection of paintings and celebrated with allegories the achievements of the Comte de Toulouse, a bastard son of Louis XIV who held the posts of Grand Veneur (Master of the King's Hunt) and Grand Amiral (Chief Admiral). This naturally provided rich allegorical material. The gallery was furnished with giltwood sofas along one wall, and console tables flanked by footstools on the other.

The Marquis de Marigny's last house, the Hôtel de Massiac on the Place des Victoires (he moved there in 1778 and died in 1781), contained a gallery in which Marigny hung paintings on walls covered with crimson moiré silk. Presumably to economize on space, he also used this room as a *salon des jeux*. His posthumous inventory records no less than thirty mahogany armchairs and twelve games tables including two tric-trac tables.

## BEDROOMS

The *chambre de parade* or *chambre du dais*, a formal bedroom which was the culmination of a grand suite of rooms in the seventeenth century, gradually ceased to be a focus of social life during the eighteenth century. It might even be used for other purposes. The Duc de Choiseul, as chief minister to Louis XV, naturally possessed one, but turned it into a *cabinet de travail* (see page 26). Blondel insisted on its importance, saying: "it must be elaborately decorated." He added that the panelling should be varnished and not painted, since white or yellow paint are colours resembling stone, and this would be inappropriate. A marble table should also face the chimneypiece to respect symmetry.

These grand bedrooms traditionally contained a bed alcove, which might be framed with pilasters or columns, such as the one at the Palais-Royal, decorated by Contant d'Ivry in 1755-8. A balustrade separated the alcove from the remainder of the room. While it was customary to hang tapestries only in the alcove, beds were no longer raised on a platform, as had been common practice in the seventeenth century.

Madame de Pompadour's bedroom at Bellevue was known as the *chambre à la Turque* on account of the Van Loo paintings of a *sultane* (said to resemble the mistress of the house), being presented with a cup of tea by a black slave girl, and working at her embroidery frame. The walls, the four-poster bed with ends *à la Turque*, crowned by a high canopy *à l'Impériale*, and the chairs, upholstered *à châssis* (with

*Chambre de parade* with its *lit à la Polonaise* at the Château d'Ussé, 1770-80.

removable panels) were all covered with Chinese silk.

The redecoration of the bedroom at the Hôtel Kinsky was no less complete than that of the *salon de musique*. Apollo and Phaeton were the subjects of the ceiling painting, and the walls were covered with rich panelling, which the Princess evidently found too simple, for in 1786 she had it further embellished with plaster flowers. The *lit à la Polonaise* bore the Princess's initials below an Imperial crown and was capped by no less than fifty-two ostrich feathers; the commode, corner cupboards and secretaire were *en suite*. The room was followed by a sumptuous *appartement des bains*.

## CABINETS

The room traditionally called *grand cabinet* or *cabinet* was still, at the beginning of the eighteenth century, the principal reception room in a private or intimate suite of rooms. Its function split into two, and it became either the *salon de compagnie*, or a boudoir. Paintings could be hung there, but during the second quarter of the century the craze for carved panelling invaded *cabinets* as well.

When describing Laborde's house in 1765, Horace Walpole emphasized the ceremonial aspect of this type of room: "Next (after *antichambres*) must be the *grand cabinet*, hung with red damask, in gold frames, and covered with eight large and very bad pictures that cost four thousand pounds . . . Under these, to give an air of lightness, must be hung bas-reliefs in marble. Then there must be immense armoires of tortoise shell and or moulu[sic], inlaid with medals." In contrast, the definition in the 1776 *Dictionnaire* tends towards the intimate aspect of the room: "A retiring room in which to work, or to talk in private, for keeping papers and books, as well as paintings or precious objects".

The charm of small *cabinets* and boudoirs derived from the care with which they were decorated. Blondel was an ardent advocate of this: "nothing must be neglected to ensure that its decoration is lively and romantic. It is here that imagination can take flight and allow one's fancy

to triumph, while in formal apartments, the strictest rules of decorum and good taste should be adhered to rigidly."

Blondel would no doubt have approved of Trémicourt's two boudoirs, and would have sanctioned the lyricism of Walpole's letter to the Countess of Ossory in September 1775: "The grand *cabinet* [of Madame de Mirepoix's house] is round, all white and gold and glasses with curtains in festoons of silk flambé, and illuminated by four branches of lilies of or-mulu, each as loose and graceful as that which Guido's angel holds in the Salutation at the Carmelites."

Madame de Pompadour's *cabinet* at Bellevue had a low ceiling, since there was a mezzanine room above, and was decorated with painted and gilt panelling by Martin, and a chinoiserie painting by Boucher. It probably contained a bidet and a *chaise d'affaire*, both pieces which reflect the intimate use of the room.

## APPARTEMENT DES BAINS

The elaborate decoration of *appartement des bains* suggests that bathing was more than a simple hygienic pastime. Indeed it seems to have been a pleasure, if a rare and principally female one. Bastide credited Trémicourt's with decoration by some significant artists, including Perrot (whose main job was as designer at the Savonnerie), Boucher, François-Thomas Germain and Bachelier. Not all grand houses of the period contained an *appartement des bains*, but it normally consisted of several rooms, starting perhaps with an *antichambre* followed by a *chambre des bains* with two bathtubs, one with soapy water and one for rinsing, and a further room for resting afterwards (see the description of the *appartement des bains* at Cirey in Appendix One).

Mademoiselle Dervieux's bathroom, like the rest of her house, was decorated in a perfect version of the *goût étrusque*. This famous actress, who married the architect Belanger in 1794, must surely have used it for more voluptuous purposes than a daily scrub. There were bas-reliefs on the walls, a round marble tub in the centre and a minstrel's gallery.

*P*ilasters, walls painted to resemble stone and trompe-l'oeil paintings by Sauvage, imitating low-relief carving, decorate this late eighteenth-century room at the Château de Compiègne, which Napoleon later used as a dining room.

# 5
# ARCHITECTURAL DECORATION

*B*oudoir from the Hôtel d'Hocqueville in Rouen, 1780s. The principal panels are decorated with painted cast plaster reliefs, while the frames are grained. The boudoir has an alcove which was designed to contain an *ottomane*.

*D*esign for the ceiling and floor of a *cabinet de parade*, by Dugourc, late eighteenth century. The floor was to be of marble arranged in geometric patterns, and the ceiling painted though not domed.

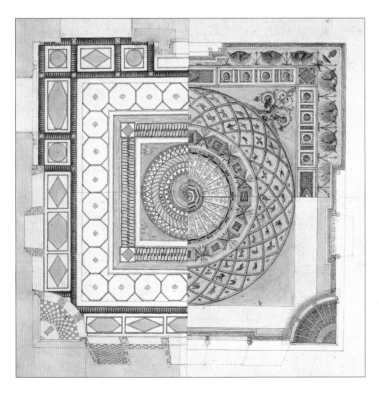

"I have seen but one idea in all the houses here; the rooms are white and gold or white, a lustre, a vast glass over the chimney and another opposite and generally a third over against the windows. In the bedchamber is a piece of hanging behind and on each side of the bed, the rest of the room is stark naked. Now and then there is a piece of tapestry of damask opposite to the windows; but surely there is nothing in which they so totally want imagination as in the furniture [decoration] of their houses. I have seen the Hôtels de Soubise, de Luxembourg, de Maurepas, de Brancas and several others especially the boasted Hôtel de Richelieu and could not perceive any difference but in more or less gold, more or less baubles on the chimneys and tables and now and then Vanloo has sprawled goddesses over the doors and at other times Boucher." Thus wrote Horace Walpole from Paris to Miss Anne Pitt, on Christmas Day, 1765.

## PANELLING

Carved and painted wood panelling formed the principal decoration of walls in important reception rooms. Textiles such as silks from Lyon, linen and cotton from France and Flanders, and more exotic or versatile materials such as paper, could provide a cheaper or more colourful alternative, but most elegant houses contained at least one panelled principal room until the very end of the eighteenth century. Carved, painted and gilt-wood panelling gradually replaced marble and gilt-bronze wall decoration in royal palaces because of the expense of these materials.

Wherever possible, panelling was arranged on every wall with symmetry, thereby conferring a noble architectural character on a room. The chimneypiece usually stood in the centre of the wall opposite the entrance, flanked by matching panels. Panels incorporating looking-glasses, with console tables below them, reflected either the chimney-

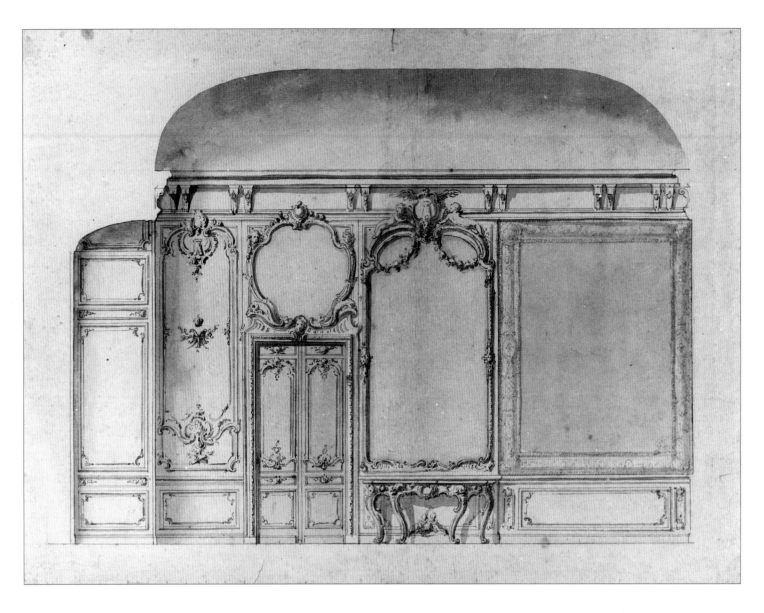

piece or the windows. There could also be mirrors and consoles between the windows. Doors were placed symmetrically; many of these are false, especially in older buildings adapted in the eighteenth century. The importance of symmetry can be judged by the engravings of Meissonier, in which he respects this principle for wall panel disposition, if for little else.

The chimneypiece and its incorporated overmantel mirror formed the principal focus of a room, and consequently received the finest and often the only decorative carving. When the entire room was to be covered in carved panelling, the chimneypiece, mirror frames and overdoors could be more finely and elaborately carved than the wall panels, and the doors were often left comparatively plain. The panels below the dado rail almost invariably bore simple mouldings, because they were likely to be hidden by furniture. When they are as elaborately carved as the rest, this indicates that a room was to contain no furniture against the wall.

Throughout the eighteenth century, plain moulded wall panelling

*D*esign by Ange-Jacques Gabriel for the decoration of a room in the Versailles apartment of the Dauphine Marie-Thérèse d'Espagne, dating from the mid-1740s. The room was intended to contain carved panelling as well as tapestry. The console table stands below a large looking-glass, which, like the carved panel to the left of the door, is surmounted by a carving of a tower, the arms of Castile. The cornice of the room can be dated to circa 1720 due to the use of paired brackets. Note the dolphins (appropriate for the Dauphin) supporting the cartouche-shaped frame of the overdoor painting.

constituted the staple diet of the workshops of the *menuisiers en bâtiments* (as opposed to the *menuisiers en meubles*). In the early part of the century, panels were rectilinear with heavy mouldings. At the height of the rococo era, they could have bow-shaped tops, and with the advent of neoclassicism square and rectangular shapes were framed with elegant restrained mouldings. Often the only decoration of panelling consisted of sculpture on the moulding itself, in the form of vivacious leaf scrolls in the rococo period, or a formal frieze such as "egg and dart" for neoclassical panelling. When a room was hung with tapestry, material or paper, this was framed by white or grey painted panelling, with gilt or painted mouldings hiding the edge of the *tenture* in the same way as they were used to frame looking-glasses.

Panelling was normally painted, often in two shades of a colour or in contrasting colours. Light colours found more favour than dark; Count Tessin's comment about the *cabinet* in the Hôtel de Richelieu in a letter of 1741 to his architect Hårleman confirms this: "nothing is as fine as far as workmanship is concerned, but nothing appears so sad; the light of two hundred candles is swallowed up, and the same number again would not survive the black lacquer and the mirrors. These days only light colours are in fashion, especially yellow and celadon." With the appearance of the *goût grec* cold colours such as pearl grey and grey blue became popular. The use of gilding was more restrained than surviving examples would imply; Louis XV carving such as that by Verbeckt on the first-floor apartment at Versailles is mostly gilded, but in private houses gilding was normally restricted to the one or two grandest rooms, contrasts of colour and texture being employed instead.

*Boiseries* or *lambris* (both meaning panelling) incorporating elaborate sculpture were the work of *sculpteurs* who were almost invariably members of the Académie de Saint Luc. Fine *lambris* represented a considerable expense and it seems that only the largest and most competent workshops regularly undertook this sort of work, particularly where the most magnificent panelled rooms of the Louis XV period were concerned.

*Sculpteurs* frequently produced their own designs, as well as implementing those provided by architects. Designs for carved decoration could be drawn life-size on the bare plaster walls, alternatives sometimes being provided from which the client or architect could make a choice. The selected drawing was then rubbed onto tracing paper which was used to mark out the wooden framed panels supplied by the *menuisiers*. Drawings of this type found recently on walls at Versailles have enabled panelled rooms to be recreated.

Carved trophies count among the most popular motifs for panelling, being found suspended on carved ribbons from the tops of panels in both the Louis XV and Louis XVI periods. The panelling of the *salon de compagnie* from the Hôtel d'Uzès, now in the Musée Carnavalet, was designed by Ledoux in 1767; it makes reference to the Duc d'Uzès's military achievements, which included having been present at Louis XV's great victory over the Duke of Cumberland at Fontenoy in 1745. Military trophies are hung, unusually, on small trees with lush and varied foliage. For the doors, a more traditional arrangement prevailed, with a ribbon-tied loop supporting trophies with shields symbolic of the Four Continents, including camels, horses, alligators and elephants. The gilt trophies stand out against the white ground, with contrasting matting and burnishing to emphasize the three-dimensional effect.

Elaborate panelled rooms were not intended for hanging paintings other than in the overdoor or overmantel panels, although some exceptions of the Louis XVI period have oval mouldings to act as portrait frames in the centre of the main panels. Many neoclassical *salons* contained decorations which are not fixed to the wall, but could have been the work of the sculptors responsible for the wall decoration. The space between pilasters could be punctuated with tapering pedestals (*gaines*) bearing busts or terracotta vases, and niches might contain freestanding

sculptures. Carved furniture, both chairs and console tables, were normally ordered at the same time in order to harmonize with the panelling and other carved, painted or gilded decorations, but survival of such ensembles is practically unknown. The *menuisier* Gontier was employed by the Princess Kinsky to provide all types of work for her Hôtel in the Rue Saint-Dominique in the 1780s, some of which was to be carved by Cauvet, or painted by Jean-Félix Watin, the author of *L'Art du peintre-doreur-vernisseur*. As well as wall panelling, Gontier supplied commodes, sofas, picture frames and a *lit à la Polonaise*. He was also responsible for the erection of scaffolding in the Princess's bedroom so that Julien could paint the ceiling.

In the first half of the eighteenth century, overdoors usually contained paintings, the frame of which formed part of the panelling.

*P*air of pedestals in gilded and painted wood, surmounted by terracotta vases representing Summer and Winter. Originally part of a set of four made before 1760 for Ange-Laurent de Lalive de Jully. The pedestals were designed by Louis-Joseph Le Lorrain and the vases were made by the sculptor Louis-Felix de la Rue, a member of the Académie de Saint Luc. They appear to have been designed *en suite* with the famous set of ebony and gilt-bronze furniture which Lalive commissioned for his Cabinet Flamand, and their role was to complement the architectural decoration of the room.

*Salon* at the Château de Montmirail (Sarthe), mid-eighteenth century. Note the traditional placing of the console table below the looking-glass, which is set into the panelling.

*L*ate eighteenth-century room panelling, installed in a bathroom at the Villa Ile-de-France, St. Jean-Cap Ferrat, in the early twentieth century. Note the manner in which the carved scrolls emerge from the panelling and join the console table, which must therefore have been provided by the same *menuisier* or *sculpteur*.

Overdoor paintings were commissioned from the finest artists of the period, such as Boucher, Oudry, Chardin and Lancret to name but a few. Suitably allegorical subjects might be chosen, such as the Seasons, hunts or the arts; for his Grand Cabinet at Versailles in 1751 the Dauphin Louis, son of Louis XV, chose his four sisters painted by Nattier as the Four Elements.

The rise of the *goût grec*, far from putting a stop to this habit, saw the overdoor become in many cases the most elaborate element of decoration in a room. Paintings continued to be employed, putti remaining a favourite motif, and Piat-Joseph Sauvage painted many in a grisaille trompe-l'oeil technique, imitating low-relief sculpture. Indeed sculpture itself increasingly predominated, with medallions, garlands and vases as well as putti carved in wood or stucco. The sculptor Philippe-Laurent Roland (1746-1816), a member of the superior Académie Royale, supplied stucco Muses for the overdoors of Marie Antoinette's boudoir at Fontainebleau in 1786.

François Roumier (circa 1690-1748) used the title of Sculpteur du Roi from at least 1721. That he was competent at designing his own work is proved by his surviving engravings for panelling decoration, picture frames and console tables, which exhibit a convoluted rococo style probably influenced by his work for the Garde-Meuble for which he was provided with designs by the Slodtz brothers. For Versailles he carved panelling, console tables, chairs and torchères, and for the Duc de Richelieu in 1732, he carved the surrounds for lacquer panels for a *cabinet chinois* (possibly for the room criticized by Tessin). A panel from this room, which survives in the Musée Carnavalet, testifies to the close stylistic links between the exotic and the rococo; the lacquer painting shows a bird being attacked by Chinamen, and Roumier's border is carved with similarly strange birds, as well as monkeys with Chinese hats.

The *livre-journal* kept by the sculptor and member of the Académie de Saint Luc, François-Joseph Duret (1729-1816), provides a useful illustration of the competence and versatility of an artist involved in in-terior decoration in the second half of the eighteenth century. Much of Duret's work consisted of elements of carving to be placed in previously designed decorative schemes, either in wood or plaster. He specialized in decorative figure sculpture, such as bas-reliefs of children, garlands of flowers, medallions and trophies, many of which were destined for overdoors. He could also provide picture and tapestry frames, and sculptural elements for furniture, as well as scale models to show to clients. He seems not to have executed the entire decoration of any one room on his own, but this was probably because architects preferred to spread the load. The question of specialization was also involved; Duret carved the figures of children for the new torchères intended for the Galerie des Glaces at Versailles in 1769. They were designed by Gondoin and the remainder of the carving was by Toussaint Foliot, who himself ordered the carving of the children from Duret. He replaced missing pieces on ancient marbles, and was once called upon to do the same for a living person, the Duc de la Vrillière, for whom he made articulated artificial hands in plaster covered with leather.

# CARVED PLASTER AND STUCCO

"Mad. de Mirepoix's house, where I supped last night is charming . . . The *salle à manger* is all of stucco, highly polished, representing white marble with panels of vert antique." Walpole's letter to the Countess of Ossory, written in September 1775, bore witness to a popular fashion. In the rococo period, carved plaster was used principally for ceiling decoration, although examples are known, especially in the country, of plaster imitating wood panelling. A frieze above the panelling could be decorated with a running motif in the same style, which was taken up for the rosette in the centre of the ceiling. Work of this sort was carried out by the sculptors who had carved the panelling. In rare cases, such as the two oval *salons* at the Hôtel de Soubise in Paris, the

*P*laster cornice in the *vestibule* of an Hôtel in the Faubourg Saint-Germain, circa 1725-30. This type of continuous decoration replaced paired brackets in cornices by 1725. Gradually, figural motifs made way for rococo scrolls and foliage.

*Salon* at the Château de Condé-en-Brie, near Soissons, painted by Giovanni-Niccolo Servandoni, mid-eighteenth century. A pioneer of the neoclassical style, Servandoni excelled in the design of theatre scenery as well as architecture.

decoration of the ceiling is more elaborate than the panelling, and different sculptors may have been employed.

Painted and polished stucco began to imitate marble from the 1750s, both in wall decoration and for vases and pedestals. This was considered appropriate for *antichambres*, dining rooms, *chambres des bains* and other rooms where marble might have otherwise been used. Stucco could also be painted with other designs, such as arabesques; these were especially popular during the Louis XVI period, since they imitated not only the colouring but the texture of ancient frescoes.

Louis Mansiaux, called Chevalier, was probably a pupil of one of the Martin family of lacquerers. His work consisted mainly of architectural decoration in imitation of marble, and he supplied stucco decoration for Versailles in this style in 1756. During that year he also provided another type of decoration for the Dauphin, comprising panels with coloured animals on a white ground and pilasters with gardening trophies. His most celebrated commission for Versailles was Madame Sophie's library of 1769, a room taken over by Marie Antoinette in 1783. Borders imitating marble of different colours framed panels with landscapes or heavy arabesques which owe their inspiration as much to the Renaissance as to Antiquity.

Chevalier's activities were not limited to wall decoration; in 1778 he delivered to the Princesse de Conti for her house in the Rue Saint-Dominique (the former Hôtel Bonnier de la Mosson) a set of stuccoed torchères in the shape of caryatids holding lyres.

The neoclassical architects François-Joseph Belanger and Claude-Nicolas Ledoux both employed stucco as an alternative to carved panelling. Nicholas-François-Daniel Lhuillier supplied for Bagatelle, which was built by Belanger from 1777, panels of stucco with arabesque relief decoration, made to the architect's designs. These incorporated small framed panels which were then painted by Jean-Démosthène Dugourc (Belanger's brother-in-law and self-proclaimed pioneer of the *goût étrusque*) in imitation of ancient cameos. Together with Alexandre

Régnier, Lhuillier carved panels of arabesque foliage with putti to Belanger's designs for the summer dining room of the Comte d'Artois at the Château de Maisons between 1779 and 1781. Membership of the Académie de Saint Luc permitted artists to work in any material, and Régnier's name is frequently found in the accounts of the Garde-Meuble as a sculptor of seat furniture.

# PAINTED DECORATION

Colourful panels of painted arabesques are found in early eighteenth century interiors; some of these decorations were executed directly on the panelling, while others were painted on canvas. Among the late examples of this technique was the Cabinet d'Angle in the Hôtel Peyrenc de Moras in the Place Vendôme, dating from 1724. The wall panels were carved by Desgoullons and Legoupil with mouldings and incorporated carved cartouches in the middle of the top and the rounded base. The panels received arabesque paintings by Claude III Audran (who also painted the ceiling in similar style), which framed landscapes enclosed by elegant painted trelliswork, in each of which was a Watteauesque figure. These landscapes and figures were painted by Nicolas

*A*rabesque panel attributed to Claude Audran in the *salon* at the Château de Réveillon. Jules-Robert de Cotte, the son of Louis XIV's Surintendant des Bâtiments, bought Réveillon in 1730, and it is likely that he commissioned this decoration at that date. The central panel contains a scene from one of La Fontaine's fables.

FOLLOWING SPREAD
*D*etail of the ceiling decoration in the *salon* of the Hôtel de Villette, Paris.

Lancret, who was also responsible for the overdoors and overmantels. By the 1730s, carved decoration had become more popular than painted panels, and it was not until the neoclassical revival that it once again came into use on plain moulded wood panelling. Arabesques remained the favourite motif, albeit in an altered fashion.

*Au naturel* painting could be particularly attractive on panelling. The Dauphine's *cabinet intérieur* at Versailles, dating from 1747, had panelling carved and painted with foliage, flowers and birds, and that of a bedroom at the Hôtel de Comminges in Paris was described in an inventory in 1751 as "painted with Indian fruits and plants on a yellow ground". In the latter part of the century this technique continued to find favour, but by then it was applied to arabesques in carved wood or stucco, as well as to plain surfaces, in a neoclassical adaptation of the arabesques of the Renaissance, which confusingly had already been used as inspiration for those of the early eighteenth century.

Charles-Louis Clérisseau designed the painted decoration of the *salon* of the Hôtel Grimod de la Reynière in the early 1770s. This was much admired at the time, prompting the Polish architect Jana Christjana Kamsetzera to execute detailed drawings of it during his stay in Paris, on the orders of his king, Stanislaus Augustus Poniatowski. Panels of symmetrically arranged scrolling foliage framed oval medallions with paintings of scenes from mythology. The *Almanach des Artistes* of 1777 applauds the harmony of this decoration, noting that the overdoors and the ceiling were in matching style, and congratulates Clérisseau for seeking inspiration from Antiquity, as well as for avoiding excessive use of gilding. The author of the *Almanach* concludes by stating that sculpture is suitable for outside decoration, while painting is more appropriate for inside.

# MIRRORS

"Madame de Marchais ... has a house in a nut-shell, that is fuller of inventions than a fairy-tale; her bed stands in the middle of the room because there is no other space that would hold it; and is surrounded by such a perspective of looking glasses [sic], that you may see all that passes in it from the first antechamber." (Horace Walpole, to George Selwyn, 16 September 1775).

Mirror glass was a highly expensive commodity. This was partly due to the fact that pieces frequently broke either during manufacture or in transit. Tessin wrote philosophically to his wife in 1741: "We are unlucky with our mirrors; I have scolded the packer, but that does not

*A*rabesque wall panel, oil on canvas, circa 1780-85. In a style close to the panels of the *salon* in the Hôtel Grimod de la Reynière, or the painted stucco decoration at the Château de Bagatelle.

*G*iltwood looking-glass carved by Nicolas Pineau and Charles Bernard, 1731. From the gallery of the Hôtel de Villars, Paris. The painting of a Sybil incorporated in the top of the frame (*trumeau*) is after Guido Reni.

**W**atercolour of a wall of the *cabinet avant la galerie* in the house of the collector Jean de Julienne, circa 1756.

give us back our looking-glass." The architect Le Camus de Mézières, in his practical and realistic guide for potential clients of architects (*Le Guide de ceux qui veulent bâtir*, 1781), explains that the maximum possible size of mirrors was 100 × 50 *pouces* (270 × 135 cm) but it was rare for the Manufacture Royale at Saint-Gobain to make these successfully, and most people had to be content with smaller ones.

In addition, defects of manufacture were so frequent that in 1753 Claude Bonnet, the Paris agent of the Court of Parma, wrote to Guillaume Dutillot, the Parmesan Prime Minister, that even the King had to make do with imperfect mirrors. Le Camus entreated his readership not to expect perfection. His practical advice was to position those mirrors with fewest flaws in the most brightly lit places.

Glass sheets were made at Saint-Gobain, by pouring molten glass on to a large iron plate, and were then taken by boat down the River Oise to Paris. The workshops of the *miroitiers* in the Faubourg Saint-Antoine polished them and coated them with mercury. Le Camus noted with concern that the *miroitiers* made themselves even more ill than the gilders on metal.

The use of mirrors must have reached exaggerated proportions, for the author of the *Almanach des Artistes* of 1777, while conceding that when they reflect something interesting, mirrors are quite delightful, castigates them as being pointless when they surround a room so entirely that all they reflect is the person standing in it.

# WINDOW GLASS

According to Walpole, writing to the Countess of Suffolk on 5 December 1765, "Each window must consist of only eight panes of looking glass [sic]." Window glass was also supplied by *miroitiers*. Again, this had to be as large as possible, and came in several shades: the best was white (*blanc*), then came half-white (*demi-blanc*) and green (*verd*). This too could be expensive: Dufort de Cheverny thought it worth recording in his memoirs that he made his friend, the Comte d'Osmont, pay for the replacement of an expensive pane of *verre de Bohème*, broken when the Comte lost his temper while playing at tric-trac and flung the dice at the window. Another activity of the *miroitiers* was to make curved glass for lanterns; sheets of glass were heated with a blow-lamp and pressed between two-part terracotta moulds.

# FIREPLACES AND STOVES

Fireplaces and stoves were the only methods of heating, and they were by no means invariably successful. Many of the guests at the Château de Chanteloup during Choiseul's exile complained about the cold, and their predicament was not unique. Some attempts were made at invisible heating using stove pipes, but these remained relatively uncommon. Dufort de Cheverny described such a system at the house of du Jonquoy de Monville, stating that hidden pipes (*tuyaux de chaleur*) fed from stoves warmed the room sufficiently to make it seem like summer. The Marquis d'Argenson, writing in 1750, echoed another of the persistent complaints of the period: "Our stay at Bellevue was not pleasant. The rooms were permanently full of smoke."

## FIREPLACES

The shape of fireplaces remained constant during the eighteenth century. Two uprights supported a frieze with a wide shelf, above which a mirror was usually placed. Inside the fireplace was a cast-iron fire-back, normally decorated in low relief with the owner's coat of arms or some other decorative motif. The firedogs (*feu* or *grilles*) consisted of iron log supports which reached to the back of the fireplace, and which were concealed at the front by sculptural gilt-bronzes. At each side were small brackets (*croissants*) to hold the firetongs and shovel. In the summer, boards could be used to mask the fireplace openings. At the 1752 Salon held by the Académie de Saint Luc, Mademoiselle de Saint-Martin exhibited one painted with a small chimney sweep going up the chimney.

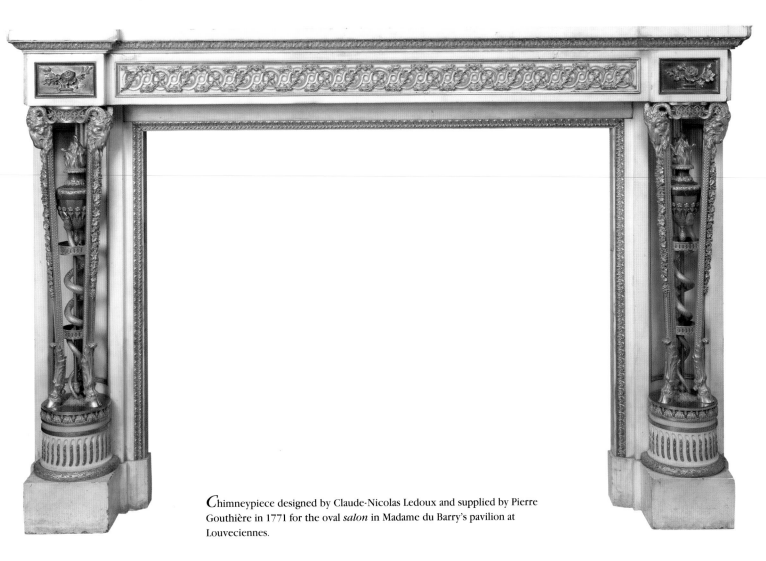

*C*himneypiece designed by Claude-Nicolas Ledoux and supplied by Pierre Gouthière in 1771 for the oval *salon* in Madame du Barry's pavilion at Louveciennes.

*M*arble chimneypiece and giltwood overmantel, of which a detail is shown above, 1730-40.

Fireplaces were made of marble or stone, and the finest marble ones were sometimes embellished with gilt-bronze. The fireplace of the Salon d'Hercule at Versailles, finished in 1730, is decorated with gilt-bronze lion masks, cornucopiae, and a mask of Hercules with a lion pelt. The Comte d'Artois's bedroom at Bagatelle, dating from 1777, has a fireplace by Augustin Bocciardi of white marble with *bleu turquin* marble cannon for uprights. The gilt-bronze ornaments were added by Gouthière.

Augustin Bocciardi, the author of the Bagatelle fireplaces, boasted of the title Sculpteur des Menus Plaisirs du Roi. Among his other work was the carved stand for the jewel cabinet supplied by the Menus Plaisirs to Marie Antoinette on the occasion of her wedding in 1770.

Members of the Académie de Saint Luc were not permitted to make vases, tabletops and fireplaces of marble. This was the exclusive right of members of the guild of *marbriers*. Notable *marbriers*, however, also possessed membership of the Académie, thereby confirming their status as artists and enabling them to broaden their activities.

Jacques Dropsy (d. 1753) became *maître sculpteur marbrier* after coming to Paris from the Hainault region, where *Rance* marble is found. He supplied a distinguished clientele, and worked for the Slodtz brothers. As well as secular work, he made numerous altars and monuments for churches. His son Jacques-François (1719-90) obtained the title of Marbrier ordinaire du Roi, and chimneypieces and tabletops from his workshop survive at Fontainebleau and at Versailles. He was succeeded in turn by his son, Jacques-Antoine (d. 1789). All three were members of the Académie de Saint Luc. They dealt directly with quarries, and some of their work was executed for stock rather than for specific clients. A particularly amusing example of Jacques-Antoine's work is to be found at the Château de Canon in Normandy. For the lawyer and *philosophe* Jean-Baptiste Jacques Elie de Beaumont, he carved quaint French, Latin and Greek mottoes in marble plaques of various colours, to be placed both in the park and above the doors of rooms in the house. The motto *qui ne sçut se borner, ne sçut jamais*

*jouir* (only by knowing your limits will you know enjoyment), was placed above the door of the room described as the dining room in the 1768 inventory.

Marble chimneypieces were designed to match the tops of commodes or tables, but even greater harmony could be achieved. The description of the *salon* in the Hôtel Grimod de la Reynière in the *Almanach des Artistes* of 1777 states that the fireplace is decorated with gilt-bronze ornaments which matched the gilt-bronze candelabra on pedestals in the four corners of the room. These, we are told, were of the same marble as the fireplace. Fireplaces of two contrasting colours of marble became popular in the neoclassical period; one such supplied by Jacques-Antoine Dropsy for Madame Adélaïde's bedroom at Bellevue in 1783 was of *sarrancolin*, and incorporated a frieze of veined white marble carved with a *cassolette* in the centre.

## STOVES

The architect Pierre-Alexis Delamair, writing in February 1719 about his proposed rebuilding of the Hôtel de Conti, included a two page dissertation entitled *Desseins de Poelles à la Françoise*. In this still unpublished manuscript, at the time of writing with a London dealer, he states that he was asked by the administrator of the Hôpital des Incurables in Paris for a method of heating the chapels which served as wards with stoves in the German fashion. The solution he suggested was as follows: cast-iron stoves in the shape of sculpture pedestals were to be placed in niches, the rounded tops of which would throw off the heat most efficiently. Upon the stoves would stand figures of the patron saints of the hospital, with the stove pipe rising up inside them. The door of the stove would be situated in a small room behind the niche, so that inside the chapel nothing would be seen other than an edifying ornament. For secular clients he proposed mythological subjects for the sculpture, such as Dido on her pyre, or a vase belching fire which would be caught by a dragon with open mouth. These were to be placed in *salles à manger* or *antichambres*.

Dufort de Cheverny described a less dignified but more entertaining version: "I was led into a stuccoed dining room, with an enormous faience stove on which stood an extremely fine figure of a woman, as black as ebony, in the pose of the Medici Venus, and similarly draped. Struck by her shapeliness, I approached and placed my hand upon a beautiful buttock; the softness of her flesh made me recoil in amazement: she was a Negress, and I had never seen one before. She threw her arms around my neck with typical abandon; it was a while before I recovered from the shock."

*Desseins de Poelles à la Françoise* (*Designs for French Stoves*) by Pierre-Alexis Delamair for the Hôtel de Conti in 1719.

*S*tove at the Château du Marais, circa 1780. The figure hides the stove pipe.

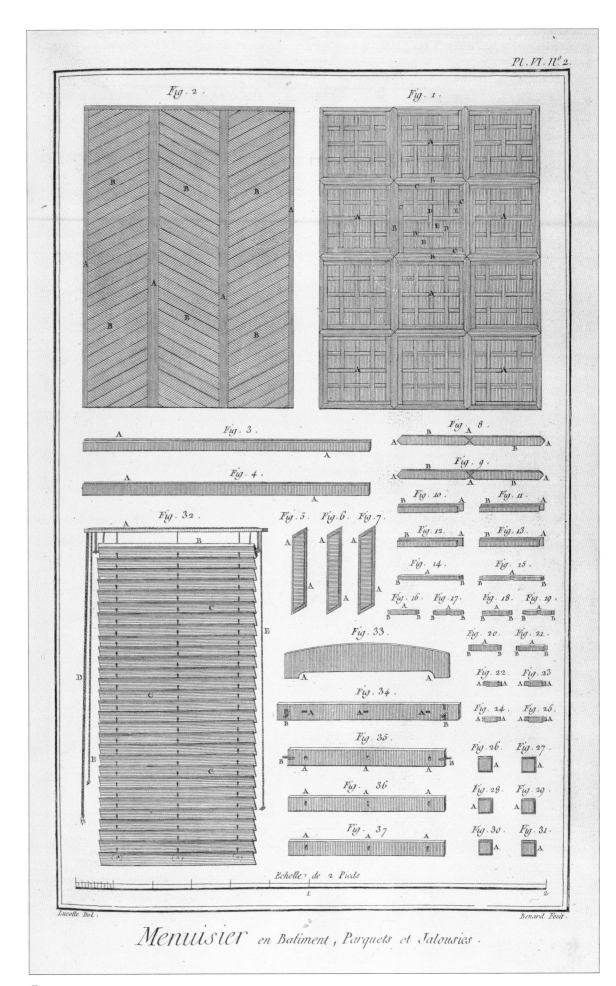

*Jalousie à la Persienne* (Venetian blind) and parquet floors. From the
*Menuisiers en Bâtiments* section of Diderot's *Encyclopédie*, 1765.

# 6
# FURNITURE

The Corporation des Menuisiers, the woodworkers guild, encompassed several specialities including *carrossiers* or coachbuilders, *menuisiers* or carpenters of two types (first, makers of architectural woodwork such as panelling, doors and console tables and secondly makers of movable woodwork, or furniture such as most chairs, beds and screens, some consoles, torchères and mirror or picture frames); and *ébénistes*, or makers of veneered case furniture. These categories were not separate by law, but had become so gradually through specialization, and it was uncommon, though not unknown, for anyone to practise in more than one.

New guild rules of 1743, confirmed in 1751, made it mandatory for members to stamp their production with their name. This seems merely to have confirmed an already well-established practice of stamping with a full name or with initials. There were, however, exceptions, notably in the case of furniture sold to dealers. Pieces verified by the *Jurés* were stamped with the guild mark "JME", standing for Jurande des Menuisiers-Ébénistes. It was illegal for anyone except a *maître* to own equipment for sharpening tools; apprentices and journeymen (*compagnons*) were theoretically therefore prevented from setting up on their own without proper qualification.

*D*etail of the *encoignure* (corner cupboard) shown on page 127.

*C*anapé from a suite made in about 1715-20 for the *galerie* in the Hôtel Crozat, Paris. The suite originally comprised twelve armchairs, two sofas, two benches and four stools. The upholstery is a rare survival, in morocco leather with applied strips edged by silk ribbon. The boar's head on the central leg is an uncommon use of animal motifs for seat furniture at this date.

# Menuiserie

The principal quarter in which the *menuisiers en meubles* operated was situated in the north of Paris, centring on the Rue de Cléry and the Rue de Bourbon-Villeneuve (now the Rue d'Aboukir). There many of the dynasties of chairmakers worked, for example the Tilliard and Sené families, and allied trades, such as sculptors, painter/gilders and upholsterers naturally gravitated to the area. Almost all of the *menuisiers en meubles* were French. Their craft was a traditional one, using well-established methods and for this reason slow to adapt to new ideas.

The techniques used by the *menuisiers* varied little during the eighteenth century. Chairs were normally of beech or walnut. Jean-François Bimont, in his *Principes de l'art du Tapissier* of 1770, states that walnut is best, but that if chairs are to be painted or gilded, it matters little what wood is employed. He adds that unless one looks carefully, the two can often be confused. In practice many *menuisiers* used both

indifferently, even for pieces with elaborate carving. Other woods are practically never found; rare exceptions include the very finely carved oak armchairs probably made by Nicolas-Quinibert Foliot and supplied to the Court of Parma in 1749.

The set of mahogany armchairs ordered by the Marquis de Marigny from the *ébéniste* Pierre Garnier in 1779 may well be the first in this wood, though it had already begun to be employed on case furniture by the mid-1760s. Georges Jacob was subsequently to make a speciality of mahogany chairs. He decorated them principally with fluting and fine mouldings, which showed off to best advantage the deep polish the wood could take.

The importance of the *menuisier* in the creation of a chair or console table varied according to how elaborate the carving was to be. For much of the basic production, *menuisiers* were able to produce mouldings and carve flowerheads, but as soon as something finer was required, a specialist sculptor was called in. These were members of the Académie de Saint Luc, and the carvings they executed could either be of their own invention, or from models provided by the architect or draughtsman if the chairs were part of a large building project. Obviously the *menuisier* and the *sculpteur* needed to work in close collab-

*Chaise-longue, circa 1740-50.*

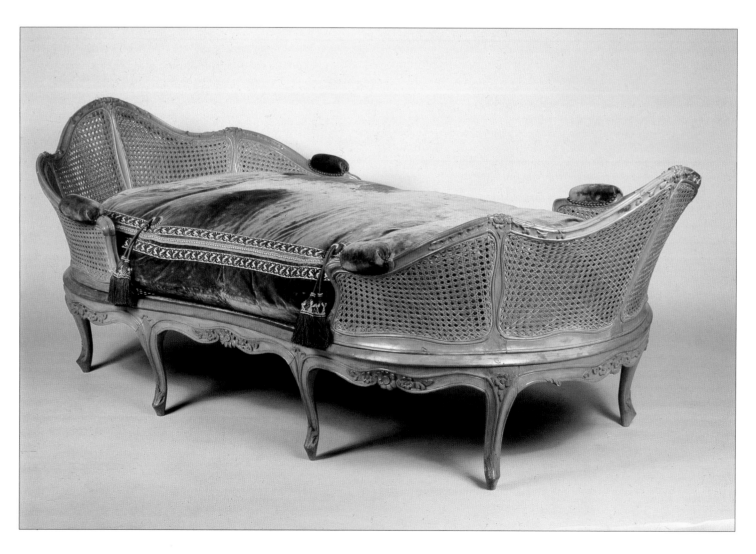

*O*ne of a set of twenty-four giltwood X-frame stools (*pliant*), circa 1740, still *in situ* in the Palais-Rohan, Strasbourg. Seats of this type were a hangover from the etiquette of the court of Louis XIV. In the eighteenth century their use was restricted to *chambres de parade* in such important houses.

oration, so that the former could provide blocks of the right size and shape for the latter to carve. Preparatory drawings might have been necessary, but unfortunately few seem to have survived and they may have been executed on the wood itself, as in the case of room panelling.

The *livre-journal* of the chairmaker Louis Delanois provides an example of the preparation of chairs. He delivered some furniture to the Comtesse du Barry (he spells the name "du Baril") in 1769, and he was careful to specify the thickness of the wood he had used for each part "so as to provide space for the carving".

There was nothing to prevent *menuisiers* from also being qualified *sculpteurs*, but in practice this rarely happened, an exception being Nicolas Heurtaut (1720-71) who, coming from a family of *sculpteurs*, became a member of the Académie de Saint Luc in 1742 (and married the daughter of a *menuisier*), settled in the Rue de Cléry and worked for various notable *menuisiers* until 1753, when he became a *maître-menuisier* himself, and was therefore able to make the frames of the chairs he carved. It should be added that he continued to carve chairs for other *menuisiers* and to subcontract the carving of his own chair-frames to other *sculpteurs*. He also provided architectural work such as frames for tapestries. Framemakers such as Jean Chérin and Etienne-Louis Infrois found it convenient to belong to both guilds, and it was as *menuisiers* that they sometimes stamped their production, not as *sculpteurs*. Toussaint Foliot, a member of a large family of chairmakers, became a *maître-sculpteur* in 1732, and worked not only for his relatives, but also for neighbours such as members of the Tilliard family, as well as for the Garde-Meuble. The names of independent furniture sculptors have rarely survived since they had no obligation to sign their work. Only in the case of the few who worked for the Garde-Meuble, such as Vallois, are their names known. This is a pity, since their role in the creation of a fine chair was infinitely more important than the *menuisier*'s.

Chairs were usually painted or gilded. This was done by specialist *peintres-doreurs* who worked not for the chairmaker but for a

*marchand-tapissier* (upholsterer). It was to the upholsterer that the client would usually go, although there were well-known exceptions, including Louis Delanois, whose *livre-journal* shows that he had a noble clientele of his own. The paint was normally matched to the rest of the decoration of a room, and often included natural colours for the carved flowers and leaves. Paint was thinly applied and protected by a coat of varnish or wax. Gilding, on the other hand, was applied on size (*apprêt*), which could dull the carving, so that a *répareur* had to sharpen up details and add further refinements such as the petals of flowers, or a fine trellis to a plain ground. In some cases, chairs were painted but had certain details gilded. Madame Victoire had at Bellevue in 1786 a set of chairs "with frames carved and painted green with gilt mouldings". The gilder Cagny's invoice for the suite of furniture sold by Delanois to Madame du Barry in 1769, as well as giving details of what sculpture was executed, adds that before gilding, the carving had to be "finely and carefully recarved . . . to revive it". Particular care was taken with this set, and Cagny justified the expense: "on account of the considerable amount of time spent by the recarvers and gilders, and the quantity and double use of the gold because of the great richness and fineness of the motifs". If a chair was to remain in natural wood, then the *menuisier* would wax or varnish it himself.

*M*ahogany *fauteuil de bureau* (desk chair) by Claude Chevigny, circa 1780. Louis XVI chairs more commonly have turned legs. From the Château de la Roche-Guyon.

*P*anelled room at the Arsenal in Paris. The Marquis de Paulmy, who was awarded this lodging by the King in 1755, is said to have installed this panelling, which may have been second-hand. The presence of musical trophies suggest the room could have been intended as a *salon de musique*. Bouchardon's *Fontaine des quatre saisons* was the inspiration for the four grisaille overdoors with putti. Paulmy's 1787 inventory records the contents of the room, which included painted and gilded console tables with marble tops and a four-leaf screen covered with Chinese paper.

*F*irescreen attributed to Nicolas-Quinibert Foliot, possibly from a suite carved by Babel and delivered to Bellevue in 1768. This is still of Louis XV shape, but is decorated with *goût grec* carving, such as pearls and palm fronds. The Bellevue suite was moved to Madame du Barry's apartment at Saint-Hubert in 1770, when it was described as upholstered with blue painted silk.

*L*ouis XVI firescreen, circa 1780-85. The Egyptian figures on the frame bear witness to the contemporary revival of interest in the ancient world. Counterweights in the uprights make it easy to raise the panel of Aubusson tapestry.

# TYPES OF PIECES

The *fauteuil* or armchair was made in a variety of different shapes and sizes. The *fauteuil à la Reine*, a large armchair with a flat back, could be pulled forward for use when needed, but usually stood against a wall, centrally placed below a panel, as much a part of the decoration of a room as the console tables and pedestals with which it alternated. Paintings of French eighteenth-century interiors often show people sitting on such chairs without having moved them. The *fauteuil en cabriolet*, by contrast, was smaller, with a curved back, and could be placed in the middle of a room among the tables. Particularly in the second half of the century, examples of both types appear as components of large sets.

The *bergère*, a large, low and comfortable armchair, had the area enclosed by the armrest filled with a panel of upholstery. This type be-

came widespread in the second quarter of the century, and at first they were not part of large elaborate sets, but were simply decorated, waxed rather than painted, and appeared in pairs. Later on, especially in the neoclassical period, they are found as parts of large suites of furniture, and it is undeniable that by this time, they had lost some of the charm they originally possessed. There were a number of variations on this theme, including the *bergère à oreilles*, with ear-shaped panels projecting from the top of the back to protect the sitter from draughts. The comfortable shape was also appropriate for invalids' chairs. The example supplied for Voltaire's use when he was staying with the Marquis de Villette in Paris in 1778, now in the Musée Carnavalet, has on one side a reading slope decorated with lacquer, and on the other a leather-topped tray.

Chairs (*chaises*) came in a variety of shapes and sizes. Those for dining were often sturdy and simply decorated. Most dining chairs sup-

the *salon de compagnie* at the Château d'Abondant, which have backs with deeply concave toprails following the outline of the lower part of the large mirror frames. The *canapé à confidents* is a variation with seats at each end separated by armrests from the main part of the *canapé*. Sometimes these ends were made separately. A report produced by the Garde-Meuble on the furniture necessary for Louis XVI's *cabinet intérieur* at Saint-Cloud states that the armrests of the sofa must be arranged so that "the King can lie down and rest his head". Exotic names were given to sofas to convey a feeling of oriental voluptousness. The *ottomane* was an example, and had two scrolled ends and no back.

The bed was the traditional vehicle for the greatest extravagances of the *tapissier*'s art. The *lit à la Française*, a four-poster with no visible woodwork, continued to be made but was gradually replaced by beds in which the work of the *menuisier* and the *sculpteur* became more important. The variety of names is considerable and confusing, but the

*Fauteuil à la Reine* from a set by Louis Delanois bought in Paris in 1766 by the 3rd Duke of Richmond. This upholstery *à châssis* is original, and the *châssis* bears Delanois's stamp. The carved laurel garlands represent an early use of neoclassical motifs in Delanois's work. He was later to supply chairs for Madame du Barry at Louveciennes.

*L*ouis XVI *fauteuil* stamped by Georges Jacob, circa 1790. From the bedroom of the Marquise de Marbeuf, and possibly designed by Dugourc in a fanciful chinoiserie style.

plied to the Garde-Meuble had stretchers to reinforce the legs. They were often caned, but could also be covered with a solid velvet called moquette. They came in large numbers, and sets of sixty or thereabouts have been recorded. As in England, it had become the practice by the 1780s to include armchairs in dining room sets, but they rarely survive together today. Chairs were also included in *meubles*, and their decoration naturally matched that of the other pieces. *Voyeuses* or *ponteuses* had a horizontal stuffed panel at the top of the back: spectators of, say, a card game sat facing the back of the chair and leaned their elbows comfortably on this.

Sofas, too, exist in many different models. These were made by chairmakers but treated as part of the decoration of a room. In some cases, this might mean that the back of a sofa needed to follow the outline of the lower part of the panelling, and during the rococo period this led to some eccentric examples, such as those of circa 1750 from

*Voyeuses à genoux* stamped by Georges Jacob, circa 1775-80, possibly made for a *salon de musique*. Jacob occasionally affixed labels to the chairs he sold, and the labels on these state they were made for the *salon* of Monsieur de Septeuil, a *fermier-général* who held the post of Premier Valet de chambre du Roi.

shape of a bed indicates where it was to be placed. In formal bedrooms (*chambres de parade*), the bed could be placed within a large enclosure at one end, usually separated from the rest of the room by a balustrade. This was generally a royal or princely practice, however, and many bedrooms were content with an alcove or *niche*; beds intended to be placed there were usually fitted with large wheels and handles on the uprights so that the bed could be pulled out to be made. The space between the bed and the sides of the alcove was known as the *ruelle*.

The *lit à la Polonaise* and the *lit à la Romaine*, with two raised ends in visible wood, had a canopy (*ciel* or *baldaquin*) resting on four uprights. In the former, the canopy was smaller than the bed and had a high dome with visible woodcarving. Bimont states that the wooden uprights supported S-shaped metal rods which curved inwards to hold up the canopy; these were to be hidden by tubes of the material used to upholster the rest of the bed. On the *lit à la Romaine*, on the other hand, the canopy was about the same size as the bed. There were variations even in this and some beds might be borderline cases. If for example the dome of the canopy was exceedingly tall, it was known as an *Impériale*. The *lit en ottomane* had two tall scrolled ends and stood sideways against the wall; a variation known as *lit à la Turque* had a tall back connecting the two ends (this was sometimes removable); either of these could also be known as a *lit en chaire à prêcher* on account of a small domed canopy fixed to the wall above, and resembling a pulpit. Delafosse's bed designs include one with bells on the canopy and a small moustachioed Chinaman with a pointed hat perched at the foot end; naturally, this is called a *lit à la chinoise*. These beds could be either freestanding or in an alcove. Hooks which remain in place high up on the walls of bedrooms in French eighteenth-century houses may indicate not only where the bed was originally placed but that it had a fixed canopy of *chaire à prêcher* type.

## MATCHING SETS

Carved furniture was normally ordered in sets, called *meubles*. For a bedroom, for example, a *meuble* might consist of a bed with canopy, bedsteps, chairs, armchairs, *bergères*, firescreens, folding screens, console tables and mirrors; the woodwork might be carved, painted and gilded *en suite*, and all the upholstery would match. This sort of unity sometimes encompassed several rooms, as at the Palais-Rohan in Strasbourg. A description of the suite delivered for Louis XV's bedroom at Fontainebleau in 1754 is given in Chapter Ten.

New chairs were delivered for Louis XVI's *salon des jeux* at Fontainebleau in 1786. The set comprised one chair higher that the others, for the King's use, sixteen chairs with fixed seats and twelve with loose cushions; the latter may have been for the ladies, as were also perhaps the four kneeling *voyeuses (voyeuses en prie-dieu)*, while the men could sit on the two *voyeuses en bidet*.

*P*air of armchairs (*fauteuils en médaillon*) stamped by Claude I Sené, 1770-80. Made on an unusually small scale, these chairs may have been intended for a boudoir. Refinements include the gilding in two tones and the upholstery *à châssis*, which is uncommon for such small chairs. The upholstery, in Beauvais tapestry, may have been *en suite* with wall hangings.

# ÉBÉNISTERIE

Most *ébénistes* worked in a different quarter, the Faubourg Saint-Antoine, east of the Bastille. It has been suggested that this was convenient because of its proximity to the river Seine, so that wood could be floated down or brought by barge. The craft of applying veneers to wood was essentially one imported from Italy and the Low Countries, and it seems to be for this reason that many of the *ébénistes* were foreign, or of foreign origin. Several came from Holland in the late seventeenth and early eighteenth centuries. Mathieu Criaerd's father was born in Brussels, and Bernard van Risamburgh I, the father of the famous *ébéniste* of the reign of Louis XV, was born in Gröningen in the northern Netherlands and worked in Paris during the latter years of

*R*andom dice-throwing machine, signed *Gallonde Invenit et Fecit Parisiis 1739*. The collector Bonnier de la Mosson owned one veneered with tortoiseshell; in the catalogue of his sale in 1745 it was stated that "it is made for the purpose of avoiding the usual noise of this game" (*il est fait à dessein d'éviter le bruit ordinaire qui accompagne ce jeu*).

*M*arquetry commode, circa 1730-35, with gilt-bronze mounts. Mounts in the shape of pagodas are a characteristic feature in the work of this unknown *ébéniste*.

Louis XIV's reign. Vandercruse (gallicized to Lacroix) is a name of Dutch origin. Later, German names begin to appear, such as those of Joseph Baumhauer or Jean-Henri Riesener, both born in Westphalia. The fluid borders between France, the Empire and the Low Countries allowed easy travel for a number of craftsmen, among them Adam Weisweiler and Bernard Molitor, who came to Paris as young men and, after an apprenticeship probably spent in the workshop of a more senior fellow emigrant, tried to set up on their own. The ideal solution was to marry the widow of one's employer: Riesener successfully won the hand of Françoise-Marguerite Oeben, and thereby control of the workshop, against what seems to have been acrimonious competition from his fellow apprentice Jean-François Leleu.

The Faubourg Saint-Antoine was not a fashionable quarter, and on the whole the clientele did not care to visit the workshops. Most *ébénistes* thus sold their production to a middleman, either a member of the dealers' guild, or a *marchand-ébéniste*, the name given to the cabinet-makers who had shops selling to the public. Some of these were in the Faubourg, such as Pierre Migeon, who subcontracted work to colleagues who were fellow guild members such as Dubois, Topino, Bircklé and others. In the case of the Ébéniste du Roi, Gilles Joubert, his subcontractors, including Marchand and Lacroix, worked from models provided, and applied gilt-bronze mounts of a standard type.

Some makers specialized in certain types of pieces: Charles Topino, for example, made small tables and also sold marquetry panels to colleagues, which they could then incorporate into their own pieces.

The principal clients of the *ébénistes* were the dealers of the Rue Saint-Honoré. They sold to the best clientele and ordered pieces to their own designs, in which the *ébéniste*'s role was merely that of executant, incorporating the various elements of decoration that were provided, such as lacquer, Sèvres porcelain, panels of Boulle marquetry or pietra dura. The dealers sold many fine veneered or marquetry pieces, but the bulk of these were sold directly by the *ébénistes* themselves, and the dealers' distinguishing speciality was to provide more exotic wares. They must have been sensitive to the varying competence of the craftsmen they employed. Bernard van Risamburgh II, Martin Carlin and Adam Weisweiler were almost always entrusted with Japanese lacquer (the best and most expensive), while Mathieu Criaerd, who worked for the same dealers, was only given Chinese lacquer. Etienne Levasseur was given old pieces with Boulle marquetry and transformed them, frequently adding new high-quality Boulle marquetry made especially in his workshop.

*Meubles d'ébénisterie* were decorated so that the carcasses should not be visible. This was an ancient tradition in furniture-making in France, dating from the Renaissance. The use of veneers concealed the construction, which often suffered as a result. Most of the more competent *ébénistes*, however, used oak as the principal wood for their carcasses, although pine is sometimes found.

Wood veneer gradually replaced tortoiseshell and brass marquetry in the early years of the eighteenth century. Ebony and other veneers were employed by Noel Gérard to make writing tables and commodes with rich gilt-bronze decoration, while at the same time he seems to have continued to decorate pieces with marquetry of tortoiseshell and metal. Indeed Boulle marquetry, as this technique was known, continued to be used throughout the eighteenth century, although for much of the first half it was employed almost exclusively on clock cases. Gérard may have signed his production with the initials N.G. The inventory after his death in 1736 gives an idea of the variety of woods available at the time; as well as ebony, he possessed *amarante* (purplewood), *pallissandre* (rosewood), *bois violet* (kingwood), and *bois de cayenne* (akin to a light shade of mahogany). These were used in sheets, in simple patterns such as quartering, in imitation of parquet floors (hence the English name of "parquetry"), or cut across the grain to form round or oval shapes, known in English as "oyster veneer". The principal practitioners of these techniques were Etienne Doirat, whose production is chiefly of commodes, and the more famous and extremely versatile Charles Cressent.

Cressent's work is highly individual. He was probably the only *ébéniste* to be a member of the Académie de Saint Luc, and his pieces are heavily decorated with sculptural bronze mounts. Because of guild restrictions, he could design his mounts, and even make the models for the moulds, but he was not permitted to employ others to carry out the

*O*ne of a pair of *encoignures* (corner cupboards) by Charles Cressent, 1740-50. They appear in the catalogue of the 1757 auction sale of his stock, where the gilt-bronze decoration is described as *deux enfans, dont l'un joue de la flûte et l'autre du tambour de basque; ils font danser un chien sur la corde* (two children, one playing the flute and the other a tambourine; they are making a dog dance while balancing on a tightrope). These *encoignures* matched commodes decorated with gilt-bronze monkeys.

manufacture of these in his own workshop. Even so, he managed to produce objects made entirely of gilt-bronze to his own designs, such as clock cases, wall lights and firedogs, as well as his furniture mounts. He also made mounts for porcelain. His furniture consists of massive commodes, bookcases, longcase clocks and large writing tables, with bold gilt-bronze frames to each panel enclosing strapwork, foliage including palm branches and ivy tendrils, and allegorical low reliefs. For example, one of the medal cabinets by Cressent in the Gulbenkian Museum in Lisbon has a scene of winged putti striking medals. He used *amarante* (purplewood), and pioneered *bois satiné* (light mahogany). His veneers give a contrasting effect: quartered for the border and parquetry for the panels, for example. They always follow closely the outline of the gilt-bronze mounts. By the time of his death in 1768 the neoclassical style was well underway, but his own style seems not to have evolved after the 1740s. Certainly he did not execute any pieces in the technique which was to become most popular in the middle of the century: flower marquetry.

*T*able de nuit (bedside table) delivered to the Garde-Meuble in 1756 by the Ébéniste du Roi, Gilles Joubert. Joubert subcontracted a substantial quantity of his royal orders, and this table is characteristic of the work of Jean-François Oeben.

*B*ureau by Jean-Pierre Latz, mid-eighteenth century. The naive dyed and engraved flower marquetry contrasts with the exuberant gilt-bronze mounts and the *mouvementé* shape.

Cressent's near contemporary, Antoine-Robert Gaudreaus, had a style so similar that one of his finest pieces, the commode in the Wallace Collection, was until recently attributed to Cressent. In fact, while Cressent designed his own mounts and kept a close eye on their manufacture, Gaudreaus, on the other hand, because he worked principally for the Garde-Meuble, was supplied with designs by the Slodtz brothers, which he executed relatively faithfully. The gilt-bronze mounts of this commode are signed by Jacques Caffiéri, and it is probable that this *fondeur-ciseleur* was responsible for the mounts on many of Gaudreaus's other pieces. They show a recognizable style featuring a heart-shaped frame for the centre of the facade of a commode, first used for the Wallace Collection piece, and found until the 1760s on furniture supplied by Gaudreaus's successor, Joubert.

## FLOWER AND PICTORIAL MARQUETRY

The adoption of the technique of flower marquetry revolutionized furniture-making in the 1740s. Like other innovations, it was probably a *marchand-mercier* who initiated it, Thomas-Joachim Hébert being a likely candidate. The name of Bernard van Risamburgh II (his stamp was his initials, BVRB), who worked for Hébert, is linked to the finest examples, but he was not alone, and two different types can be distinguished: the first, both in time and in quality, was end-cut flower marquetry, which was practised by BVRB, Jean-Pierre Latz, Jacques Dubois, Antoine-Mathieu Criaerd and Joseph Baumhauer, and the second, marquetry of ordinary pieces of wood dyed and engraved to achieve the intended effect seems to have been practised slightly later, generally by lesser *ébénistes*, such as Pierre Roussel and Léonard Boudin. By the 1760s, end-cut ("impressionist") marquetry made way for a better quality of "realist" or "pictorial" flower marquetry, the principal specialists in this field being Roger Vandercruse-Lacroix (his stamps were LACROIX or the initials RVLC), Jean-François Oeben (and his workshop after his death in 1763) and, later, Jean-Henri Riesener.

*Bois de bout* or end-cut marquetry uses the grain of the wood to create an effect, such as the movement of a leaf or petal. This is applied to a quarter-cut background of a different shade, such as *bois satiné* (light mahogany) or *bois de rose* (tulipwood), producing a lively and stylized impression. The serrated bronzes of the work of Latz complement this type of marquetry to perfection. This *ébéniste* had mastered the other method as well, and a *cartonnier* (filing cabinet) by

*Régulateur de parquet* (longcase clock) by Ferdinand Berthoud, 1752; the case, which is decorated with end-cut marquetry, perhaps by Jacques Dubois. Berthoud's pride in this, his earliest equation clock and first major horological achievement, induced him to fix an engraved plaque inside the case, stating that "This equation and composite verge clock is the work of Ferdinand Berthoud, clockmaker in Paris, who has designed the equation movement, and who has submitted it to the Royal Academy of Sciences in Paris in 1752" (*Cette pendule à Equation et à Verge composée, a été faite par FERDINAND BERTHOUD, Horloger à Paris, qui en a inventé l'Equation, et qui l'a présentée en 1752 à l'Académie Royale des Sciences de Paris*). The Academy's transactions for that year include a detailed description and an engraving of the movement.

Latz in the Wallace Collection has end-cut branches, with dyed and engraved flowers. End-cut marquetry may not have been inspired by engravings, but realist flower marquetry often was.

In the 1760s, with the advent of the neoclassical style, came new types of marquetry. *Ébénistes* copied the engravings of Jean-Charles Delafosse and others, executing not only flower panels but also trophies of all sorts (hunting, gardening or music), and landscape scenes, classical ruins proving especially popular. Some makers added details in ivory and other materials. Panels of this type could be bought from specialists such as André-Louis Gilbert and Daniel Deloose. As well as producing marquetry of flower sprays and garlands, Charles Topino decorated small pieces such as *bonheur-du-jours* with marquetry of teapots, cups and saucers, small vases and other objects, in an oriental style which may have been derived from motifs found on Chinese lacquer.

The natural colouring and figuring of the wood was used to good effect in these marquetry pictures, alongside staining and engraving. Unfortunately, time has weathered much of the colour, and the engraving has been worn down by zealous restorers, so that it is only possible to get an idea of the original brightness of these by looking at paintings of the period. The portrait of Madame de Pompadour by Drouais in the National Gallery in London shows an early neoclassical worktable by Oeben of bright red and green colour (see page 22). Today it would have faded to yellow and brown, but the insides of some pieces such as secretaires, when they have been rarely opened, can still convey an impression of the original vivid tones.

Another type of marquetry to find favour during this period

*P*iano by Sébastien Erard, circa 1780. Erard, the pioneer musical instrument maker of the end of the eighteenth century, managed to obtain the authorization to make his own cases. This piece is traditionally stated to have belonged to Marie Antoinette.

consisted of repeated small-scale patterns. Oeben made a speciality of this, notably with interlocking lozenges of contrasting colours creating an effect of receding stacked cubes, or a fish-scale pattern. Riesener created even more elaborate patterns, such as single flowerheads within trellis frames, some of which bear an uncanny resemblance to patterns in black and gold on the borders of the doors or the insides of seventeenth-century Japanese lacquer cabinets. It is probable that they were copied directly from these, which are the parts of a lacquer cabinet least likely to be of use to an *ébéniste* for veneering. A notable exception is the commode by Adam Weisweiler in the Swedish Royal collection, for which he has used strips of an elaborate seventeenth-century Japanese lacquer border to create a frame for a Gobelins pietra dura panel.

*Ébénistes* continued to use elaborate marquetry patterns during the 1770s. Martin Carlin employed trelliswork as well as symmetrical scrolling foliage. But gradually plain panels of carefully chosen veneers replaced these. Claude-Charles Saunier's pieces are often veneered with *bois de rose* but for other *ébénistes* mahogany was soon to predominate. This could be plain or of an interesting pattern, such as plum-pudding mahogany (*acajou moucheté*). Oeben had made the first pieces in plain mahogany in the early 1760s for Madame de Pompadour, and his successor Riesener followed his lead in this, but without abandoning trellis and flower marquetry, as some of his pieces of the mid-1780s show. By this time, however, its character had changed and it now had finer borders, with lozenges of sycamore or *bois satiné*. The cylinder desk and worktable he made for Marie Antoinette's boudoir at Fontainebleau in 1786 are, exceptionally, covered in trelliswork of silvered copper enclosing mother-of-pearl lozenges.

The use of exotic materials by *ébénistes* stemmed from the competitiveness of the *marchands-merciers*. Since the days of Louis XIV, lacquer, pietra dura, metal and tortoiseshell had all decorated furniture. Boulle marquetry furniture ceased to be made (with the exception of cartel clock cases) from circa 1720, but existing pieces continued to be displayed, especially in grand interiors. By the middle of the century many of them required restoration, explaining the presence of *ébénistes'* stamps on some late seventeenth- and early eighteenth-century pieces. Demand must have overtaken supply, and certain *ébénistes*, as well as repairing or altering pieces, made new versions. Some were direct or close copies of Louis XIV models, but others were of contemporary type. Most of this work was carried out for *marchands-merciers*, who bought old pieces in sales (for example those of the Garde-Meuble of the mid-eighteenth century). Etienne Levasseur made a speciality of Boulle pieces, many of which were ordered from him by the *marchand-mercier* Julliot, one of the purchasers at the Garde-Meuble sales.

# MOUNTS FOR FURNITURE

The gilt-bronze frames used by the *ébénistes* of the late Louis XIV period did not cease to be applied when wood veneer replaced Boulle marquetry circa 1720. Indeed for a while gilt-bronze was to become the principal ornament of furniture. Moulded frames for drawer fronts and panels, masks, corner mounts with female heads and leafy scroll feet were all part of the traditional repertoire, and individuals added their own variations. Etienne Doirat applied symmetrical heart-shaped frames of leafy scrollwork to the facades of commodes, while an unknown but original *ébéniste* used gilt-bronze pagodas and dragon corner mounts. Charles Cressent and Antoine-Robert Gaudreaus were the acknowledged masters, the latter using bold rococo scrolls and leafage.

When flower marquetry and lacquer came to be used on furniture in the 1740s, gilt-bronze had to be more restrained in order not to encroach on the main panels of decoration. Attention was lavished on the frames of panels, on corner mounts, *sabots* or foot mounts, and on apron mounts, as well as on handles, although these started to be incorporated into the framing of the facade (Cressent and Gaudreaus had pioneered this). Latz's repertoire of motifs is particularly inventive, incorporating batwings and ivy tendrils in addition to leafy scrollwork.

The *bronziers* adapted to the neoclassical style faster than most *ébénistes*. This accounts for furniture dating from the 1760s, by Roussel and others being in the rococo style but mounted with neoclassical gilt-bronzes, a discrepancy that also serves to show such *ébénistes* bought bronzes ready-made. Baumhauer, however, arguably the first *ébéniste* to work in the new style, used heavy architectural bronzes which are perfectly integrated and specially designed.

During the Louis XVI period, gilt-bronze was used for the friezes of commodes, secretaires and writing tables, either in the form of a continuous leafy scroll, or of a Greek key or other classical pattern. The engravings of J. F. Forty appear to have provided inspiration for the friezes on furniture by Weisweiler. That most commonly found has a central Bacchante mask flanked by rams, cymbals and satyr children playing trumpets. Hanging garlands of flowers tied with a ribbon were used as corner mounts, panels were framed in gilt-bronze cast with bead or stiff-leaf motifs, and milled collars and bands began to be employed.

# SHAPES OF PIECES, THEIR ORIGIN AND USE

At the beginning of the eighteenth century, case furniture was principally intended for use in small, intimate rooms, such as bedrooms and *cabinets*. With the gradual merging of the formal and informal suites of rooms, however, *meubles d'ébénisterie* found their way increasingly into the principal rooms, and they became more lavishly decorated as a result.

The two pieces delivered by André-Charles Boulle for Louis XIV at Trianon in 1708 are often considered to have been the first "commodes". These have two drawers, one above the other. Chests of drawers had certainly existed before this, but these may be among the earliest to have two rows of drawers instead of three. They were described as *bureaux* at the time, possibly a sign of uncertainty as to their belonging to one or other category. Other commodes made for Louis XIV in that year are, however, specifically referred to as "commodes"; they were destined to become the principal piece of case furniture of the eighteenth century, and were, therefore, the pieces on which

*C*ommode by Bernard van Risamburgh, dated between 1748 and 1753, and delivered for the use of Louise Elizabeth, Duchess of Parma. The lacquer appears to be Japanese, of the finest quality, although it is uncommon to find mirror-image symmetry in Japanese lacquer motifs.

*M*id-eighteenth-century marquetry commode by Jean-Pierre Latz.

the most elaborate decoration was usually lavished.

By the 1760s, many commodes were made *en suite* with secretaires, and intended for bedroom use; *encoignures* or corner cupboards were also made to match. As the use of rooms changed during the century so did their contents, and commodes were increasingly to be found in principal reception rooms, such as *salons de compagnie* and *cabinets*. In houses where the principal reception room was used as a *salon des jeux* a commode could be employed to store cards and counters, but the principal incentive to placing a commode,

secretaire, or other piece of lavishly decorated case furniture in the main reception room of a house was undoubtedly the fact that it was normally the most expensive and therefore prestigious piece of furniture its owner would possess.

Large rectangular writing tables were called simply *bureaux* (they are now known as *bureaux plats*). They usually contain three drawers in the frieze, which pull from the same side, while the other side has false drawer fronts. They were used in *cabinets de travail* or other rooms where their owner might work, such as bedrooms, and were not intended for reception rooms. A *cartonnier* was often placed at one end, either on a cabinet of the same height as the table with doors opening at the side, or directly on the end of the desk, in which case it was called a *bout de bureau*, and was sometimes surmounted by a clock. The Présents du Roi ordered such a set from the *marchand-mercier* Hébert in 1745 to give as a present to the Empress of Russia; it included a desk, a *bout de bureau* and a *cartonnier* surmounted by a clock, and was probably the work of BVRB.

In the early 1760s there appeared a variation on the theme of the *bureau plat*: the *bureau à cylindre*. The upper part consists of a curved cover which slides back into a nest of shelves, revealing a writing surface which on some examples comes forward as the cylinder goes up. Most of these date from the Louis XVI period. In the earliest ones, principally the work of Oeben, the cylinder consists of slats of wood on a canvas backing, which roll up behind the drawers. The *bureau du Roi*, ordered from Oeben in 1760 and finished by Riesener nine years later, is the most elaborate of this type. It contains a clock, candle branches at

*O*ne of a pair of *encoignures* (corner cupboards) of circa 1765-70, stamped RVLC, the expanded initials of Roger Vandercruse-Lacroix.

*C*ommode à vantaux (commode with doors) attributed to Adam Weisweiler, circa 1785. Veneer of burr-thuya, gilt-bronze bas-reliefs. The fluted and tapering corner columns are a hallmark of some of the finest of Weisweiler's work, as is the construction of the doors – the centre panel is part of the right-hand door, and swings back on a double hinge. This piece may have been sold by Daguerre. Bas-reliefs of fountains also appear on a commode in the Swedish Royal collection which has lacquer borders taken from a seventeenth-century Japanese close stool. The close stool had been delivered to Daguerre by the Garde-Meuble in 1784, and lacquer from it was veneered on to a secretaire for Louis XVI and a writing table for Marie Antoinette by Weisweiler. Indeed a similar commode, which, like this, was also formerly at Mentmore, bears Versailles marks.

each side, and has a clockwork mechanism which opens the cylinder at the quarter turn of the key. It was the mechanism, a speciality of Oeben, that was particularly prized at the time, rather than the lavish marquetry or bronzes. Riesener delivered many of these (on a smaller scale) to the Garde-Meuble in subsequent years, either in marquetry, or, later, in finely figured mahogany. François-Gaspart Teuné specialized almost exclusively in this type of piece, normally of large size and decorated with marquetry.

The appearance of the *secrétaire à abbatant* or *secrétaire en armoire* in the 1730s, together with the *bureau à dos d'âne* or *bureau en pente* shortly afterwards, marks a new departure in working furniture. The first *bureau en pente* mentioned in the *Journal du Garde-Meuble* was made by BVRB and delivered by Hébert for the Dauphine at Versailles in 1745. These were not pieces for serious work, but they responded to the need for letter-writing furniture, which was to increase considerably thereafter. When Blondel stated that *antichambres* should not contain anything precious, it was because of the large number of servants who were always in attendance ready to deliver a constant stream of letters, and furniture suitable for this purpose was to proliferate. The *marchands-merciers* met the demand with energy, providing many types of small table, all of which have one drawer fitted out with divisions for ink-pot, sand-box and pens. It was the responsibility of the

*Bureau* with its *bout de bureau* (writing table and filing cabinet) stamped by Nicolas Grevenich, 1770-80.

*S*ecretaire stamped by Martin Carlin, and decorated with Sèvres plaques, which are dated 1776 and 1777. Carlin was the *ébéniste* normally employed by the *marchands-merciers* Poirier and Daguerre to mount porcelain plaques on furniture, and this piece is likely to have been made on Daguerre's behalf. The drapery frieze and the hanging bunches of foliage are typical of Carlin's work.

*C*ylinder desk by Jean-Henri Riesener, delivered to the Garde-Meuble on 24 December 1774. The curved legs recall the *bureau du Roi* of 1760-69, but the marquetry and gilt-bronzes are totally neoclassical. Riesener's attention to detail extended to using purplewood (*amarante*), a dark wood, for the borders to provide a contrast with the gilt-bronze mouldings (*pour faire fond à la dorure*).

dealer to provide these. Variations in shape of desk and table were continuous; a famous example, the *table à gradin* or *bonheur-du-jour* dates from the 1750s. Pieces of this type were often provided by *marchands-tabletiers*. Writing furniture was needed in every room; in 1778 a marquetry *table à écrire* was delivered by Riesener specifically for use in Madame Elizabeth's Pièce des Bains at Versailles. It is now preserved at Waddesdon. It may have suffered from the damp in its original position, since its elaborate marquetry top with *un groupe du Tems* has now vanished.

The fashion for gambling pervaded every level of society, from the Court downwards. Tables were required for this activity, but they do not seem to have survived in any great quantity, suggesting that many may have been simple pieces, covered with a cloth. The principal *ébénistes* did not habitually produce them, with the exception of tric-trac tables, of which there are several extant examples by Riesener, among others. The *marchand-tabletier* could supply these along with the accessories required, and a number of tables, dating from the very end of the eighteenth century, include fittings for every sort of game, including roulette, chess, and *jeu de l'oie*.

From the 1730s, new shapes of specialist furniture began to proliferate, such as worktables and *toilettes* (dressing tables). Some *ébénistes* made a speciality of these. Canabas, for instance, produced from the 1760s a large number of *rafraichissoirs* of the same model.

Made of solid mahogany and standing on four gently curved legs with casters, these incorporate spaces for two wine coolers and cutlery, as well as a marble top for hot dishes.

Larger pieces of case furniture were often made with specific purposes in mind. Armoires were more common during the reign of Louis XIV, but they and cabinets (*bas d'armoires*) continued to be made; the Dauphine Marie-Josèphe de Saxe purchased an armoire five *pieds* (1.62 m) high from Lazare Duvaux on 15 June 1754, with veneered surrounds to the lacquered doors. Bookcases were usually incorporated into the panelling, but some large examples in marquetry survive.

*M*arquetry *bonheur-du-jour* in the style of Roger Vandercruse-Lacroix, circa 1770-75.

*T*able with pietra dura panels by Martin Carlin, circa 1775-85. Although his principal speciality was the mounting of furniture with Sèvres porcelain plaques, Carlin also made a few pieces incorporating pietra dura panels, some of which must have come from the large cabinets formerly in Louis XIV's collection. The central landscape on this example is most probably Florentine, but panels with birds such as these were also made for Louis XIV at the Gobelins in Paris by craftsmen imported from Italy.

*M*ahogany *armoire*, and detail, stamped by Jean-Henri Riesener, circa 1780.

FOLLOWING SPREAD
*S*alon in a Paris Hôtel with panelling installed in the mid-eighteenth century.

During the reign of Louis XV, console tables were of carved wood, but later on *consoles d'ébénisterie* with marble tops made their appearance. Saunier produced many of these with turned tapering fluted legs in mahogany, and a lower shelf. These might have rounded ends with open shelves, as on some of his commodes, in which case they were called *commodes à l'anglaise*.

Some *ébénistes* made clock cases. During the rococo period, these were bracket or mantel clocks covered with Boulle marquetry, wood veneer or French *vernis*. Cartel clocks entirely of gilt-bronze were also made at the time, and by the beginning of the Louis XVI style these replaced wooden clock cases completely, except for longcase clocks (*rég-*

*ulateurs de parquet*). Balthazar Lieutaud made a speciality of these, and examples of his work are found both in the Louis XV and Louis XVI style.

The fashionable Geneva-born doctor, Théodore Tronchin, known for his eccentric prescriptions, usually called his patients hypochondriacs and recommended that ladies should sweep floors to get a little exercise. He seems to have been responsible for the introduction of a new type of writing table, which was known as a *table à la Tronchin* in his honour. Writing in 1759 to the Comte de Vergennes, Louis XV's ambassador to Constantinople, he prescribed: "If you really must work . . . you must write at a raised desk, while resting against a tall stool." The appearance of tall writing stands with a sloping surface in the 1750s may be connected to Tronchin's recommendations. In the latter part of the century, these increased in size, and usually take the shape of large writing tables, with metal rods inside the legs and a ratchet mechanism so that the whole top can be raised. A reading and writing slide then lifts out of the top, supported on a bracket.

# 7

# GILT-BRONZE

Bronze has been gilded since Antiquity. The illusion it creates that the whole mass is made of gold and not simply the surface must have provided a certain incentive from the very beginning, but by the seventeenth century no one was taken in by the great gilt-bronze motifs in the interior decoration at Versailles. Louis XIV had imported craftsmen from Italy to work at the Gobelins in Paris producing Florentine-style furniture, which included gilt-bronze framing

*Chimneypiece wall in the Salon d'Hercule at Versailles, 1730. The gilt-bronzes are by François-Antoine Vassé, who practised mainly as a decorative sculptor despite being a member of the Académie Royale.*

*Commode with elaborate gilt-bronze decoration, probably the work of Antoine-Robert Gaudreaus, about 1740-45.*

to the inlaid hardstone plaques, as well as architectural and symbolic ornaments. For the great marble-clad rooms of Versailles, gilt-bronze was used for the bases and capitals of columns and pilasters, as well as for huge trophies applied to the marble walls. The shine of the gold and the massive scale of this decoration achieved its intended effect, which was to humble visitors before the Temple of the Sun King.

In 1729, Louis XV ordered the completion of the decorative scheme in the Salon d'Hercule at Versailles, begun by Louis XIV shortly before he died, including in gilt-bronze the moulded bases and composite capitals of the marble pilasters, as well as the allegorical motifs on the chimneypiece, which consisted of a mask of Hercules with his lion pelt, framed with foliage and massive cornucopiae (see opposite). Use of gilt-bronze on such a scale became very rare in the eighteenth century, and wood panelling with gold leaf on the carved ornament provided a

cheaper and more versatile alternative. The rococo movement and the neoclassical revival made use of this highly adaptable material in an amazingly inventive manner, as decorative mounts for furniture, ceramics, and marble, as well as for objects entirely in gilt-bronze, principally for lighting and heating purposes, and for clocks. Gilt-bronze replaced silver in a number of these cases.

Since the material has little melt value, there was no temptation to destroy it in times of hardship, or with the evolution of styles and fashions. This accounts for the high survival rate of French eighteenth-century gilt-bronze objects, while silver of the period is now extremely rare.

# USES

"He has a lot of bronzes for sale, to be used for the decoration of rooms, such as candelabra, wall lights, firedogs and candlesticks of all shapes and sizes, decorated with figures . . . and clock cases ready to receive movements." The *Sieur* Hubert, who made this announcement in the *Mercure de France* in 1767, has summed up neatly the stock of a Paris *bronzier*. After emphasizing the use of gilt-bronze in interior decoration, he goes on to describe the types of object he manufactured and sold. These fall into three different categories: light fittings, fireplaces fittings, and clocks.

## LIGHTING

Candles were the principal source of light and required holders. These could be of several different types, including candlesticks (*flambeaux*) for one candle, and candelabra which were no more than candlesticks with detachable branches. These were light enough to carry around and are frequently seen in paintings, either on tables or on chimneypieces. Movable candlesticks rarely appear in paintings of interiors during the day, suggesting that they were brought out for use and then put away.

Large candelabra (*girandoles*), which carried as many as eight or ten candles, stood on torchères (*guéridons*), console tables or chimneypieces, so that their light could be reflected by the looking-glass behind.

*M*eissen porcelain stag with gilt-bronze base and candle branches, about 1730-35. Now in the Residenzmuseum, Munich. The *ébéniste* and *sculpteur* Charles Cressent is thought to have mounted porcelain objects in gilt-bronze. Although none have so far been identified with certainty, the mounts on this piece are in a style close to those on his furniture, and it seems likely that these are his work, especially since Charles-Albert, Elector of Bavaria, who was probably the original owner, was one of Cressent's clients in the 1730s.

*P*air of *rocaille* gilt-bronze candlesticks. The model was designed by Meissonier for the Duke of Kingston, and a silver example (with candelabra branches), dating from 1734-5 and bearing the Duke's crest, is preserved in the Musée des Arts Décoratifs, Paris. Meissonier published his engraved design, which must have been used by the anonymous *bronzier* who manufactured these.

They were frequently hung with glass or crystal drops and decorated with porcelain flowers, in the manner of contemporary chandeliers (see following page). Dutillot complained to Bonnet in 1760 that he only had "four crystal candelabra with porcelain flowers" and begs for eight more to be able to light a large room. The design by one of the Slodtz brothers for Louis XV's medal cabinet, executed by Gaudreaus, shows a crystal-hung pair, in the correct position. In the neoclassical period, these *girandoles* grew in size and importance. They were modelled as scantily draped females holding candle branches, or as Antique tripods or vases. In the Duc de Choiseul's posthumous sale of 1786 were four "life-size female figures carrying lily branches with five candle nozzles, to use as torchères". These were ten *pieds* (3.25 m) in height and said to be suitable for a *magnifique salon*. Also in the sale were four "white marble vases carrying lily branches to be used as fine five-light candelabra; they are mounted with rams' heads, fluted friezes and garlands of fruit and foliage, all on a round base of stucco imitating granite."

Wall lights (*bras de lumière*) were fixed on either side of looking-glasses, as close as possible in order to multiply the light. They normally have between two and five branches. In the Louis XV period, they were shaped as a flowing succession of rococo curves and foliage, some of the early examples being decorated with dragons or Chinamen. With the start of the neoclassical era, they began to be constructed out of architectural elements, such as fluted tapering pedestals, classical vases and lyres, with stiff-leaf ornament and garlands of laurel. Some wall lights could be integral to the decoration of a room, such as those made

circa 1756 by François-Thomas Germain for the Duchesse d'Orléans at the Palais-Royal, which were supported on bronze putti seated at each end of the chimneypiece. Madame de Sérilly's boudoir, now in the Victoria and Albert Museum in London, has false wall lights carved and gilded in low relief on the panelling.

Gilt-bronze lanterns became extremely popular during the reign of Louis XV. Usually with five or six sides and glass of serpentine section, they contained a multiple candle holder (*chandelier*), and were surmounted by a glass disc (*chapiteau*) to prevent soot from staining

*O*ne of a pair of massive candelabra, circa 1780.

*D*esign for a crystal-hung *girandole*, probably by one of the Slodtz brothers. From the Garde-Meuble album in the Bibliothèque Nationale, Paris.

*G*ilt-bronze and rock crystal *girandoles*, circa 1740.

the ceiling. They were normally hung in rooms with architectural decoration, such as *salons*, or to light staircases, but Duvaux, who sold a large number, supplied many small ones, for *garderobes*, for example. He naturally also provided cords (*cordons*) from which to hang them; these might be of crimson silk with tassels, or could have counterweights and pulleys to make it easier to change the candles. Louis XVI lanterns are normally round with pilaster uprights.

The two great Louis XV gilt-bronze chandeliers signed by Jacques Caffiéri (now in the Wallace Collection), which once had matching wall-lights and which belonged originally to Louise Elizabeth, Duchess of Parma, are by no means typical. The traditional chandelier consisted of a pear-shaped frame of silvered or gilt-brass, with glass or crystal drops

*O*ne of a pair of gilt-bronze and enamel candlesticks, late 1780s. These candlesticks, in an exotic version of the Etruscan or arabesque style, bear Spanish royal heraldic devices on the nozzles and must have been among the objects supplied to the Court of Spain by the clockmaker François-Louis Godon, who was appointed to the post of Relojero de Camara (Court clockmaker) in 1786. Godon employed Dugourc as a designer, and it is likely that Dugourc drew these, and that the gilt-bronze is by François Rémond. The enamel was executed by Joseph Coteau, who provided Godon with enamel clock-faces. Coteau must also have been responsible for the raised jewelling seen here, a technique he perfected for Sèvres in 1780. Jacques-Joseph de Gault, who started his career as a painter at Sèvres in the late 1750s, specialized in painting enamels in the style of ancient cameos for the lids of gold boxes, and the cameo-style painting here is probably his work.

Gilt-bronze *bras de lumière* (wall light), one of a set of four. Mid-eighteenth century, in a pure rococo style. Possibly brought back by the 4th Duke of Bedford from his Parisian embassy in 1762-3.

which were sometimes coloured. An especially splendid example was delivered by the dealer Delaroue for the Cabinet du Conseil at Versailles on 29 May 1738. This was five *pieds* (1.62 m) tall and 42 *pouces* (1.13 m) in diameter, and carried twelve nozzles in groups of three. Its frame was shaped as four curving palm branches, from which hung flat drops and spheres, and which supported crystal palmettes, vases and pyramids. Inside was a large crystal vase below a hanging sphere. Above was a crystal stem, and the nozzles and drip pans were also of crystal. From each element hung a bewildering array of crystals, either singly or as garlands, cut as fruit, lyres and cabochons.

After the description of this sumptuous construction, the delivery note adds that ninety-eight of the pieces of crystal were supplied by the Garde-Meuble, which had bought them two years previously. The note states that as a result there are only forty-two pieces left in store. A number of pieces of crystal, including the substantial pear-shaped terminal (described as *très belle*), were provided by Delaroue. The

widow Girault had supplied on the previous day a cord for the chandelier. This measured 6.5 *aunes* (7.8 m) in length, included in its weave an intricate pattern resembling lace (*point de Milan*), and was decorated with tassels. The entry in the *Journal du Garde Meuble*, states, amazingly, that it was of fine gold (*or fin*).

In the neoclassical period, wall lights in the shape of half chandeliers of crystal were hung on looking-glasses. The ones visible on the Moreau le Jeune watercolour of Louveciennes, dated 1771, may be among the earliest examples, and Marie Antoinette's boudoir at Fontainebleau is similarly equipped.

*G*ilt-bronze lantern, circa 1790.

*O*ne of a pair of *girandoles* for outside use, circa 1780. These may have been among the objects bought from Daguerre by the Comte and Comtesse du Nord in 1784.

*G*ilt-bronze *feu* (firedogs) with military trophies, circa 1735.

*L*ouis XV gilt-bronze *feu*.

# FIREPLACE FITTINGS

Firedogs or *feu* had acted as vehicles for decorative sculpture since the Renaissance. In the eighteenth century, pairs of firedogs were placed inside fireplaces, the gilt-bronze decoration concealing wrought-iron log supports, called *grilles*. Early eighteenth-century examples were sometimes shaped as sculptures on pedestals, but with the advent of the rococo the pedestal and the sculpture merged into one continuous motif. The *doreur* Le Lièvre delivered many to the Garde-Meuble, including some on 10 June 1754 for the Château de la Muette: "Fire-irons with four polished iron rods of 22 *pouces* (60 cm) in length, decorated on the front with a bear hunt and a boar hunt, of gilt-bronze, with shovel, tongs and pincers also of polished iron, with gilt knobs, and tin protective covers with woollen linings". A pair of this type, delivered by Le Lièvre to Louise Elizabeth in Parma, has survived in Italy. The gilt-bronze elements were often detachable from the iron log-supports, so that they could be removed when a fire was lit. An example is clearly visible in Boucher's *La Toilette* (see page 50). In this case they had no

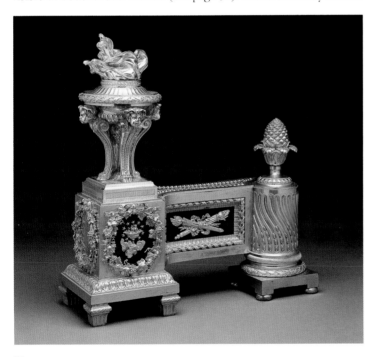

*Feu* attributed to Pierre Gouthière, circa 1780.

other support at the back and had to be leant against the side of the fireplace. Architectural bases returned to favour with the Louis XVI style, surmounted by vases or figures, few of which are as exotic as the pair made by Gouthière for Marie Antoinette at Fontainebleau, with camels reclining on socles decorated with arabesque scrolls on a blued steel background.

# CLOCKS

King George IV almost invariably had the movements of the French clocks he bought replaced by English ones. This overt contempt for French horology would not have been justified in the case of clock-

*G*ilt-bronze cartel clock, dial signed by Jean-Baptiste Baillon, case stamped with the crowned *C* mark, 1745-9.

makers such as Stollewerck, Berthoud (see page 129), Lepine or above all Breguet, but it has to be admitted that French clocks were and are principally appreciated for the decorative appeal of their cases rather than the quality of their works. The makers of clock cases, however, were normally employed by the clockmakers, and it was these latter who sold clocks directly to the public (and to the Garde-Meuble), having commissioned *ébénistes* and *bronziers* to supply them with cases, to which they fitted their movements.

There were numerous types of clocks in France in the eighteenth century, and gilt-bronze formed a major part of the decoration of most of them. Wallclocks (*cartels*) made entirely of gilt-bronze began to appear in the 1720s, the *ébéniste* and *sculpteur* Charles Cressent being

*G*ilt-bronze musical mantel clock with mechanism by Stollewerck, dated 1756.

*G*arniture of Sèvres porcelain and gilt-bronze, 1770-80. The mounts were probably made by Jean-Claude Duplessis fils.

responsible for some characteristically large and vigorous examples, decorated with putti, figures with scythes emblematic of Time, and Apollo masks amid jagged rockwork and serrated foliate scrolls. Jacques Caffiéri and others followed suit in a lighter but still asymmetric rococo style. Such clocks were habitually hung just above eye level, either on walls or on a looking-glass incorporated into panelling; such an arrangement can be seen in the gouaches of the Choiseul snuffbox, painted circa 1770. The arrival of the *goût grec* in the 1760s heralded a sudden change, and cartel clocks of this period are decorated with the vases, lion masks and symmetrical acanthus foliage characteristic of this style, while retaining the same basic shape, incorporating an enclosed space below the clock face for the pendulum, and a swelling above for the bell. Cartel clocks gradually declined in the early 1770s, being replaced by an increased variety of mantel clocks.

Bracket or mantel clocks entirely or mostly of gilt-bronze had been introduced by André-Charles Boulle around 1700, and countless variations of these were produced throughout the eighteenth century. The

*marchands-merciers* of the second quarter of the eighteenth century added Meissen or Oriental porcelain figures to act as supports to the dials or to stand on the gilt- or lacquered bronze plinths, which often had porcelain flowers emerging from trees at the back. Cases entirely of bronze, in the style of cartel clocks, were decorated with dragons or supported by Chinamen, some of which were lacquered by Martin.

*P*atinated and gilt-bronze clock, circa 1770, with movement by Lepaute. The case was designed by Charles de Wailly, an architect who returned to Paris from Rome in 1756, and the figures by Houdon.

*C*lock with Vestal Virgins, circa 1785. Attributed to Pierre-Philippe Thomire, from a design, probably by Dugourc, now in the Musée des Arts Décoratifs, Paris.

Clocks supported on animals made their appearance circa 1745; a rhinoceros, a wild boar or, most frequently, an elephant of patinated bronze stands on a rockwork base and carries a dial on which sits a monkey or a putto. Jean-Joseph de Saint-Germain manufactured some with a large plinth containing a musical movement, as well as others with a mythological theme: a patinated bronze bull flanked by scantily draped young ladies supports a dial garlanded with flowers and surmounted by a figure of Europa.

Figure clocks reached a zenith of popularity during the neoclassical era. At first, clocks became victims of some of the more extreme manifestations of the *goût grec*, being shaped as vases, and without a dial; the time was told by the hanging forked tongue of a serpent coiled around the vase, which pointed at a spot on two friezes engraved with

the hours and the minutes, and rotating at different speeds. Elaborate clocks became fashionable, incorporating the movement in a vase or in a truncated column, and resting upon a marble base inset with a gilt-bronze frieze, with figures of putti holding garlands of flowers, women reading, or mythological scenes, of gilt- or patinated bronze, marble or biscuit porcelain. Towards the end of the eighteenth century other types were introduced, including the portico clock, with its face balanced between two columns or obelisks of marble, and the lyre clock, sometimes of Sèvres porcelain.

# MAKERS AND TECHNIQUES

The several stages in the manufacture of gilt-bronze objects – the design, the making of the mould, the casting, the chiselling and the gilding – involved a number of craftsmen belonging to different guilds. Members of the Académie de Saint Luc owned the exclusive right to provide models, in a variety of materials, including carved wood, wax, plaster, terracotta or lead. Casting could only be undertaken by a member of the guild of founders (*fondeurs*), who were forbidden to

*G*ilt-bronze and Sèvres porcelain clock, late 1780s. The porcelain is close to designs by Lagrenée.

*G*ilt-bronze model of a fire engine, circa 1765-70. A *goût grec* toy.

usurp the right of members of the gilders' guild (*doreurs*) to gild. Large numbers of lawsuits between the various guilds endeavoured to deal with some of the grey areas, the main one stemming from the difficulty of deciding who had the right of *ciselure* (chasing). This was at various times claimed by the *fondeurs*, who would describe themselves in documents as *fondeurs-ciseleurs*, but the *doreurs* normally managed to retain the upper hand, and as a result were often known as *ciseleurs-doreurs*. After the finance minister Turgot's short-lived attempt at abolishing the guilds to encourage free trade at the beginning of Louis XVI's reign, the *fondeurs* and the *doreurs* merged into one guild in 1776, thereby resolving the problem once and for all.

It is misleading to consider this situation as entirely one of conflict, since members of the two guilds needed to cooperate extremely closely in the manufacture of individual objects, and, in the usual manner of craft and trade at this period, families could include members of both guilds. It may even have been possible for individuals to belong to both guilds. Quentin-Claude Pitoin, at any rate, appears to have done so, as well as being a member of the Académie de Saint Luc, a sensible precaution which enabled him to carry out every single stage in the design and manufacture of an object. Another way around the restrictions of the system was offered by a Royal appointment; the Caffiéris and Antoine Le Lièvre were among those who benefited from this useful loophole. Many *bronziers* seem to have been content to belong to just one of the two, and to subcontract work to members of the other. Such was the case of Robert Osmond, a *fondeur* who was among the few to sign his pieces.

Ownership of models provided a splendid pretext for litigation; a furniture mount could itself be used as a model, for example, and for this reason a registry of designs was established in 1766 by the *fondeurs*' guild, with the intention of offering protection from unauthorized copying.

## MANUFACTURE

The *fondeur* pressed the model into fine sand in a box, molten bronze being poured into the resulting depression. The extremely rough casting which emerged was cleaned up, imperfections removed, and unintended holes filled. Large bronzes, cast in several places, were braised together at this stage. The cleaning-up process, known as *reparure*, was the work of the *fondeur*, but the *doreurs* lived in perpetual fear that it might overspill into creative work or *ciselure*.

The object then passed to another specialist craftsman, the *ciseleur* (chaser), who was employed by the *doreur* or the *fondeur*. He began by setting it in a block of tar, a fixing preferable to a vice which might distort it. The *ciselure* of a bronze was of extreme importance in that it gave the surface its final character and style. Bronze was chased with chisels of varying types, depending on the surface intended. A matt surface was obtained by the use of a chisel with tiny points on the end of its blade. The graining of a leaf or a branch could be achieved by a chisel with parallel lines of points, giving a directional effect to the surface. In

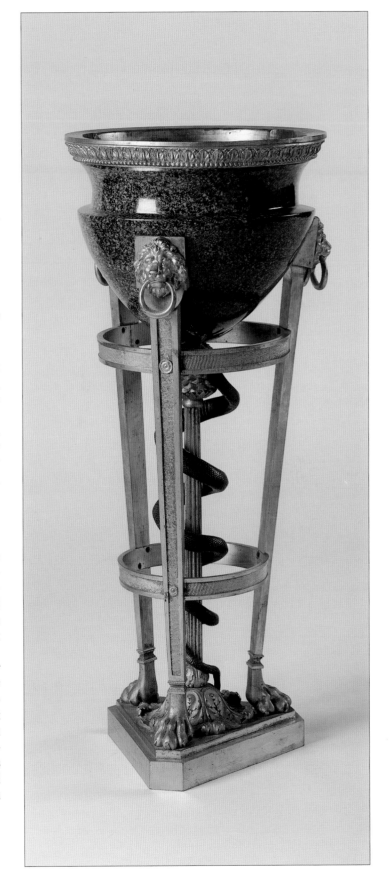

*O*ne of a pair of late eighteenth-century gilt-bronze and marble tripods of *Athénienne* shape.

*G*ilt-bronze and blued steel *miroir de toilette*, circa 1780. The arms of Louis XVI and Marie Antoinette may have been added, but the birds and garlands of flowers echo the gilt-bronze frame made by Gouthière for the glazed panel of the door of Marie Antoinette's Cabinet de la Méridienne at Versailles.

the rococo period, fairly rough matting chisels were used to give a naturalistic feeling, but with the neoclassical style came finer matting chisels, which emphasized the delicate nature of flower petals, for example. Flat surfaces were smoothed down and burnished with an agate, both before and after gilding, producing a slightly rippled effect.

The technique of gilding bronze is a complex and costly one; and alternative finishes were often preferred. The *ébéniste* Charles Cressent, writing in the catalogue of the auction of his stock and collection in 1749, comments on the highly elaborate bronze mounts on two bookcases, representing the Four Seasons and the Four Corners of the Earth: "They have only been given a gold colour because of the great expense [of gilding them]; whoever buys them can be confident that they are totally suitable to be gilded". The *couleur d'or* process involved dipping the bronze in acid to remove all dirt and tarnish, and coating it with a varnish intended to preserve and protect the very shiny

surface. The varnishes were usually clear, but they could be slightly tinted, often yellow, to imitate the colour of gilding. This technique was extremely widespread, particularly in the first half of the eighteenth century, but because varnish either rubbed off or could be chipped, many pieces originally varnished have subsequently been gilded.

The most common method used to gild bronze in France in the eighteenth century is thought to have been known at least since Roman times. Its French name, *dorure d'or moulu*, or gilding with powdered gold, was adopted in England as "ormolu". The technique consists of applying to the acid-cleaned bronze surface a paste made with powdered gold and mercury. These two metals amalgamate easily, and the liquid mercury acts as a vehicle to deposit the gold thickly onto the bronze surface. The paste often spilled onto the back of the pieces, and these spills can still be visible today. The piece is then heated to burn off the mercury and allow the gold to seep into the grain of the bronze. This is the dangerous part of the operation, mercury fumes being especially poisonous. The process might be repeated several times, to produce a progressively richer effect. At the end of the gilding operation, to further enhance the crispness of the chasing, the matt parts were gone over again with chisels, and the smooth parts were burnished with agate burnishers to achieve a sparkling appearance.

*P*erfume fountain delivered to Louis XV by the *marchand-mercier* Thomas-Joachim Hébert in 1743. The design survives in the Bibliothèque Nationale, Paris.

*M*id-eighteenth-century Chinese porcelain vases, with gilt-bronze mounts of about 1770, the early neoclassical period.

Pierre Gouthière claimed, probably rightly, to have been the inventor of a refinement to this technique, known as *dorure au mat* (matt gilding). This became popular during the reign of Louis XVI, and involved coating the areas intended to remain matt with a special chemical, heating the piece, and then plunging it into cold water. The resultant effect is of a very finely and evenly grained surface, achieved without chasing. Patination was also used at this period. The contrast between gilded and patinated bronze was particularly appreciated, because of the "Antique" impression it conveyed.

Bronze mounts for furniture were at first fixed with surprisingly little attention to the visibility of the fixings. Under Louis XV, rococo furniture mounts had holes drilled in them, and were attached with screws or nails in an indiscriminate manner, even by the finest *ébénistes*, such as Bernard van Risamburgh, but by the beginning of the neoclassical period such rococo carelessness had given way to considerable ingenuity in hiding the fixings, by braising lugs to the backs of the mounts, and attaching them from behind. *Ébénistes* practised double standards even in this, however, by hiding the fixings of some of the bronzes on a piece and not of others.

At the beginning of the eighteenth century, the mounts of vases maintained a pretence of being removable; the uprights forming the handles were hinged to the base and rim, so that the removal of the pins could in theory allow the dismantling of the mount; but by the 1730s extravagant rococo mounts were screwed or bolted together. Bases and collars could be made in several sections, with a leaf or other ornament hiding the join and its fixing. The fixings of bronze mounts on vases are usually well hidden; probably because the craftsmen who made the mounts also had the task of applying them.

## CROWNED "C" MARK

A small hallmark, a *C* (for *cuivre*) with a crown above it, is found on some gilt-bronzes, usually on pieces of the first half of the eighteenth century, although a few earlier bronzes also bear this mark. In February 1745, Louis XV issued an edict instructing that all objects made wholly or partly of copper should have their copper content verified, and be hall-marked. The reason for this was ostensibly to prevent copper being alloyed with cheaper metals, but it is probable that economic considerations were uppermost; France was deeply embroiled in the War of the Austrian Succession, and an additional hallmarking tax was always useful. Practical disadvantages of poor alloy included less resistance to fire in copper saucepans, and a reduction in the quality and durability of gilding. The edict ordered that all new and old copper objects in the trade should be marked. Thus the mark is found on everything from gilt-bronze furniture mounts to seventeenth-century bronze sculpture. A further edict of February 1749 abolished the practice. As a method of dating, it is only satisfactory to confirm with precision the date of objects which are stylistically compatible with this period, and all others must be assumed to have been in the trade during those four years.

*M*id-eighteenth-century perfume burner of gilt-bronze, lacquered metal, Meissen figures and Vincennes flowers. The chimney in the farmhouse is fitted for burning perfume. A characteristic example of an assemblage invented by a *marchand-mercier*.

*G*ilt-bronze and Sèvres porcelain inkstand, circa 1780. A typical *marchand-mercier* object, decorated with plaques and vases especially ordered from Sèvres.

*Salon* with Régence panelling in the Abbot's palace at Chaalis, built in the early eighteenth century by Jean Aubert. The tall panels still retain the proportions of pilasters, and giltwood mouldings frame the looking-glass and the panels of crimson damask.

# 8

# PORCELAIN

"*Que l'on fuïe le lourd et le trivial, qu'on donne du leger, du fin, du neuf et du varié. Le succès est assuré.*" (Avoid heavy or obvious motifs, but use instead lightness, subtlety, novelty and variety, and you cannot fail.) This was the recommendation of Hendrick Van Hulst, artistic advisor to the Vincennes porcelain factory, writing to the factory's director, Jacques-René Boileau, on 21 September 1751.

## ORIENTAL INFLUENCE

In 1686, Louis XIV, his family and ministers received lavish gifts from the Siamese embassy sent by Constantine Phaulkon, a Greek merchant established in Bangkok. Several thousand pieces of porcelain were included, and these were added to the already important collections owned by the King and his son, the Grand Dauphin, as well as being distributed to various members of the Court. Chinese porcelain had been reaching Europe in some quantities since the mid-seventeenth century, and the first major manifestation of interest in Oriental porcelain had been the so-called "Trianon de Porcelaine", built for the King in the gardens of Versailles in 1670, and decorated with glazed earthenware tiles and vases from Delft, Rouen and Saint-Coud, in a blue and white colour scheme. The fashion for porcelain pioneered by Louis XIV, both for use at table and in interior decoration, was to flourish during the eighteenth century, and Oriental porcelain objects found an honoured place in France, despite competition from European factories.

Continuing the tradition of mounting precious objects in silver or gold, Chinese and Japanese vases were frequently mounted in gilt-bronze, and used to decorate chimneypieces and console tables. The

*A* Chinese celadon vase mounted in gilt-bronze and filled with flowers, from a painting by Anne Vallayer-Coster dated 1774. Oriental porcelain vases may frequently have been intended as flower vases, and Anne Vallayer-Coster produced many paintings of them, some of which she provided as cartoons for the Gobelins or the Savonnerie.

description of the pieces placed by Madame de Pompadour at Bellevue (see Chapter Four) provides a good example of the use of gilt-bronze mounted Oriental porcelain. Pieces were adapted for European use; a Chinese chamberpot might have its handle removed to turn it into a decorative bowl, and many tall vases were cut down to be mounted with a footrim and collar, as well as with two scrolling handles. Oriental porcelain was also incorporated into more elaborate confections, such as pot-pourris or perfume fountains, together with lacquer and other porcelain, including European. By the 1760s, the Sèvres factory had begun to produce imitation Chinese vases for mounting, in plain-coloured, green or dark blue porcelain, on order from *marchands-merciers* such as Dulac or the Poirier-Daguerre partnership, who may have been unable to get enough Chinese porcelain to satisfy the demand.

The difficulty in finding the required quantities of Oriental porcelain may have been one of the factors to actuate Rodolphe Lemaire, who in 1729 managed to persuade Augustus the Strong, Elector of Saxony, to allow some pieces of Japanese porcelain from his collection to be copied at the Meissen factory. That Lemaire, a shrewd French businessman, was intending to pass off the porcelain as Oriental is evident from the fact that he insisted that pieces made for him should not be marked with the familiar crossed swords. They were designed for the French market, and the question remains as to whether the French were deceived. The Prince de Condé, whose Japanese porcelain collection at Chantilly inspired the Chantilly porcelain factory, may even have unwittingly owned some, so that some Chantilly pieces could conceivably be copied not directly from Japanese originals, but via Meissen.

At any rate, by the 1740s Meissen was available in Paris through *marchands-merciers* such as Duvaux, whose day-book records the sale of a large quantity of pieces. Some of these were sold as they were, such as tea services, while others were mounted up, such as figures, which might be raised on gilt-bronze bases, incorporated into wall lights with Vincennes flowers, or used to support a gilt-bronze clock case.

In 1747, following the death of his first wife, the Dauphin Louis, son of Louis XV, married Marie-Josèphe, daughter of Frederic Augustus II, Elector of Saxony, the son of Augustus the Strong and protector of the Meissen porcelain factory. On this occasion Marie-Josèphe was presented by her father with some of the finest wares that the factory could

produce: "The porcelains are considered as the masterpieces of our factory, and are used to decorate the chimneypieces in the magnificent rooms in the Dauphin and Dauphine's apartment," wrote Loss, the Saxon envoy, to Augustus's minister Bruhl. There were vases and clock cases painted in green *camaieu* (monochrome) to match the decoration of the rooms, which had been lacquered by Etienne Martin. Marie-Josèphe's apartments were quite obviously being used as a showcase for her father's beloved porcelain. She received further presents of porcelain, including, upon the birth of her first child in 1750 (a daughter named Marie-Zéphirine), a series of white-glazed figures representing Apollo and the Muses, which the Duc de Luynes, in critical mood, accused of looking like bleached wood. By 1765, the Dauphine herself recognised the superiority of Sèvres over Meissen. Writing to her brother Xavier to thank him for sending her Meissen figures, she complained that they suffered from "an uncomfortable and affected appearance, which deprives them of elegance; . . . I prefer the porcelain made here, and I wish it were copied in Saxony." This is all the more surprising since Sèvres never competed seriously with Meissen in the manufacture of glazed figures and groups.

# FRENCH PORCELAIN

Research into the manufacture of porcelain was being carried out in France soon after the middle of the seventeenth century, and had begun to bear fruit by the time of the Siamese embassy's presentation at court.

*P*air of Mennecy beggars, mid-eighteenth century. This factory, which was established by François Barbin, produced charming pieces, both sculptures and more utilitarian (mostly *toilette*) wares. The whiteness of Mennecy paste is close to that of Vincennes.

*S*aint-Cloud *seau à bouteille* (bottle cooler), circa 1730. The shape and moulded decoration is taken from a traditional Louis XIV *seau*. Gilding is used here for the Oriental figures in an unusually lavish manner.

The most preposterous theories about the nature of porcelain – that, for example, it was made by burying a variety of alchemical materials, such as lobster shells and plaster, in the ground for eighty years – had been discounted by this time, but it was not until the 1760s that the discovery in France of the essential material, kaolin, permitted the manufacture of true (or hard paste) porcelain of the type made at Meissen or in the Orient.

Continuous experiments in various places including Rouen, Saint-Cloud, Nevers, Paris, Chantilly and Mennecy, produced a variety of different pastes made of strange ingredients, which when fired and covered with a glaze could be slightly translucent, in various shades of off-white. This type of porcelain was known as soft paste. Many small factories were established to produce pieces in this technique, and they met with varying rates of success.

Of all the factories or workshops which produced soft paste porcelain in the eighteenth century, Saint-Cloud and Chantilly stand out because of the quality and originality of their work, but they both ultimately succumbed to Sèvres, even though they attempted to compete with it by imitating its production.

## SAINT-CLOUD

At the beginning of the eighteenth century, only one major porcelain factory existed in France. Saint-Cloud, established as a faience factory, had supplied tiles for the Trianon de Porcelaine, and continued to make faience (tin-glazed earthenware) until its demise in 1766. Its porcelain production at first consisted of pieces in imitation of Louis XIV silver shapes, with decoration in blue in the style of the applied or engraved lambrequin motifs of Louis XIV silver. Gradually new influences increased the variety of Saint-Cloud's work. Blanc-de-Chine shapes were copied, with relief-moulded foliage, and these mixed with Louis XIV influences to produce charming pieces such as *seaux à bouteilles* (bottle coolers) of silver shapes with grotesque masks and applied flowering branches in the Chinese style. Polychromy and gilding appear to have been developed by the beginning of the eighteenth century. At first simple, bright colours such as yellow and green were used to imitate

*C*hantilly *déjeuner* (tea service), circa 1730-35. The pieces are shaped in the form of stylized leaves, with Kakiemon decoration.

Chinese and Japanese decoration, such as *famille verte* and Kakiemon. Gilding was sparingly employed, but a number of small pieces survive with gold-leaf figures and foliage applied in a raised technique akin to that used for enamels. The fashion for chinoiserie during the Régence period inspired Saint-Cloud to produce its own series of Oriental figures, in the same style as those found in carved wood or on gilt-bronze objects at this epoch.

The Saint-Cloud factory was run by various members of the Trou and Chicaneau families, and their disagreements resulted in the establishment of an associated workshop and retail outlet in Paris. An advertising leaflet of 1731 conveys an impression of the variety of Saint-Cloud's production, although it is not clear whether this includes goods from the Paris workshop as well. It proudly proclaims itself a Manufacture Royale, on account of the various Privilèges it had successfully obtained. It also gives details of the objects available at the shop in the Rue de la Madeleine, which included barbers' bowls, ewers and basins, candlesticks, components for the *toilette* and for tea services (stated to be "relief moulded like those from Japan"), pot-pourri vases and some table wares including wine coolers and tureens. The sculptures are described as *figures grotesques*. The factory's success undoubtedly lay in its ability to produce attractive, colourful and reasonably priced alternatives to silver, in shapes especially adapted for useful purposes. Some of the objects available in the Paris shop were made to be mounted, including "Tree trunks, for making candelabra". The château at Saint-Cloud belonged to the Orléans family, and the protection of the Regent and his son extended to financial assistance, as well as helping to obtain the renewed Privilèges necessary to preserve the factory from loss of secrets or workers. From the 1740s, the rise of Vincennes spelt disaster for Saint-Cloud, and Saint-Cloud's director, Henri-François Trou, unsuccessfully petitioned Louis XV in 1766 to be appointed as successor to Boileau, the Sèvres factory's director.

## CHANTILLY

Ironically, it was under the protection of the Prince de Condé (known as "Monsieur le Duc"), arch-rival of the Orléans family, that Ciquaire Cirou, a porcelain painter who had been associated with Saint-Cloud, started a porcelain factory at Chantilly in the mid-1720s. Cirou's patron, suffering in gilded exile at Chantilly after his failed stint as Louis XV's chief minister from 1723 to 1726, appears to have taken an active interest in this and other scientific activities on the estate. The production in the

early years consisted of charming imitations of Japanese Kakiemon pieces, probably directly from the Prince's substantial collection, but also through the engravings of Jean-Antoine Fraisse, who held the title of Peintre de S.A.S. Monsieur le Duc. Fraisse published a set of engravings in 1735, representing various fanciful Oriental scenes and motifs allegedly drawn from originals in Monsieur le Duc's collection. Whether he invented some of these himself can unfortunately no longer be verified, but at any rate they occasionally appear to have inspired Chantilly (and Mennecy) porcelain, as well as various faience and textile workshops.

*P*air of Chantilly seated wolves, circa 1740. The Chantilly factory started to produce sculpture and wares not inspired by Oriental prototypes at about this date. Another example of this model is naturalistically coloured.

Unlike Saint-Cloud, Chantilly sought its inspiration almost entirely from the East, albeit often indirectly or inaccurately. Shapes of cups and saucers, jugs or wine coolers were consistently light and graceful, and the decoration they normally bore, in a limited polychromy, was sparingly applied in the Japanese manner, but with a fine black outline. Elaborate naturalistic or fanciful pieces became a speciality: cups and saucers shaped like leaves, and pot-pourris with pierced lids held by bald smiling Chinamen. Indeed Oriental figures and animals count among Chantilly's most successful productions, whether left in the white, to show off the modelling, or brightly coloured, with richly patterned costumes.

Monsieur le Duc died in 1740, and Chantilly's fortunes began to waver. Cirou could not count upon the support of the Prince's heir, a minor, and may have faced financial difficulties as a result. This period also coincided with the rise of the Vincennes factory, and Chantilly's production, in an attempt to evolve, began to abandon the Oriental inspiration that had constituted its particular charm, concentrating instead on poor imitations of its powerful rival, often decorated with monochrome blue sprigs of flowers. Bonnet wrote to Dutillot in Parma in 1760 that: "The Chantilly service is for the secondary tables, everyone prefers it to Indian [meaning Chinese] porcelain, and everyone wants some. This manufacture has reactivated itself, I am not sure whether it will be able to survive, to make my service they have used new and very expensive moulds made in imitation of those of Sèvres."

## SÈVRES

The soft paste of Vincennes, the result of the researches of Claude-Humbert Gérin, was the whitest of all the soft pastes. It was this whiteness that in the 1740s encouraged various investors and shareholders ("Messieurs les Intéressés"), some of whom were well placed in the favour of the King and of Madame de Pompadour, to establish succeeding companies which sought and successfully obtained Privilèges enabling them to place the Vincennes factory on a sound financial footing, by stifling the competition from the other, longer-established concerns.

*V*incennes *pot de chambre ovale* with chinoiserie decoration, probably taken from an engraving after Jean Pillement. Unmarked, dating from the second half of the 1740s.

*G*lazed Vincennes group, *L'Heure du berger,* circa 1748-52. This ambitious group is close to an engraving by Jean Pelletier after Boucher, called *Le repos de Diane,* but probably antedates it, suggesting that the model was copied directly from a drawing provided by Boucher himself. Pelletier's engraving is a reversed version of the group.

While still in private hands, the factory moved to Sèvres in 1756, and was finally sold to Louis XV in 1759. It has remained state property ever since.

While the nature of the soft paste remained fairly constant at Vincennes-Sèvres from the earliest days, research continued into the production of different colours and gilding, as well as into the shaping and calibration of pieces through the use of specialist machinery. Jean Hellot, the head of the Académie des Sciences, who had already submitted to the Academy a treatise on textile dyes (*Théorie chimique de la teinture des étoffes*) in 1740-41, was called in and perfected a greater variety of enamel colours, ground colours, and, most importantly, shades within colours. This work, accomplished by Hellot and some of the porcelain painters, contributed to the factory's success by placing it apart

*V*incennes flower vase on original gilt-bronze stand. Bearing the date letter *c* for 1755 and interlaced *L*s, the royal cypher which the Vincennes factory appears to have started using in the late 1740s, before Louis XV took an active interest in it, perhaps because it was lodged in a royal castle. This was probably one of the first shapes designed by Duplessis in about 1750. The *bleu céleste* ground colour is applied mostly to the back (below right), which indicates it may have been intended to sit in front of a looking-glass. Its original name has not been identified, but it may have been called a *cuvette Roussel*, in which case it is tempting to identify it with the example given by the factory to Boucher as his yearly present in 1756.

Vincennes *caisses carrées* of 1754 with *bleu céleste* ground and scenes of birds in landscapes by Armand l'Aîné, the factory's best bird painter. They were bought from Duvaux by the dealer Madame Lambert in December 1755, on behalf of Lord Hervey (later the 3rd Marquess of Bristol).

from its competitors, whose range of colours was limited and who were prevented by the various Privilèges from endeavouring to imitate Vincennes's new technical advances.

The quest for hard paste finally met with success in the 1760s, through the work of men such as the splendidly eccentric Comte de Lauraguais. His friend the Comte de Ségur, though he complained about Lauraguais's exaggerated womanizing, claimed that Lauraguais lost most of his fortune not on women but through his scientific experiments, which included endeavouring to discover whether it was possible to dissolve diamonds. In contrast to this magnificently wasteful pastime, Ségur proudly affirmed that Lauraguais perfected the science of making true porcelain. However, biscuit medallions in the style of medals are all that is known to survive from Lauraguais's short-lived production.

The Sèvres factory was to employ kaolin from Saint-Yrieix near

Limoges successfully from circa 1769. Unfortunately, some of the technical advances made at Vincennes and Sèvres for the decoration of soft paste were never completely successful in their effect on hard paste, and even specially developed techniques did not manage to create pieces in hard paste of such aesthetic harmony. Soft paste continued to be produced until the end of the eighteenth century, and most of the factory's finest work is in this medium even after the advent of hard paste, despite the fact that hard paste was much cheaper to make and easier to work. Many of the colours developed for soft paste would not work with hard paste, and those that did never blended with the glaze in the same pleasing manner.

Vincennes could not have taken off and eclipsed its rivals without more than simply technical superiority, and it was fortunate that the shareholders were men well placed to bring to the factory the finest available artistic talents. Of the several artists involved, three stand out on account of their predominant role: Duplessis, Bachelier, and Boucher. Their work created a style completely divorced from that of the other factories, whose staple diet consisted in charming but comparatively simple pieces inspired more or less directly by Oriental prototypes, some via traditional French silver shapes and faience decoration. By applying to Vincennes-Sèvres porcelain the stylistic developments of the most up-to-date branches of the decorative arts, such as those of gilt-bronze, carved panelling and decorative painting and engraving, these artists were to create something with a spark of new invention which differed completely from all that preceded it.

At the very beginning, however, in the early 1740s, Vincennes produced pieces in the same style as those made at other factories such as Saint-Cloud, for example vases with relief-moulded branches of flowers. Meissen was also imitated, with flower-painting or figures in elaborate landscapes, but by the mid-1740s porcelain flowers modelled and painted to imitate real ones undoubtedly formed the first serious commercial success of the new venture. This success was protected, as always, by a Privilège which prevented other factories from making or painting flowers "in imitation of natural flowers". These had a ready use in interior decoration, being fitted to lacquered metal branches which were placed in vases or were added to wall lights and lanterns. Lazare

Vincennes *pot à eau et bassin* decorated with birds in reserves on a *bleu lapis* ground, and a gold mount for the lid. Dated 1753, it is probably the example sold by Duvaux to Madame de Pompadour in the following year.

*S*èvres *seau à liqueurs du Roi*, 1758. The shape was designed by Duplessis in 1752, probably for Louis XV's *bleu céleste* service. The scenes of hunters in blue coats are reminiscent of the Oudry cartoons for the Gobelins tapestry series of the *Chasses du Roi*. This *seau*, with decoration described as *Rose chasses*, was part of a service that may have been sold to Louis XV by the *marchand-mercier* Madame Lair, who bought it from the factory in late 1759.

Duvaux supplied his clients with objects decorated with Vincennes flowers as early as 1748, and in May the following year he delivered and fitted in the *petit cabinet* of the Dauphine Marie-Josèphe de Saxe at Versailles (the room with the white and green Meissen) two pairs of wall lights with naturally coloured branches mounted with Vincennes flowers of specified types, including tulips, hyacinths, narcissi, roses, anemones, violets and *oreilles d'ours*. The drip-pans were also of Vincennes porcelain; only the nozzles were made of gilt-bronze.

As with many other branches of the decorative arts, the *marchands-merciers* were heavily involved. Duvaux began to be employed by the factory to mount flowers onto branches, as well as doing so on his own account, and it may be noteworthy that Duplessis was among the artists he commissioned to model and make gilt-bronze mounts.

Jean-Claude Chambellan called Duplessis (circa 1695-1774), as a member of the Académie de Saint Luc, was able to model gilt-bronze mounts or provide any sort of decorative design, and in addition could

*S*èvres *marronière* (chestnut basket), dated 1758. Possibly the example bought by Madame de Pompadour at the end-of-year sale at Versailles in 1760.

make gilt-bronze objects that bear witness to a rococo inventiveness akin to that of his fellow Torinese Meissonier. By the early 1750s, he was employed as a regular designer, and all the elegant rococo pieces produced by the factory at this period appear to have been his work, notably the shapes for the Louis XV *bleu céleste* service, the designs for many of which survive to this day in the factory's archives (see page 39). His designs for utility objects, such as plates and sauceboats, were gradually simplified, probably because they were too elaborate and expensive to produce, and these modified shapes continued to be employed for service and tea wares until the end of the eighteenth century. Vases designed by Duplessis in the early 1750s, such as the aptly named *vase Duplessis*, were of sufficiently extravagant rococo shapes that they were gradually replaced in the early 1760s by ones in an equally exaggerated version of the *goût grec*, in some cases still Duplessis's work.

"Outlandish taste is the hallmark of mediocrity . . . Stick to jasmine, daffodils . . ." ranted Diderot at Bachelier as a result of the latter's attempt at serious painting for the 1765 Salon. Jean-Jacques Bachelier

*S*èvres biscuit bust of Louis XV, on a green-ground pedestal with gilt trophies, circa 1759-60. These were produced to celebrate Louis XV's purchase of the factory, and are probably from a model by J. B. Lemoyne. The *marchand-mercier* Poirier bought two green-ground pedestals with busts in early 1760, and may have sold them to the Duke of Parma. Claude Bonnet wrote to Guillaume Dutillot in April 1760 to inform him he was sending "The portraits of the King and Queen also in biscuit porcelain, on small pedestals which are used for flowers when the busts are removed" (*Le portrait du Roi et de la Reine aussi en biscuit sur des petits pieds-destaux qui servent a mettre des fleurs lorsque l'on ny met pas les petits bustes*).

*P*air of Sèvres *vases à têtes d'éléphants*, 1760. The shape was designed by Duplessis, and the idea for the elephants' heads may have come from a Chinese porcelain vase. The Chinese figures, painted by Charles-Nicolas Dodin, are taken from Boucher engravings. These vases, which have lost their candle nozzles, may have been bought by Madame de Pompadour in 1762.

*T*wo Sèvres biscuit groups from the service given by Louis XV to the Duchess of Bedford in 1763. They were intended to form part of the table decoration. The left-hand group, *La maitresse d'école*, was modelled by Falconet after a Boucher engraving, as was the right-hand group, *Le sabot cassé*.

(1724-1806) never attained a reputation as a serious painter, but his work for Vincennes-Sèvres showed the way for the factory's painters for the next fifty years. Unfortunately none of the drawings he made for the factory have survived, but he is known to have provided panels of flowers to be copied directly on to porcelain; examples of several pieces of porcelain all painted with the same panel, clearly from one of his models, testify to Bachelier's competence in this field. He must also have supplied allegorical trophies; the large trophies he painted on canvas for the Hôtel des Affaires Etrangères at Versailles in the early 1760s bear many of the features of allegorical painting on Sèvres of the same period, including putti, painters' pallets, helmets with

*S*èvres teapot, 1758, with the painter's mark (a crescent) of Armand l'Aîné. An uncommon decoration, with peacock feathers instead of the more usual painted reserves. It was probably part of a tea service. In the nineteenth century, the pink ground colour became known as *rose Pompadour*, and, later, *rose du Barry*.

multicoloured plumes, martial trophies, medallions, flags and foliage. As well as his own designs, Bachelier supplied a wide variety of engravings to the factory, notably sets of Teniers village fetes. The porcelain painters used these inventively, taking details with a few figures from these large engravings. François Boucher's engravings suffered the same fate; the painter André-Vincent Vielliard specialized in lifting individual putti from these and bringing them together, sometimes clothing them and placing them in landscapes.

Boucher also contributed to Vincennes-Sèvres in a more direct manner during the 1750s, supplying drawings which were copied by the painters or turned into biscuit groups by the factory's modellers. Most of these were of children, some taken from the tapestry cartoons he had supplied for Beauvais some years earlier.

White glazed sculpture had been among the factory's first productions, but by the early 1750s biscuit (unglazed porcelain) figures largely replaced it. The absence of glaze preserved the sharpness of the modelling, and the texture was akin to that of carved marble. Biscuit figures and groups, many of which were taken from Boucher's designs, were destined for use on table centrepieces, and therefore sold in quantities with dinner services, as well as on their own and in pairs. They were modelled by specialist workers at the factory, who were only entitled to do so because the Privilège exempted them from the requirement that modelling could only be carried out by members of the Académie de Saint Luc. On occasion, however, outside modellers were called in: in 1772, the decorative sculptor François-Joseph Duret provided the models for a centrepiece comprising several groups taken from Van Loo's *Concert Espagnol*, to the order of the *marchand-mercier* Madame Lair, who specialized in services and table decoration.

"He [Louis XV] made us unpack his beautiful blue, white and gold service from Vincennes, which had just been delivered from Paris, where it had been placed on show. It was one of the first masterpieces of this new porcelain manufacture, which was seeking to surpass and bankrupt Meissen." The Duc de Croÿ, who was present on this auspicious occasion in February 1754, has summed up neatly the production and aspirations of the factory at that moment. Armed with its

Privilège, which gave it the exclusivity of producing pieces not only decorated with human figures but also gilded, in the Meissen manner, the Vincennes factory's growing output was to reduce substantially the quantity of Meissen imported into France, despite the persistent efforts of the Dauphine's father.

In addition to new shapes and designs for the panels, one of the major innovations of the 1750s was undoubtedly the development of ground colours, in imitation of Chinese and Meissen porcelain; these were used until the end of the eighteenth century and beyond. The bodies of pieces such as vases, cups and saucers and teapots and the edges of plates were covered in a colour, reserving one or more areas in white, which could then be decorated. Since the colours were often uneven at first, especially on the edges, increasingly elaborate gilded borders were employed to frame the reserves. The first attempts, in 1752, resulted in a blotchy underglaze blue which became known as

*Sèvres tobacco jar with spoon, circa 1765. Gold snuffboxes, an important fashion accessory, were refilled from porcelain jars of this type.*

*Sèvres tea service. Part of the porcelain purchased by the 3rd Duke of Richmond while British ambassador in Paris in 1766, and still preserved at Goodwood. Unusually, it matches a dessert service bought at the same time.*

*P*ieces from a Sèvres dessert service commissioned by Lord Melbourne in 1770. Only the larger pieces are painted with putti, while the others bear trophies by Charles Buteux, Sèvres's specialist trophy artist.

*bleu lapis*. This was soon followed by a turquoise, known as *bleu Hellot* or *bleu céleste*, used first on Louis XV's service (see page 12). Yellow and violet also appeared at this date, but were discontinued, either for technical or commercial reasons. The next campaign of research into ground colours took place in 1756-7, with green, pink and a pale green known as *petit vert*. Over the next few years, several ground colours were employed together on pieces, with a main colour overlaid by scrolling ribbons of another. Pink grounds were covered with patterns in blue and gold, to create marbled effects. This was to lead in the early 1760s to another major stylistic development, the *fond Taillandier*, named after one of the factory's most talented flower painters; small

white discs in a regular pattern over a ground colour (often a modified *bleu céleste*) are edged with gilt or coloured dots and contain a stylized flowerhead. Increasingly elaborate border patterns came into use with the neoclassical movement; continuous flower scrolls or vases of flowers competed with the ground colour on the borders of plates, for example. During the 1760s, *bleu nouveau*, a deep navy-blue ground colour, replaced the slightly purple *bleu lapis* and became the most popular colour, especially for vases and other pieces with elaborately decorated reserves.

Gilding was one of the major strengths of the Vincennes-Sèvres factory, and successive Privilèges sought to establish the Manufacture Royale's monopoly of this technique. Introduced in 1748, gilding was at first employed to outline borders of shapes and decoration, but gradually it was seen as a suitable vehicle for decorative motifs, and was used as such in the borders of reserves. The earliest versions of this resemble the lambrequins of Meissen gilding, but soon wild rococo patterns predominated, with palm fronds, flowers, birds and trelliswork. Two coats of gilding were normally applied to provide relief, and, after firing, the surface was tooled with a point to achieve contrast, for example, in the petals of flowers or the feathers of birds. Gilding became more restrained at the end of the 1750s, with simple wide lines tooled with contrasting motifs, and the *goût grec* saw gilding

*S*èvres cup and saucer (*gobelet litron*), 1770-80. This cylindrical shape was most popular for cups and saucers at Sèvres throughout the eighteenth century. The decoration applied to them was extremely varied and mixed sets were frequently purchased for display rather than use.

*S*èvres vase, probably known as a *vase Bachelier à feuilles d'acanthe*. Unmarked, about 1775-80. The scene of Turkish lovers was probably taken from an engraving by Jean-Baptiste Le Prince.

Garniture of Sèvres biscuit figures on blue-glazed stands with gilt marbling, circa 1780. The marble version of the centre figure, called the *Baigneuse Falconet*, was exhibited by Etienne-Maurice Falconet at the 1757 Salon of the Académie Royale and the first porcelain models appeared in 1758. The outer pair, known as *Amours Falconet*, were first produced in 1758 (boy) and 1761 (girl). Many of the earlier examples stand on low octagonal bases. Truncated column bases such as these are a neoclassical innovation.

Sèvres *beurrier anglais* (English butter dish), 1788, with arabesque decoration.

being employed for classical features such as Vitruvian scroll friezes. Increasingly, gilding sought to imitate gilt-bronze, especially on relief-moulded decoration, but garlands of flowers and borders tooled like the gold frames of snuffboxes persisted as the most frequent use of this striking technique. One splendid but fragile variation, jewelling, was introduced in 1780. This consisted of elaborate patterns stamped out on gold, which were applied to the porcelain and covered with blobs of coloured enamels simulating precious stones set in mounts. The Geneva-born enameller Joseph Coteau, whose principal speciality was the painting of enamels for clock faces, was responsible for introducing this technique at Sèvres, although his stay there was short-lived.

Large vases formed highly decorative ornaments for chimneypieces and console tables, but other shapes were used for this purpose as well, notably *cuvettes* (bowls for flowers); even cups and saucers were acquired as much for display as for use (including jewelled ones, which were totally impractical). They and other types of objects were therefore manufactured with this primary purpose in mind, to such an extent that when Louis XVI ordered his great *bleu nouveau* dinner service in 1782, he was not intending to eat out of the plates decorated with mythological scenes and commissioned another set without any painting at all in the wells.

Shapes for objects in current usage were practically all developed by the time of the factory's move to Sèvres in 1756. Table service and *toilette* component shapes (such as *écuelles* and ewers and basins) were close to the silver equivalents, a fact which is hardly surprising in view of Duplessis's involvement; he was to be appointed Orfèvre du Roi in 1758 after spending several years begging for this privilege in payment for supplying a machine of his own invention that ensured pieces were of uniform thickness. Shapes changed little until the end of the eighteenth century, variety being provided by ever-changing decoration.

It was in the design of vase shapes that the factory was continuously to show the most considerable ingenuity. Some of the early shapes endured in popularity, such as the *vase Hollandois*, a flared bulb vase of oval section socketed into a flat base, but other were produced in small numbers, notably highly elaborate ones such as the *pot-pourri en vaisseau* (better known by its nineteenth-century name of *vaisseau à mât*), a boat-shaped vase on a scrolled rococo base with a tall superstructure of complex rigging surmounted by a swirling flag, which is first found in the late 1750s. As well as being sold singly or in pairs, vases were put together to form *garnitures* (sets). These normally consisted of one, or two different, pairs of vases for either side of a chimneypiece, with a more elaborate vase for the centre. The centre one might be for pot-pourri, and the side ones for lighting; in 1758 the Prince de Condé bought a *garniture* (decorated with a pink ground and putti) consisting of a central *pot-pourri en vaisseau*, with a pair of *vases à tête d'éléphant*, both fitted with two candle nozzles on the end of each trunk, and a pair of matching *vases à oreilles*. All these shapes were designed by Duplessis.

Bachelier also designed shapes in addition to his other duties, and the *vase Bachelier* (see page 177) is one of the factory's most elegant. The *goût grec* was responsible for some boldly shaped vases with the usual classical motifs applied, and often gilded. With the abatement of this style in the 1770s came new, more sleek and elegant vases, typically of elongated egg shape standing on concave bases, with scroll-shaped handles covered in gilding to imitate gilt-bronze. As the end of the century approached, they were increasingly actually made of gilt-bronze, either by Pierre-Philippe Thomire working as the factory's gilt-bronze fitter, or by one of Daguerre's fitters, who included Thomire and Rémond.

Painted decoration rapidly went beyond flower, bird or putti reserves. Vielliard copied engravings both of children and of trophies after Watteau in the 1750s, and subsequently concentrated on landscapes strewn with attributes of gardening, such as watering cans and wheelbarrows. For the finest vases, the factory's best painter, Charles-Nicolas Dodin, provided panels with pastoral or mythological scenes taken from engravings and paintings. Dodin had started his career painting putti like Vielliard, but his talent was quickly spotted and he was soon employed on the most ambitious pieces, including, circa 1760, Chinese-style scenes which may have been inspired by Canton enamels. The acquisition of new models for painting was a constant preoccupation, and Louis XVI sanctioned the purchase of two major collections for use by Sèvres: the studio of the painter François Desportes in 1784, and the Baron de Non's collection of Ancient Greek vases in 1786. In the event, these proved of little general use, but the arabesque style of the 1780s was fully exploited by Masson, who designed the "Arabesque"

*O*ne of a set of Sèvres hard-paste vases with lacquer-style decoration, circa 1785-90.

service, supposedly in the style of the Renaissance, and Lagrenée, whose work on Marie Antoinette's Laiterie at Rambouillet is among the most original of the factory's production. In the tradition of the porcelain rooms of the seventeenth century, porcelain was used here as the principal decorative element, with shapes of Antique inspiration decorated with friezes of goats and other animals in cold monochrome grey, outlined in bright colours such as yellow.

*Marchands-merciers* counted among Sèvres's principal clients, and it was hardly surprising that their requirements started to influence the factory's production. Mountable objects, of which porcelain flowers were among the first, were produced to the design or order of the *marchands-merciers* until the end of the eighteenth century. Poirier led the demand for furniture plaques, and Dulac may have been the first to commission *vases à monter*, although Daguerre's role became so predominant in this field that some of these became known simply as *vases Daguerre*. The factory realised the commercial good sense of complying with the dealers' demands; it also commissioned its own gilt-bronze mounts for vases, as well as lacquer or tôle trays for tea sets once it was seen how successful these were. Indeed the *bronzier* Thomire began to order porcelain plaques, altar-shaped tripods and vases to mount into clocks and candelabra on his own account.

In 1783, the Comte d'Angiviller, who as Directeur des Bâtiments was ultimately responsible to the King for the Sèvres factory, was able to report that "French [Sèvres] porcelain, along with precious objects [meaning furniture and gilt-bronzes], mirrors and other objects of art have placed French workmanship in a unique position in all European Courts. Chinese porcelain has lost the exclusive superiority it possessed in this Kingdom, which was the cause of our ruin and shame."

Sèvres's clientele was essentially royal and aristocratic. Much of the yearly production was geared to the New Year exhibitions, which from 1758 were held in the King's private apartments on the first floor at Versailles; new models and decorations were elaborated especially for

*O*ne of a pair of commodes with Paris porcelain plaques, probably designed by the architect François-Joseph Belanger. They were made by the *ébéniste* Godefroy Dester, and delivered by the *marchand-mercier* Delaroue on 17 November 1785 for the bedroom of the Comte d'Artois at the Palais du Temple in Paris. The porcelain plaques were probably made at the Dihl & Guérhard (the Duc d'Angoulême's) factory. The commodes were seized by the revolutionary authorities in 1792, and one of them was offered as a prize in a lottery held by the Convention on 29 Germinal-8 Prairial an III (18 April-27 May 1795): *Une commode porcelaine de Sèvres, à fleurs et arabesques, garnie de cariathides et autres ornements de bronze doré d'or moulu, et à dessus de marbre blanc* (A commode with Sèvres porcelain decorated with flowers and arabesques, mounted with caryatids and other ornaments of gilt-bronze, with a white marble top). The quality of the painting on the plaques (see right) deluded the lottery's organizers into thinking that they were Sèvres.

*D*inner service with cornflower trails and monograms, a typical product of the Manufacture de la Reine, Rue Thiroux factory in Paris, of about 1780-85.

this event, which accounted for up to half of the total yearly turnover. Another major use for Sèvres was satisfying the demand for lavish diplomatic presents which both Louis XV and Louis XVI gave to foreign princes and their ambassadors. In some cases, this resulted in orders from foreign courts, such as the service of entirely new shapes ordered by Catherine the Great in 1776. The Sèvres factory's serious financial problems during the revolution stemmed from the massive emigration or execution of a substantial proportion of its regular clientele.

## PARIS MANUFACTURERS

By contrast, several of the best Paris factories survived the revolution comparatively unscathed. The discovery of kaolin on French soil had led to the founding of a number of new porcelain factories and decorating workshops, all of which were hampered by various aspects of the stringent restrictions placed upon their activity by Sèvres's Privilège. In 1779, for example, Leboeuf (Manufacture de la Reine, Rue Thiroux) and Deruelle (Manufacture de Monsieur, Clignancourt) were fined for making painted and gilded porcelain. They nevertheless benefited from Sèvres's technical and artistic knowledge, as d'Angiviller was quick to point out in his 1783 report to Louis XVI: "the private establishments, which have profited from the discoveries made by the Sèvres factory, have in the last twenty years made the use of French porcelain more common on our tables than was the use of faience for our ancestors one hundred years ago."

The Paris factories sold to a different, less prestigious clientele than Sèvres, who did not require pieces of such elaborate shapes and decoration. Nevertheless, some factories endeavoured to steal designs from Sèvres: this was the case of Locré, the owner of the Rue Fontaine-au-Roi or La Courtille factory, who in 1777 produced biscuit sculptures from models by Boizot, which had been intended for Louis XVI's apartment at Versailles. Parent, the Sèvres factory's director, begged d'Angiviller to have Locré properly punished, and stated that colours and gilding were also being stolen with the connivance of workers at Sèvres, who were generally less well-paid than their Paris counterparts.

As a means of sidestepping the restrictions imposed upon them by the Sèvres Privilège, the Paris porcelain manufacturers sought the nominal protection of members of the Royal family, in much the same manner as Saint-Cloud and Chantilly had enjoyed the patronage of the Duc d'Orléans and the Prince de Condé respectively. The protection they obtained was at first purely nominal, as in the case of Dihl & Guérhard, whose factory in the Rue de Bondy was placed under the patronage of the Comte d'Artois's son, the Duc d'Angoulême, who was aged six when the factory implored his protection in 1781. By 1787, however, the stratagem had paid off, and these factories were granted limited permission to manufacture certain types of objects in a more elaborate style than hitherto.

Naturally, it was the *marchands-merciers* who sold the Paris factories' products; Granchez stocked those of two of the most important ones, the Rue Thiroux and Clignancourt factories, and advertised in the *Mercure de France* in May 1775 "a selection of new pieces of Clignancourt porcelain, including sets for chimneypieces, tea sets, clocks, candlesticks, vases, bulb pots etc. mounted with matt gilded bronze".

On 12 February 1791, the London auctioneer James Christie held a sale of "A Capital and Valuable Assortment of Porcelaine, of Monsieur Locré's Manufactory, Of Paris, the only one having the King's Patent". Locré or one of his agents was clearly trying to get rid of stock at a difficult time. The sale included only services and tea sets, with decoration of blue cornflowers, groups of flowers, "blue and white" and "white and gold". This unexciting mixture probably reflected the limited range of Locré's production, despite the claim in the catalogue that the pieces were "of the most Elegant and beautiful Patterns".

*L*arge covered bowl, perhaps a stewpot. Paris, Clignancourt factory, about 1780-85.

# 9
# LACQUER, TÔLE AND WALLPAPERS

## ORIENTAL LACQUER

Lacquer from the Far East had been imported into Europe from the sixteenth century, and immediately became fashionable due to its decorative appeal and exotic character. A varnish made from the sap of the tree *Rhus vernificera*, lacquer could be coloured and incorporate gold leaf. It was applied in many layers to form a shiny and hardwearing surface. Screens, cabinets, coffers, trays and other shapes reached Europe in increasing quantities, and were adapted for use in European interiors. Cabinets might be mounted on European stands, for example.

By the beginning of the eighteenth century, the requirement for harmony in decoration meant that there was no longer a place for cabinets on stands, and they began to be dismantled, the individual panels of lacquer being used to veneer onto the surfaces of commodes, *bureaux plats* and secretaires. The tops, sides and doors of a cabinet might be used for the front and sides of a commode. The panels were not usually large enough to cover the whole front of a commode, and the familiar breakfront facades of these pieces readily accommodated three lacquer panels used together. Lacquer screens from China were also used, and with these it was possible to have one continuous decorative surface, although the divisions of the leaves are sometimes visible, as on a commode by van Risamburgh in the Musée des Beaux-Arts in Caen. The drawers inside lacquer cabinets could be employed as well; the probate inventory of the *ébéniste* Jean-François Oeben in 1763

*Médailler*, about 1730, decorated with Chinese Coromandel lacquer, of which a detail is shown left, and gilt-bronze. The lacquer framing the Chinese panels and on the cornice is a French imitation. This piece, of traditional *armoire* shape, was made as a coin-cabinet for Joseph Pellerin, the greatest eighteenth-century French coin collector. The collection was bought for Louis XVI's Cabinet des Médailles in 1776, but Pellerin was so fond of this piece that he refused to surrender it, and it was finally sold by his heirs in 1784. Still in the Cabinet des Médailles, Bibliothèque Nationale.

lacquer pieces with gilt-bronze or gold mounts, some of which have chinoiserie motifs. Her *cabinet intérieur* at Versailles was decorated with these, as well as with Japanese porcelain and mounted hardstone vases. A *cage aux laques*, probably a display cabinet, contained a group of Japanese black and gold lacquer boxes of various shapes, including a fan-shaped one. On 10 October 1789, fearing the worst for her collection, she entrusted it to the *marchand-mercier* Daguerre, who had probably been responsible for supplying or mounting a substantial proportion of the objects. He was asked to repair some and fit leather cases, so that they could be transferred to Saint-Cloud. The Queen was never to see them again, and after her death, Daguerre and his partner Lignereux petitioned the revolutionary authorities to take this embarrassing deposit off their hands.

The lacquer room at the Hôtel du Châtelet in Paris, finished by 1776, is a typical example of the use of large quantities of lacquer in interior decoration, in this case Chinese red and gold lacquer from screens. There were nine tall lacquer panels around the room, two of which served as doors, as well as four armoires, one commode and a curious double-fronted cylinder desk with its *cartonnier*. These all had borders of *bois de rose* and *bois satiné*. The Lenormant sale in 1767 included "a magnificent twelve-leaf screen, with leaves thick enough to be split to form the complete panelling for a room". Screens could, however, be employed intact to keep out draughts, or even for less avowable purposes; the painter Greuze caught his wife in a compromising posture with a *conseiller au Parlement* "behind the screen in the *salon de compagnie*".

*Early seventeenth-century Japanese lacquer coffer on a French giltwood stand of about 1725. A very late example of this type of juxtaposition. After this date lacquer objects were generally dismantled, but Japanese lacquer of this early date was infrequently employed on furniture.*

*Bureau à cylindre, early 1770s, decorated with red lacquer. From the lacquer room at the Hôtel du Chatelet.*

*Pair of late seventeenth-century Japanese lacquer ewers, mounted circa 1780 in gilt-bronze. These vases were among the objects Marie Antoinette entrusted to Daguerre at the revolution.*

mentions "An old cabinet of antique lacquer, with no drawers or other ornaments, . . . the two sides and the top in antique lacquer". Indeed the entire carcass of a lacquer cabinet was sometimes turned into a commode with short legs, veneered on the outside. Examples survive from both the Louis XV and Louis XVI periods; Madame de Pompadour owned two, probably by BVRB, and one formed part of the furniture delivered to Earl Spencer by Dominique Daguerre in the 1790's.

Screens, however, were still used to keep out draughts, although the temptation to cannibalize them was strong. Other smaller objects were adapted by being mounted in gilt-bronze. A Japanese lacquer cylindrical wine pot now in the Louvre was turned into a pot-pourri vase circa 1750 by the removal of its handle and spout (the marks are still clearly visible) and the addition of gilt-bronze base, collar and scroll-shaped handles.

It has been argued by some specialists that the fashion for lacquer waned with the rise of the neoclassical style. Nothing could be further from the truth, as the large surviving number of neoclassical objects and pieces of furniture decorated with lacquer clearly testifies. Indeed, the taste for the exotic continued to the very end of the eighteenth century. Marie Antoinette, in addition to having many pieces of lacquer-decorated furniture at Saint-Cloud, owned a collection of Japanese

The role played by the *marchands-merciers* in this trade was as predominant as usual. It was they who purchased lacquer objects and organized their transformation into pieces with a ready appeal. A Japanese lacquer wine pot might be a curiosity, and as such, collected by a small number of connoisseurs, but a pot-pourri vase with gilt-bronze mounts and a decorative body made of Japanese lacquer was a desirable object for which there was a ready use in any smart household. The quest for lacquer was by no means an easy one. Gersaint, who made long trips to Holland, wrote in the sale catalogue of the Chevalier de la Roque in 1745 that "Choice pieces are extremely hard to find, especially old ones. They sometimes fetch surprising prices, even in Holland." The Dutch East India Company had a monopoly on trading with the Japanese, and Holland was therefore the obvious place to seek out lacquer. However, Japanese export lacquer had been priced out of the market by Chinese imitations, and ceased to be imported into Europe at the end of the seventeenth century, so that the Japanese lacquer used in French furniture and objects in the eighteenth century was often as much as one hundred years old.

Lacquer was of variable qualities, Japanese being the finest, with the various grades of Chinese lacquer following far behind. The Père

*I*nkstand decorated with Japanese lacquer and gilt-bronze, 1745-9. The gilt-bronzes bear the crowned *C* mark. It was made by using the concave sides of the lid of a seventeenth-century Japanese lacquer sarcophagus-shaped box.

*W*riting table by Martin Carlin, circa 1783-5. Carlin was employed by the *marchand-mercier* Darnault to make matching suites of furniture, decorated with Japanese lacquer, for the apartments of Mesdames Adélaïde and Victoire at Bellevue. Some of the lacquer he used came from two Japanese cabinets bought by Darnault at the Duc d'Aumont's sale in December 1782. Most of the furniture is now in the Louvre, but it is likely that this table formed part of the suite. The lacquer on the drawer-fronts must have been taken from the drawers inside a Japanese cabinet, as a close examination of them reveals plugged holes marking the position of the original Japanese drawer-handles.

Mid-eighteenth-century commode stamped by Jean Demoulin. The lacquer appears to be Chinese, with some colour and gilding added in France. Traditionally stated to have belonged to the Duc de Choiseul at the Château de Chanteloup.

d'Incarville, a Jesuit missionary to China in the 1750s, sent a *Mémoire* to the Académie des Sciences in Paris, in which he states that "however accomplished the gold painting applied to lacquer in China, it cannot compare with beautiful Japanese lacquer," a sentiment echoed in Europe by Gersaint's statement in the Angran de Fonspertuis sale catalogue in 1748: "There is no comparison between the finest Japanese lacquer and the best ever made in China. In fact the latter, in the eyes of connoisseurs, is of absolutely no interest."

The *marchands-merciers* employed *ébénistes* to dismantle Oriental cabinets and cut up screens, and fit the pieces on to carcasses of commodes, writing tables and secretaires. Bernard van Risamburgh was a pioneer in this field, again for the dealer Hébert. The commode he delivered for Marie Leczinska at Fontainebleau in 1737 (now in the Louvre) is one of the earliest pieces known and shows that the technique was still in its infancy. A central Japanese lacquer panel with a raised cartouche-shaped border, from the flat top of a Japanese coffer, is clumsily framed with gilt-bronze, and branches of French *vernis* decorate the ends of the front.

Within a few years van Risamburgh had perfected the formula. The elaborately decorated tops of Japanese lacquer cabinets of the first half of the seventeenth century were used for the central panel of the front of commodes; the two doors were placed on either side; a gilt-bronze frame encircled the three panels as well as concealing the joins between them. The sides of the cabinet were veneered on to the sides of the commode. The surrounds could be in black *vernis*, or be veneered with ebony to harmonize, or a light wood to contrast. This basic formula was repeated until the end of the century. The drawer-fronts of Japanese cabinets became the drawer-fronts of writing tables. The holes left by the removal of the original handles are usually quite clearly visible, although the *ébénistes* always tried to hide them. The two great specialists of this technique during the reign of Louis XVI were Martin Carlin

and Adam Weisweiler, who worked for the dealers Daguerre and Darnault.

Chinese lacquer is found on pieces by lesser but still highly competent *ébénistes*, such as Adrien Delorme (and probably his father before him), Jacques Dubois and Mathieu Criaerd. For the most part they used cut-up screens; and the vertical divisions here are more likely to be concealed with French *vernis*.

# EUROPEAN LACQUER

A workshop for "Ouvrages de la Chine" had been set up at the Gobelins in 1672, and in 1713 Jacques Dagly, an experienced German lacquerer, came to direct it, but none of its work has so far been identified. Dagly is thought to have worked in a largely Oriental style while in Berlin, but it is possible that when he came to France he also created pieces inspired by the chinoiserie designs of Jean Bérain and Claude Audran. The painter Antoine Watteau may also have executed some panels in this style for him. Dagly was succeeded at the Gobelins by Pierre de Neufmaison, who bore the title Directeur des Ouvrages de la Chine en peinture et dorure. He died in 1752, leaving his secret to Pierre-Robert Tramblin. Tramblin had a reputation as a decorator of theatres and of carriages, and it was this type of work, along with wall painting, furniture and small objects, which was undertaken by French *vernisseurs*. In addition to the decorative, there were practical benefits to their work: a good varnish could ensure, for instance, that the bodies of carriages were waterproof; and snuffboxes made of lacquered papier maché were a decorative and cheap substitute for gold or enamel.

Many independent *vernisseurs* operated in Paris in the eighteenth century, and as well as having their own guild, a number of them were

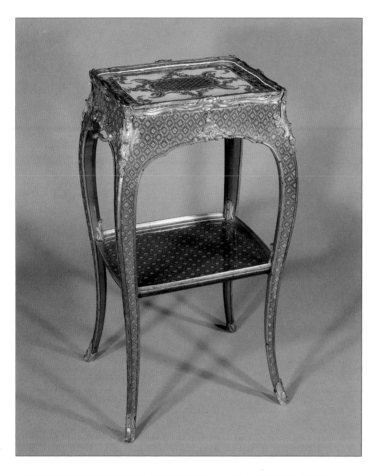

members of the Académie de Saint Luc; this probably indicates that painting and lacquering were related specialities. Indeed much of their work was in a European style, although they endeavoured to imitate Oriental lacquer, especially on furniture, and with varying success. Restoration and embellishment of Oriental lacquer seems to have been practised by them too; Japanese lacquer was sometimes considered too sparse for French tastes, and extra motifs have been found added on in French *vernis*, such as trees, mountains and birds.

## VERNIS MARTIN

On 21 April 1738, the *Sieur* Martin, Vernisseur du Roi, delivered to the Garde-Meuble for the King's *cabinet de retraite* at Marly "A corner cup-board of Martin lacquer, green ground, with a serpentine front, the (locking) door with a Chinaman sitting on a carpet, playing a sort of guitar, and a bare-headed boy next to him; within a cartouche of gold-ground mosaic; having a top of *brèche violette* marble . . . on a separate stand . . . lacquered and gilded in the style of the corner-cupboard . . . A superstructure with three shelves of the same green ground lacquer with Chinese work."

The brothers Etienne-Simon and Guillaume Martin obtained a Privilège for the manufacture of lacquer in 1730, which received

*T*able à café by Bernard van Risamburgh, bearing his stamp BVRB. The Sèvres plaque is dated 1766. Poirier, who probably commissioned this piece, may have sold tables of this type with tea services that matched the decoration of the porcelain trays. Originally, the lacquer also matched the border of the table top, but it has yellowed with age.

*C*ommode by Mathieu Criaerd, delivered in 1743 by the *marchand-mercier* Hébert for Madame de Mailly's bedroom at Choisy. The lacquer decoration, in an entirely European style (shown in the detail, right), is likely to be the work of Martin himself, since his decoration of the Dauphine's *cabinet* at Versailles a couple of years later was in a similar colour scheme. All the bronzes in the bedroom were silvered, including the *feu*, which was decorated with *enfants chinois* and flowers in blue and white enamel.

confirmation in 1744, and guaranteed them (and various other members of their family) the exclusive right to make a lacquer "with raised decoration in the Japanese and Chinese style". This assured them protection from competition in this field alone, and Voltaire's oft-quoted statement:

> Ces cabinets où Martin
>
> A surpassé l'art de la Chine

proves how successful they were (Voltaire was one of their clients and had a former apprentice from the firm working for him at Cirey), but they also produced lacquerwork in a European style, both for furniture and notably for interiors at Versailles and at Potsdam. The *Inventaire Général des Meubles de la Couronne* of 1760 records the existence of a "commode in light green lacquer by Martin... with yellow monochrome in panels", which is clearly not in imitation of anything Oriental.

Their work at Versailles included a *cabinet* with *petit vert* decoration on a white ground. As well as the walls, the furniture, including chairs and screens, was decorated to match.

The Martins also made small boxes and other pieces, including objects for the *toilette*, such as a "mirror frame... with gold and aventurine lacquer" for a client of Duvaux's. That they lacquered carriages is confirmed by a letter from Madame de Pompadour to the Comtesse de Noailles in 1748: "Have you been to Martin's to see my new carriage, as you said you would? I have forbidden him to spoil it with lascivious scenes, of the sort that make honest people blush." Most of the Martins' work for Madame de Pompadour through Duvaux consisted of repairs, both to commodes and to oriental lacquer cabinets.

While the Martins were by no means the only lacquerers working in Paris in the eighteenth century, the name *Vernis Martin* was

*P*air of tôle *seaux à bouteille* with mask handles imitating gilt-bronze. An identical pair sold in London by Sotheby's (5 July 1985, lot 62) was signed *François Louis Dorez fecit à Lille 1734*. Dorez was a member of a large family of Lille *faïenciers*, and moved to Valenciennes to set up a faience workshop in 1737, at which date he was trying to sell a lacquer commode. It could be that this too was tôle.

subsequently universally applied and is now synonymous with all French lacquer of the period.

# TÔLE

Lacquered tin, known as "tôle", was used as a cheap substitute for Oriental lacquer and Sèvres porcelain, and a great variety of work was undertaken in this field, both for decorative objects and furniture. Lazare Duvaux had added lacquer trays to tea sets in the 1750s, and the Sèvres factory soon began to copy him. None have so far been identified, but possibly they, like some of the small table-tops sold by the Sèvres factory, matched the porcelain in decoration. By the 1770s, the trays supplied by Sèvres were of tôle, which must have been specially ordered and which were therefore probably matching.

The *ébéniste* Pierre Macret is the author of several commodes and corner cupboards with large tôle panels which have a dark coloured ground and central cartouches with Oriental-style landscapes. These date from the late 1760s, but panels of the same type continued to be used by Claude-Charles Saunier for commodes into the 1780s. Saunier was working for Daguerre at the time, applying Japanese lacquer and Sèvres porcelain to furniture, and it may be that Daguerre also supplied him with tôle.

The dealer Granchez did not sell Sèvres porcelain, but he tried to imitate it by taking as a model the rectangular gilt-bronze Sèvres-mounted inkstand devised by his rival Poirier, and mounting it with tôle plaques painted in Sèvres style. One such piece, painted with putti and bearing Granchez's label, appeared in the Doucet sale in Paris in 1912.

The *Sieur* Gosse, "master painter, sculptor and lacquerer", invented a *vernis* for metals, and in 1767 his widow and their son-in-law François Samousseau obtained a Privilège, valid for fifteen years, to manufacture this product, which was stated to protect iron from rust, to be resistant to fire and acids, and to be odourless and of a "fine black colour"; these qualities having been tested by the Académie des Sciences. They were given permission to apply it to metals, and also to wood, leather, cardboard, paper, terracotta, earthenware and porcelain. Since they were also enjoined to sign their production, it is surprising that not a single object bearing a signature appears to have been recorded. It may be that they were responsible for the lacquered metal panels on the Macret or Saunier commodes, or the Granchez objects, and that the *marchands-merciers* discouraged them from signing, or scraped off their mark.

# CHINESE AND FRENCH WALLPAPERS

"At the Sign of Fame, Rue St. Jacques, opposite the Fontaine St. Severin, Langlois, dealer, keeps a stock of genuine Indian [meaning Chinese] paper of all sizes, with figures, landscapes, flowers and birds, to decorate fine suites of rooms; *Cabinets de toilette*; overdoors, folding screens and firescreens, and will arrange them with the ultimate care; very pretty sheets for trays; flock papers of chopped wool, and painted English paper, imitating textiles, such as Utrecht velvet, damask, satin, moiré, Chinese and Persian silk, all sorts of calico; paper imitating real glazed tiles for closets and bathrooms; painted paper for panelling, in all sizes, and generally all sorts of small hand-painted papers for wallcovering; marbled paper of the most refined colours for dining rooms, lavatories and fireplaces, to be used in panels; papers painted to look like tortoiseshell and veneer of different colours, to imitate marquetry; finely gilt paper to frame drawings, etc. Paris, 1772." Langlois was the successor of Jean-Michel Papillon, the author of a *Traité historique et practique de la gravure en bois*, who had been asked by Diderot to write the section entitled *Tapissier en papier* for the *Encyclopédie*.

Coloured paper had been used in France instead of more expensive wall decoration, such as leather, tapestry, wood, or marble; and as a liner for the inside of cupboards, drawers and screens. The catalogue of what could be imitated with paper is extensive; besides the uses mentioned, wallpaper imitating pointed stonework has been found in the entrance halls of eighteenth-century apartments in Paris.

Lazare Duvaux's day-book contains many mentions of paper of all kinds, and these were used not to decorate the walls of principal rooms, but to line screens and cupboards, as well as for the walls of small and subsidiary rooms such as bathrooms and passages. These papers are described as English, Chinese, Indian (meaning Chinese), from Paris,

and *papier tissu*.

Wallpapers imitating textiles were made in England, and were imported into France until the outbreak of war between the two countries in 1756. Undeterred, French wallpaper manufacturers accelerated their efforts to copy them, including one Aubert, who must have been among the first, since his tradecard is dated to that year. He "... informs the public that he has discovered the correct way of manufacturing flock or English papers, in the manner of damask or Utrecht velvet, in one or more colours" (*... donne avis qu'il a trouvé la véritable façon de fabriquer les papiers veloutés ou papiers d'Angleterre en façon de damas & velours d'Utrecht, en une ou plusieurs couleurs*). The engraver Jean-Gabriel Huquier the younger, who with his father is famous for the series of prints he produced after Boucher, was among those who set up factories to produce such papers. These "flock" papers were called *tontisses*, and imitated damask or cut velvet. Felt dust was glued on to

*D*omino or lining paper. First half of the eighteenth century.

the paper in patterns, in one or several colours. Papillon noted in the *Traité historique* that they were extremely difficult to apply to walls, since they disintegrated when wet. Not surprisingly, these sorts of paper have rarely survived. They were often nailed to the frames of screens; Lazare Duvaux supplied Madame de Pompadour with English paper mounted in this way, for unglamorous purposes such as *garderobes*, mezzanine rooms, and a bathroom at the Château de Champs.

French printed lining papers, called *dominos*, had been in use since the sixteenth century, and by the eighteenth were colourfully patterned, with geometric designs and flowers (see previous page). They were made by *dominotiers*, and are to be found inside cupboards, drawers and on the backs of screens.

Papers in the style of textiles had also been made in China, and must have reached France, for Papillon explains that "The Chinese make a most extraordinary sort of paper . . . which looks like a knitted fabric," but he reluctantly admits that "we do not yet know exactly how it is made." Chinese painted wallpapers started being imported into Europe in the late seventeenth century, and were used for the same

*C*hinese wallpaper, from a complete set of panels delivered in 1753 for a room in a château in the Vosges.

*P*anel of wallpaper by Réveillon, 1780s, from the Wallpaper Room at Clandon Park, Surrey. The design was known as *Les Deux Pigeons*.

purposes as European papers, but Langlois's tradecard confirms that they could be designed to hang in large rooms (see left); indeed examples are known in which the pattern is continuous from one roll to the other all the way round a room. They could also be used on screens.

In the Moulin (mill-house) built in 1783 for the *hameau* of Mesdames Adélaïde and Victoire at Bellevue, Robert, Papetier du Roi, created a print room in the English manner. On walls covered with English green-ground paper mounted on stretchers, he stuck ninety-five Chinese prints supplied by the two Princesses, and applied a false cornice printed on paper with "foliage, English green ground, acanthus leaves, egg, pearl and ribbon motifs". Paper strips imitating mouldings and decorated with arabesques and cameos were fixed to doors and overdoors, window and mirror surrounds. The furniture was painted to match and upholstered in apple-green silk.

Other types of paper imitated leather hangings. Gold- or silver-coloured metal foil was made to adhere to the paper when it was passed through a heated press. It was then printed or painted with flowers or other designs. Gilt leather could also be copied in other ways: in 1762, one Stoucard advertised his "toile factory, in the style of gilt leather, with gilt and silvered flowers and multicoloured patterns".

Jean-Baptiste Réveillon was the principal paper manufacturer in Paris in the second half of the eighteenth century. Following the common trend of the times, he applied industrial processes to wallpaper printing, and in 1783 successfully sought the title of Manufacture Royale. His production encompassed all the traditional fields, as well as the copying of Chinese papers, but he is best known for his multicoloured arabesque papers. These imitated Lyon woven silks, and wall decorations of the type of the Grimod de la Reynière *salon* and of the stuccoes at Bagatelle. Complete room sets were made, with panels of individual but connected subjects, such as the Five Senses. Some of these are close to designs produced for Sèvres by Jean-Jacques Lagrenée, and it may be that Réveillon employed the services of designers from other fields, for example Dugourc, who was himself to set up as a wallpaper manufacturer in 1791. Réveillon has been accused of stealing the designs used by Oberkampf to print toiles at Jouy; surviving Oberkampf toiles, including "Indiennes", are identical to Réveillon papers, but it seems more likely that the two collaborated to produce coordinated toiles and papers, the former for the curtains and bedhangings, and the latter for the walls.

# LEATHER HANGINGS

Leather hangings may have been more common in France in the eighteenth century than the few surviving examples *in situ* would suggest, but contemporary records confirm their existence. The 1752 inventory of the Château de Choisy, which had been decorated for Louis XV in the 1740s, mentions gilt leather hangings "with panels and Turkish and Persian figures". Some were delivered to Compiègne in 1755 by a supplier named Delfosse, the principal specialist in this field. Bimont informs us in his *Principes de l'art du Tapissier* of 1770 that leather hangings are only suitable for *antichambres*, and the inventory carried out by the Garde-Meuble upon Louis XV's death records no less than seventy sets.

# 10
# TEXTILES

The role played by textiles in interior decoration in France in the eighteenth century was a capital one. During the reign of Louis XIV, the efforts of his minister Colbert had ensured that French tapestry, the worthy descendant of the great northern tradition of tapestry weaving, became the finest in Europe. Similarly, the French silk industry, born to imitate products from Italy and further afield, assumed a leading role in Europe. Just as it had done with other products of French industry, the civilized world supplied itself with French textiles, which were exported as far afield as China and Peru.

## THE SAVONNERIE

Workshops producing carpets *velouté façon de Turquie* (like velvet, with a thick knotted pile) were established at the Louvre in the early seventeenth century as part of Henri IV's initiative to revive industry and the arts after the Wars of Religion. By 1671, these had moved to a disused soap works (hence the name Savonnerie) at Chaillot on the western outskirts of Paris. From 1714, there was a single workshop, managed by an *entrepreneur* (contractor).

The early production of these workshops consisted of carpets for floors and tables, with flowers on a dark background, but, by the time of the summit of Louis XIV's reign in the 1680s, they were already being woven to designs provided by the great team which, under Charles Le Brun, created a unified style in art as a means of glorifying the King.

PREVIOUS SPREAD
**W**hile British ambassador in Paris in 1765, the 3rd Duke of Richmond obtained some Gobelins tapestries from a *tenture* of *Don Quichote* of some twenty *pièces*. These had been woven between 1762 and 1764, and were intended for Marly, but were not all purchased by Louis XV. They are still preserved at Goodwood.

**S**avonnerie tapestry of the 1720s, with allegorical emblems of Spring, and contemporary chairs and chair covers. The tapestry is a rare example of a Savonnerie wall-hanging and forms part of a set of four showing the Seasons. It was a private commission and bears the arms of Count Franz-Joseph Czernin von Chudewitz and Isabella Maria de Mérode, who were married in 1717.

From then on, designs were supplied almost exclusively by artists working for the Crown, and fulfilled a double function, playing a part in the general decorative scheme of a project, and, more importantly (once a design had been approved and was found to be successful), being woven again and again, even if fashion had changed, until the cartoon became so worn that it was no longer usable.

Carpets formed the principal production of the Savonnerie, but other types of objects were woven there as well, such as panels for folding screens and firescreens, covers for chairs and benches, pictures copying oil paintings, including portraits, and *portières* (door curtains). The Savonnerie made more of these in the first half of the eighteenth century than during the neoclassical period, when woven silks, the principal competition for Savonnerie in these fields, became even more popular.

Fortune did not always favour the Savonnerie. The Duc d'Antin reported to Louis XIV in 1708 that it was on the point of collapse (*"cette belle Manufacture est sur le point de sa chutte"*), and that he intended to reverse this situation. In the event, the Louis XV period marked a high point. The King, in the company of Marigny and Gabriel, was generally personally involved in the choice of designs, and annotated alternatives bear the royal *"bon"* in his own hand, in addition to the phrase *"bon à choisir"*, the formula signifying that a design was worthy of being submitted to him. The lack of interest shown by Louis XVI and Marie Antoinette in the Savonnerie may have contributed to the fact that in carpet design the Louis XV period was more successful than that which followed.

Most of the Savonnerie's production was intended for the King. Carpets and other pieces went to the Garde-Meuble where they were kept until they were needed, either for a room in one of the palaces or to be given to foreign dignitaries. Savonnerie carpets featured among the splendid presents given by Louis XV to the Ottoman Sultan in 1742; not only did he want to show the Sultan that his country could manage without Turkish carpets, he also wanted to impress him with the quality and richness of French carpets, woven on this occasion with borders of gold thread. The gesture was somewhat ironic since Turkish carpets (like English ones) were the subject of almost prohibitive customs duties upon entry into France, and were therefore uncommon.

*S*avonnerie *paravent* (screen) of the first half of the eighteenth century, one of a pair. At 2.73 m, these represent the tallest of the screens woven by the Savonnerie, and were probably intended for a *salon* or large *antichambre* in one of the royal palaces. The cartoons for this screen were provided in 1714 by François Desportes for the birds, and by Jean-Baptiste Blain de Fontenay for the surrounds.

*P*ainted design, circa 1720, by François Desportes, for the leaf of a Savonnerie screen.

Other clientele could aspire to owning such prestigious works of art, but it has been estimated that not more than fifty carpets were woven as private commissions by the Savonnerie during the eighteenth century. Marigny, as Directeur des Bâtiments, was naturally well placed to own some, and a design survives for a carpet he commissioned in 1769 in imitation of tiger skin. Among complete outsiders was William Beckford, who arrived from England in 1792, at a moment when the Savonnerie was delighted to find someone who took an interest in their expensive product. Two small carpets, intended for his father's Adam house, Fonthill Splendens, were woven to designs executed especially for Beckford, and in keeping with the Adam interiors.

The Duvivier family, *entrepreneurs* at the Savonnerie from 1743 to 1826, took an active part in every aspect of the production, including translating sketches into detailed cartoons. Pierre-Josse Perrot was the artist responsible for many of the finest cartoons of the Louis XV period; his panels framed by scrolls with flowers and leaves are among the happiest inventions of the eighteenth century. Soufflot, the architect who had accompanied Marigny to Italy in 1749, became *inspecteur* at the Savonnerie in 1755; it was, however, a little-known artist called Michel-Bruno Bellengé who was to interpret neoclassicism for the Savonnerie in a set of fluent cartoons making use not of architectural detail but of arabesques incorporating elegant vases and garlands of flowers.

*S*avonnerie carpet, woven in the Duvivier workshop, from a cartoon by P. J. Perrot. Similar carpets were woven for Fontainebleau and Choisy between 1744 and 1756.

# WOVEN TAPESTRY

The great tapestries of the seventeenth century were slightly out of place in the new interiors of the eighteenth, but they nevertheless continued to be hung in rooms for which solemnity was the prime requirement; for example at Versailles, where seventeenth-century and even Renaissance tapestries decorated the Grands Appartements until the end of the *ancien régime*.

Tapestry increasingly tried to imitate paintings in order to fit in with modern decoration, to the extent that dyes were multiplied to provide an increased number of colours and shades within colours, and the borders of tapestries were woven to resemble giltwood picture frames. Indeed some tapestries were woven without borders: "Borders can be applied to these tapestries, but they can also be framed in giltwood, if you prefer not to have tapestry borders," wrote Cozette, one of the Gobelins *entrepreneurs*, to Claude Bonnet in 1754.

Many of the finest painters provided cartoons for tapestry weaving, but two names are of paramount importance, to the Gobelins and to Beauvais as well as indirectly to Aubusson: Jean-Baptiste Oudry and François Boucher.

## THE GOBELINS

Louis XIV's furniture and tapestry workshops, lodged in a building formerly occupied by the Gobelins family (hence the name) had closed in 1694 for economic reasons, but reopened in 1699. It had the status of Manufacture Royale, and much of its production was intended for the King, either for decorating one of the royal palaces, or as presents. The workshops within the Gobelins had some degree of independence, and others could approach one of the *entrepreneurs* for private commissions.

Cartoons were ordered from leading painters. These consisted of a number of paintings, from which *tentures* (sets of hangings) were woven; some of these comprise a large number of tapestries. The cartoons were kept, to be used repeatedly for a period of many years. The designs for the borders of the tapestries, usually in the style of giltwood picture frames, were periodically updated, so that an early *tenture* of a subject may have a different border to a late one.

During the reign of Louis XIV, ponderous subjects such as the King's victories were chosen for tapestries, but the eighteenth century saw a greater variety, in a more charming and exotic vein, as the art of tapestry became increasingly associated with interior decoration rather than forming part of the architecture. *L'Ambassade Turque* of 1731, after cartoons by Charles Parrocel, represented an attempt to retain the grand manner, but with the elegance of the new age; in the event, it was discontinued, and in 1733 Oudry was asked for cartoons for a new and

*"Le* Triomphe de Vénus", Gobelins tapestry from a cartoon by Noel Coypel. Inspired by a sixteenth-century original, it was woven in the *haute lice* workshops of Jans the Younger, and was part of a set begun in 1705 and completed in 1713. In 1717 the *tenture* was housed in the French embassy in Sweden, and from 1748-91 in the French embassy in Rome.

different *tenture*, the *Chasses du Roi*. In the same year he was appointed Inspecteur sur les Ouvrages at the Gobelins. The *Chasses du Roi* was one of the Gobelins' great successes; *L'Ambassade Turque* had been an unruly jumble of figures on horseback, but here the occasional figure, dressed in the blue of the royal hunting uniform, is glimpsed against the beautiful royal forests, a background reminiscent of the lush foliage of traditional *verdure*. The cartoons' enduring popularity is proved by the fact that Louis XVI had them copied on porcelain by Sèvres in 1782 for his dining room at Versailles.

Charles-Antoine Coypel provided the Gobelins from 1714 onwards with a set of twenty-eight paintings for the *Histoire de Don Quichote* which continued to be woven until the revolution. A set of these could comprise several large *pièces*, as well as other smaller ones and overdoors. This *tenture* signalled a new departure: the picture in the centre has become smaller, and is almost a mere pretext for a breathtaking *alentour* (border) incorporating a background of one-colour damask (red or yellow), brilliantly patterned, upon which elaborate gilt frames, trophies and garlands of flowers, peacocks with tails outspread, cornucopiae and coats of arms completely overshadow

*L*ouis XVI armchair, probably by Jean-Baptiste-Claude Sené, covered in Gobelins tapestry. The seat cover is identical to those on chairs that match the first *Tenture de Boucher*, woven in 1764 for Lord Coventry (now in the Metropolitan Museum of Art, New York).

"*L*es Noces d'Angélique", Gobelins tapestry of a scene from the opera *Roland et Armide*, from the *Tenture de l'Opéra*, finished in 1749. The cartoon was painted by Charles Coypel, who exhibited it at the Salon in 1737, and the tapestry was woven by Monmerqué. The borders, simulating a giltwood picture frame, were designed by P. J. Perrot. Presented by Louis XV in 1763 to Paul-Jérome, Duc de Grimaldi, the Spanish ambassador to Paris.

the central shaped panel, which is nevertheless highly exotic, with figures in Spanish costumes indulging in scenes of total buffoonery taken from the great novel by Cervantes. The designs for the borders varied, and several artists were involved in each, including Michel Audran and Alexis Peyrotte.

Upon Oudry's death in 1755, Boucher, who had already painted two of his greatest pictures, *Le Lever du Soleil* and *Le Coucher du Soleil*, (now in the Wallace Collection), as cartoons for tapestries to be woven by the Gobelins for Madame de Pompadour in 1752, was named Surinspecteur there by Marigny, and ceased working for the Beauvais factory. His major work for the Gobelins consisted of a set simply known as the *Tenture de Boucher* for which he provided paintings of Olympian gods, often as pairs of lovers. These were designed along the same principles as the *Histoire de Don Quichote* for the picture is confined to a central oval again surrounded by a frame imitating giltwood (as does the outer border). The whole seems to hang from the ceiling on brightly coloured ribbons tied in a knot at the top of the tapestry, on a damask background with garlands of flowers. Maurice Jacques was responsible for the designs of these borders, with the assistance of Louis Tessier for the flowers.

Designed to form the complete decoration of rooms, these *tentures* comprised tapestries for each wall panel, even the small ones at the side of the chimney and overdoors. They also included complete sets of seat and screen covers, some of which have oval scenes within them while others are merely decorated with garlands of flowers. The first set was woven from 1764, and was bought by an Englishman, Lord Coventry. There is nothing surprising in this, since the end of the Seven Years War had drawn the English to Paris in large numbers, but it does seem strange that every single version of this particular set went abroad, some being sold and others given, such as the set given by Louis XVI to the Comte du Nord. Madame de Genlis was to complain that it had become the fashion to relegate Gobelins tapestries to storage and replace them with English blue paper, and perhaps the Gobelins' production was more at home in foreign palaces than in Paris houses and apartments.

As well as weaving pictorial tapestries, the Gobelins was responsible for *portières* (door curtains). These were often armorial, with elaborate borders, but one of the Gobelins' first and most successful patterns was the *Portières des Dieux* followed in 1727 by the *Portières aux Armes de France* for which the cartoons had been provided by Perrot, in a style similar to the work he was executing for the Savonnerie at the same time.

## BEAUVAIS

The Beauvais factory benefited from the same status of Manufacture Royale as the Gobelins, but with greater independence, since most of its production was for public sale. In the early eighteenth century, Beauvais underwent financial problems, but nevertheless managed to produce splendid sets such as *L'Ile de Cythère ou le Temple de Vénus*, a *tenture* of six *pièces*, from cartoons by Jacques Duplessis in 1724. Brightly coloured exotic coastal landscapes with classical buildings contain figures in Eastern costumes, putti and classical gods. Elaborate trophies

of love abound in the borders, incorporating quivers, lyres, putti and swans.

Jean-Baptiste Oudry's involvement with tapestry weaving began in 1726 when he began to supply cartoons to the Beauvais factory; in 1734 he became the factory's director, in partnership with one of the great silversmiths of the first half of the eighteenth century, Nicolas Besnier. His cartoons mainly showed nature in various forms, but he could venture into new ground, providing, for instance, a set after Molière, and one of *Métamorphoses*. Upon his appointment as Surinspecteur at the Gobelins he ceased to paint cartoons for Beauvais himself, but successfully found other painters to do so instead. Felicitously, his choice fell upon the young Boucher, whose first *tenture*, the *Fêtes*

"*L*e jardin chinois", one of the five *pièces* of a Beauvais *Tenture Chinoise* of 1750-54, from cartoons by Boucher. There is little that is Chinese about this lady at her *toilette*, except perhaps her hairstyle and the blue-and-white vases, but the luxuriant vegetation, the parasol and the colourful costumes all convey an exotic and Utopian feeling. The original oil sketch for the design, now in the Musée des Beaux Arts, Besançon, is larger and incorporates further Chinese figures and a Chinese pavilion.

LEFT

*E*arly eighteenth-century panels of Beauvais tapestry with decorative and allegorical motifs.

*B*eauvais carpet of arabesque style and in tapestry weave, late 1780s. De Menou, the director of the Beauvais factory, also produced such carpets in Savonnerie weave.

RIGHT
*M*id-eighteenth-century Aubusson tapestry.

*Italiennes* (four *pièces*) of 1734-5, showing groups of figures in landscapes (some of which were used by Vincennes for biscuit groups), was followed by *L'Histoire de Psyché* in 1736, and a *Tenture Chinoise* in 1741 (see page 207). After Boucher joined the Gobelins his cartoons, as well as Oudry's, continued to be employed at Beauvais, on account of their popularity, and because Beauvais found it difficult to obtain cartoons by competent artists. When Jean-Baptiste Le Prince exhibited at the Salon in 1767 a set of cartoons for Beauvais for a *tenture* to be called *Les Jeux Russiens* (as usual there was little that was Russian about it) Diderot complained of the poor composition and of a "dirty colour".

While still producing wall tapestries such as Huet's *Pastorales à draperies bleues et arabesques* during the reign of Louis XVI, Beauvais turned to the manufacture of two other specialities of note; seat covers and carpets. Large suites of Louis XVI seat furniture, normally by the *menuisier* Henri Jacob, have survived with Beauvais tapestry covers of garlands of flowers and ribbons, but other subjects were also attempted, notably a set comprising wall tapestries as well as seat covers. These were woven in the late 1780s to the designs of Jean-Jacques-François Le Barbier with scenes symbolizing the role played by France in the War of American Independence. It was ordered by Louis XVI to give to George Washington, but sadly seems not to have reached him.

In 1780 the new director at Beauvais, de Menou, who had come from the Aubusson factory, started production of carpets in the style of the Savonnerie; Aubusson had been engaged in this activity since the mid-eighteenth century, and he realised that Beauvais too could imitate the Savonnerie cheaply. Carpets of tapestry weave as well as *façon de Perse* (woven with a pile) enjoyed considerable success in the years preceding the revolution.

## AUBUSSON

To revive the independent tapestry workshops at Aubusson in central France, which had been seriously depleted by the mass exodus consequent upon the Revocation of the Edict of Nantes in 1685, a painter, Jean-Jacques du Mons, and a technical adviser from the Gobelins were both sent there in the 1730s, and until the end of the eighteenth century Aubusson was to produce charming tapestries of pastoral scenes, some woven from discarded cartoons of the Gobelins and Beauvais, and some with subjects drawn from the engravings of Boucher and others. *Verdures* remained popular, and Aubusson competed with Flanders in this field. As well as tapestries, Aubusson began to weave cheaper versions of Savonnerie carpets in the mid-eighteenth century, sometimes to designs pilfered from the Savonnerie itself.

# UPHOLSTERY: SILK AND OTHER TEXTILES

Jean-François Bimont, a *maître-tapissier*, published in 1770 an updated version of an upholsterer's manual he had written some years previously. In this work, the *Principes de l'art du Tapissier*, he seeks to instruct his colleagues about current practice in upholstery, both on the nature and use of materials, and in the technical aspects of the craft. He insists on the importance of knowing how to use the patterns woven or printed on a material: "the principal flowers should be placed centrally on walls, and at eye level", "the principal flower panel must without fail be placed on the back of chairs." If the pattern is too big to fit entirely on the back of a chair, the lower part of the bouquet should be placed on the seat. When using striped materials, care should be taken to ensure that "two stripes of the same colour should not be sewn together", and lengths of it should be used sideways to form borders at top and bottom. The gilt nails used to fix materials to chairs should have a small space between them, and should not be placed too close to the edge of the frame in order not to damage it when they are hammered on. Another useful tip given by Bimont concerns curtains; to avoid getting them dirty they should always be fitted with pulls. Realistically, he concludes his advice with the comment that the work can only be as good as the budget is large.

Damask, Bimont tells us, is the material most frequently employed in upholstery. It may be plain coloured, or have a background of one colour and one or more colours in the pattern. This is appropriate to cover a *meuble d'hiver* (winter set), as is tapestry, while for a *meuble d'été* (summer set) a *taffetas à fleurs ou chiné* is preferable.

Curtain, wall and furniture upholstery could be changed with the seasons. This extravagant practice took place at Versailles twice a year, the autumn change happening during the Royal household's yearly stay at Fontainebleau. Lesser households often included a servant called a *valet de chambre tapissier* whose job it was to carry out this change, but

*S*ketch by François Desportes for a velvet cushion with gold braid and tassels. Oil on paper, first half of the eighteenth century. Desportes painted some of Louis XV's dogs seated on similar cushions.

*R*ed, green and cream silk damask, mid-eighteenth century. An example of one of the most widely used upholstery materials.

FOLLOWING SPREAD
*M*arie Antoinette's *salon des jeux* at the Château de Compiègne, 1786.

*P*elmet from a bed or window, wool embroidery on linen, about 1720-30.

Bimont is happy to advise those on a budget to fit loose covers of, say, white silk with flowers, for the summer. Some of the finest seat furniture of the Louis XV and Louis XVI periods is built so that the upholstery can be removed; the back, seat and armrests are upholstered on to frames which unclip and can be replaced by others covered in a different material. This type of chair is known as *à châssis*. While it may have been usual to have a *meuble d'hiver* and a *meuble d'été*, occasionally more are found. Bonnet wrote to Dutillot in Parma in 1749 to tell him that he had ordered designs for "three different [sets] . . . for winter, spring and summer".

Lyon weavers produced the finest silks of the eighteenth century (many of them for the Garde-Meuble), but with interruptions which periodically brought the industry to its knees. In 1730, the first major royal orders since the reign of Louis XIV revived the Grande Fabrique, as the weavers working for the Crown were known.

The earliest sets of silk hangings woven in the 1730s for the Garde-Meuble were executed in a traditional style, with patterns reminiscent of those of the Louis XIV period. On backgrounds of crimson or blue were symmetrical arrangements of leaves, scrolls, flower garlands and strapwork in gold and silver thread. Since these were to be used for covering surfaces of varying sizes and shapes, the patterns were woven accordingly, with different repeats for chair seats and backs, and separate vertical and horizontal borders for the wall hangings. This practice was to remain current throughout the century for luxury materials, and during the Louis XVI period, when seat upholstery became more angular, thin strips of matching border were woven for the edges of seats and backs.

On 28 September 1754 the *tapissier* (upholsterer) Le Queustre

delivered a set of bedroom furniture for the Chambre du Roi at Fontainebleau. This very large and elaborate *ameublement* (suite) is a perfect if exaggerated example of usual practice in the eighteenth century. It comprised a bed, two armchairs, two *carreaux* (thickly stuffed cushions), twelve *pliants* (X-frame stools) one firescreen, one folding screen, wall hangings (including an overdoor panel) and curtains, all in Lyon silk with gold flowers on a blue ground, edged with gold braid, apart from one curtain which for some reason was of white damask. The silk had been woven in Lyon in 1731 to designs by Lallié, and the Duc de Luynes approvingly noted that "the more one contemplates this room, the more splendid it seems."

The bed, described as a *lit à l'Impériale et à la Duchesse* (not only was the canopy domed but it was of square outline) was extravagantly upholstered: valances with added gold embroidery and elaborate fringes were surmounted by four gilt helmets each bearing thirty loose white feathers and an *aigrette* (plume). The curtains, lined with plain blue satin, were garnished with *paillettes* (sequins) and other ornaments, and the shaped backboard was enriched with leaves and ornaments of raised gold embroidery. The King slept on no less than four mattresses, and was kept warm by a white satin quilt. The matching furniture, as well as its upholstery of the same silk, bore loose covers of another heavy blue silk, and the firescreen was fitted with a cord of blue and gold with a lead-filled pear-shaped tassel.

In the first half of the eighteenth century, silk designers native to Lyon provided most of the models for the weavers. An exception was the design for the pilaster-shaped vertical borders of a *tenture* made by Barnier between 1730 and 1733. These were the work of the

*S*ilk woven with a pattern of coral and flowering branches designed by Philippe de Lasalle, 1765-70.

RIGHT

*L*yon silk *lampas* with silver thread, circa 1735. A characteristic example of
the work of Jean Revel, with exotic motifs symbolizing Love, making this a
suitable fabric for the upholstery of a bedroom in a *petite maison*.

*C*hiné velvet by Camille Pernon, 1788. Ordered from Pernon for the Court of
Spain, some of this material is still in place in the Casita del Principe in the
Prado.

celebrated silversmith Thomas Germain. In 1725, the Lyon silk weavers petitioned the King to obtain protection from plagiarism of their designs. They stated that they spent considerable sums on training their designers, and that every year they sent them to Paris to observe the latest fashions, but that many of them tried to sell their designs to more than one weaver at the same time, or, worse, to foreigners.

From the mid-eighteenth century, many of the designs for Lyon silk were provided by the Garde-Meuble's own designers, such as Peyrotte and Gondoin, and later Dugourc. Multicoloured garlands of ribbon-tied flowers on light and bright backgrounds gradually adopted a more symmetrical appearance with the advent of neoclassicism, becoming enclosed in frail arabesques. A new style emerged for the 1780s, exemplified by the *salon des jeux* of Louis XVI at Fontainebleau in 1786. This was upholstered with panels of shiny blue silk with pale arabesques incorporating cyclops, winged seahorses, river gods and spaniels. At three *aunes* (3.57 m), the repeat (*rapport*) followed the general rule, which was to be as long as possible, testifying to the virtuosity of the weaver as well as affording a more varied appearance. The hazy and elegant appearance of *chiné* silks and silk velvets, with warp dyed before the weaving, ensured their continued popularity. At the end of the eighteenth century, Dugourc's designs, in a striking Etruscan style, proved to be a new departure.

Philippe de Lasalle (1723-1804), undoubtedly the most famous of the Lyon silk weavers of the eighteenth century, rarely worked for the Garde-Meuble. In addition to silk designing and weaving, he became a silk merchant in Paris and Lyon, and the technical improvements he introduced to weaving brought him much praise, although they also earned him the opprobrium of his colleagues. His varied clientele included the ex-king of Poland, Stanislas Leczinski, for whom he supplied a *tenture* in traditional style in the early 1760s, with flower garlands and ribbons, but he is perhaps best known through his work for Catherine the Great, that voracious consumer of the products of French genius. Indeed it was through the most brilliant personification of such genius that Catherine first heard about Lasalle in 1771. Voltaire owned a silk portrait of the Empress by Lasalle, an embroidered monochrome profile surrounded by woven garlands of flowers, and he wrote about it to her in glowing terms: "it is a masterpiece of the arts practised in the city of Lyon." She was to employ Lasalle to weave some fabulous silks, including a *tenture* to commemorate the battle of Chesmé, the first Russian victory in a sea-battle for nine hundred years. Lasalle rose to the challenge with a design incorporating a ship on a stormy sea, enclosed within trelliswork of flowers and ribbons in his favourite style.

In eighteenth-century descriptions and inventories, painted silks abound but, perhaps hardly surprisingly, very few seem to have survived to this day. The name *Pekin peint* was normally employed to describe painted silk, which suggests that it was Chinese, but in fact it was often made in France, although Chinese examples are known, including panels in the Victoria and Albert Museum of flowers painted on blue silk, but with European borders of white silk painted with a

*D*etail of a painted silk panel by Cardin, for Louis XVI's Cabinet du Conseil at Compiègne. One of a series with military scenes; the borders show how close the neoclassical style could be to Louis XIV baroque.

continuous frieze of scrolls and flower trails. White and yellow silk was woven in Lyon and painted there, to be sold in Paris, At first, designs imitated Chinese originals, with flowering trees or Oriental figures, but gradually a French style predominated, and a series of panels of painted silk of the 1780s in the J. Paul Getty Museum are in a wholly French arabesque style. Many competent artists, including those working for the Garde-Meuble, painted silk upholstery for walls and chairs, often possibly *in situ*, and the *bronzier* Quentin-Claude Pitoin advertised himself as a "painter on textiles in the Indian style".

Velvet, both plain and cut, including *velours d'Utrecht*, which was made in Northern France, was normally only used for chairs and door-hangings, according to Bimont, who tells us that this is the same sort of material as is used for women's dresses and men's jackets, and that it is suitable for *bergères, fauteuils à la Reine, cabriolets*, or chaise-longues but not normally for *meubles à demeure* (fixed seat furniture) such as sofas and *ottomanes*.

Moquette, a type of solid velvet with a strong pile, is only good, in Bimont's eyes, for chairs in *antichambres*, or for placing on the floor. This is the ancestor of fitted carpet, and began to be used as such in the eighteenth century. The floor of Marie Antoinette's box at the Théatre Français, decorated when the theatre was new between 1780 and 1782, was of moquette, with a crimson, green and white mosaic pattern.

Painted or printed cottons from the East, principally from India, had become so popular in Louis XIV's reign that it was judged necessary in 1686 to ban their import, on the grounds that they deprived the nascent French printed-cotton industry of a living. The French industry itself was banned in turn, at a time when the economic hardships of the end of the seventeenth century prompted Louis XIV to issue a variety of sumptuary laws, but both French-made products and imported cottons continued to be widely, though illegally, employed (see page 18), until various challenges brought the ban to an end in stages during the 1750s, and a number of workshops throughout France began to produce printed cottons, for example at Nantes or Bourges. Naturally, the *enclos privilégiés* had acted as refuges for cotton printers during the ban, and Bimont records the existence of one at the Temple in Paris. That the ban was unevenly enforced is evident from the fact that even royal palaces contained printed cottons; the 1752 inventory of the Château de Choisy mentions "a canopy bed, upholstered in calico, of sandy-coloured ground with bunches of flowers in red". The curtains and valances were edged with silk ribbon.

"Siamoises", "Indiennes", and "Masulipatam" were all exotic names given to various types of Eastern printed or painted cottons, but the names continued to be employed for the imitations made in France. They were decorated with luxuriant flowering foliage in red, brown and blue, with matching borders. These cottons could be produced much more cheaply than silks, and their highly colourful and exotic nature made them extremely popular. Bimont considered them suitable for beds, walls and curtains, but not for chairs, except as cushions.

In 1760, Christophe-Philippe Oberkampf started a factory producing printed toiles at Jouy-en-Josas near Versailles, the enormous success of which has led to the generic name "toiles de Jouy" being applied to all French printed toiles of the late eighteenth century. Oberkampf, a typical example of an entrepreneur of the early industrial era, printed toiles in the traditional calico "Indienne" style and in loose imitation of Lyon woven silks. He also developed a distinctive style of his own, the monochrome printing of pastoral and allegorical scenes taken from the engravings of Huet and others, in blue, red or purple. In 1783 Oberkampf was granted a Privilège, which allowed him to call his factory a Manufacture Royale, as was Réveillon, the printed-paper manufacturer with whom Oberkampf may have collaborated.

"Painted toiles can be used for fine upholstery, especially in the country." This comment by Bimont is intended to emphasize the rustic aspect of toile, but Marie Antoinette employed it for rooms in her private apartments at Versailles, such as the *cabinet de retraite*, which in 1784 contained a *bergère*, a *lit à la Turque* and door and window curtains upholstered in "toile de Jouy" with applied borders, and lined in white taffeta.

Instead of woven tapestry chair covers, *tapissiers* could supply the equipment for ladies to execute their own *petit-point* or embroidery panels. Tessin sent some to his wife in Sweden in 1741 "six armchairs of tapestry to be filled in, with the necessary wool, in a pattern imitating one colour damask". Mesdames Adélaïde and Victoire were ardent embroiderers, ordering silks from Mademoiselle Dubuquoy in the Rue Saint-Honoré, which they applied in various patterns including arabesques and a "design of drapery and cartouches". Being well-organized princesses, they ordered the chairs before starting work. These were delivered, with white upholstery, carefully scrutinized *in situ*, and then stored away until the work was done.

*Louis XVI, restaurateur de la Liberté.* Toile de Jouy designed by Huet in 1789. Toiles printed with monochrome patterns such as this were the mainstay of Oberkampf's production.

FOLLOWING SPREAD
*W*all panelling in the *salon* of the Hôtel de Villette, Paris.

# 11
# SILVER

The taste for ostentation, at the apogee of Louis XIV's reign, was responsible for the creation of some remarkable if impractical and ephemeral baroque pieces of silver. The silver furniture of Louis XIV, an assemblage of tables, *guéridons* (torchères) and objects such as vases, firedogs, ewers and tubs for orange trees, was really an excuse for displaying great wealth, which, when the need arose, had to go to the mint to help pay for the King's disastrous wars, along with much of the finest table and buffet silver belonging both to the King and to the aristocracy. It is undeniable that the great melting of 1689-90, together with subsequent ones, as well as occasional sumptuary laws, contributed in no small measure to the expansion of a variety of rival specialist crafts, such as glazed earthenware, porcelain or pewter to replace the great sideboard ewers and dishes, plates and tureens, and giltbronze to replace firedogs, frames, candlesticks and chandeliers. Nevertheless, despite the terrible toll of hardship and bankruptcy such political decisions caused among the silversmiths, especially those who worked for royal and princely clients, the noble metal continued to be employed throughout the eighteenth century, albeit rarely on a large scale, and almost exclusively for objects connected with the dining table and the *toilette*.

Fine French eighteenth-century silver is rare today. Meltings, such as that of 1760, caused the disappearance of quantities of pieces (though these were often rapidly replaced). The revolution witnessed the melting of much plate, but probably the biggest single cause of melting was the ordering of newly fashionable pieces. When new silver objects were made, it made sense for the client to return the old ones, and it was not until the nineteenth century that antiquarian interest in the subject protected surviving pieces. Almost no French eighteenth-century royal

silver survives, so that the finest pieces to be seen today are those ordered by foreign royalty, such as Catherine the Great of Russia, John V of Portugal, Christian VII of Denmark or George III of England, or other grandees including the English Duke of Kingston and the Swedish Count Creutz, Gustav III's ambassador to Paris. It is questionable whether these represent accurately the silver made for French use. Nevertheless, the finest artists were employed in the design and manufacture of these great services, so that they do at least act as witnesses to the inventiveness and skills of Parisian eighteenth-century silversmiths.

## TABLE DECORATION AND EATING PRACTICE

Elaborate banquets formed a major part of court and social life. One of the main purposes of such feasts was the display of wealth, in the form of silver, both on the table and on the great multi-tiered buffets of painted wood or marble which are seen in the paintings of Desportes. For the table, serving dishes, bowls and tureens were arranged in patterns around a central *dormant* (centrepiece). These could be of several types. The fashion for the *surtout* (an elaborate silver ornament created for Louis XIV and designed to hold the oil and vinegar bottles, the salt, sugar and spices, as well as candlebrackets when used in the evening) waned during the reign of Louis XV, and by the middle of the century its place was largely taken by the enormous silver or Sèvres tureens which were made as matching parts of dinner services. Silver *surtouts* were rarely found except on royal and princely tables, and most of the ones made for foreign courts were the work of the French King's goldsmiths, whose workshops were situated within the Louvre. Other more colourful and ephemeral decorations were also employed, notably the *sablé* patterns of multicoloured sand arranged on shaped pieces of mirror glass. For the court's stay at Rambouillet in 1784, a document preserved in the Archives Nationales describes in some detail the eating arrangements for the various members of the household. M.M. les Maîtres, the senior officers, were entitled for both meals

*Buffet d'Orfèvrerie* by François Desportes, circa 1730. The importance attached to the decoration of the buffet in the early eighteenth century, which is conveyed in this magnificent painting, was gradually to fade, leaving such paintings as the only testimonies to the variety of objects that could be found on grand tiered buffets. In this case they include hardstone vases, some of which are mounted, Japanese porcelain bowls and important silver, all garlanded with flowers. Desportes was employed by Louis XV, and the quality of the pieces portrayed here make it likely that they belonged to the King.

to a table with "five pieces of mirror glass with coloured sand and decorated with groups and vases with natural flowers". Here figures and vases, probably of biscuit porcelain, were used together with the *sablé*. The lesser officers had to be content with a *dormant* for their supper only, as well as a less varied selection of dishes.

This type of table centrepiece followed an earlier tradition, as did the decoration for the banquet celebrating the wedding of the Comte and Comtesse d'Artois in 1770, of which a contemporary description survives. It was a masterpiece of the genre, with a "marvellous mechanism" invented by Blaise-Henri Arnoux, described as a *machiniste plein d'imagination*: "The centre was a river which gushed inexhaustibly throughout the meal. Small ships decorated its course . . . The glitter of the diamonds . . . gave the impression of a fairy palace." Figures and groups of sculpted sugar had traditionally been employed for table decoration, and they could naturally be consumed at the end of the meal. When Louis XV's dissolute friend the Duc de Richelieu was sent to Dresden to collect the Dauphin's second bride, Marie-Josèphe de Saxe, in 1747, he gave a banquet there for which the centrepiece consisted of sugar sculpture. When at the end of the meal he instructed the spectators to help themselves from the centre of the table, they took not only the sugar but the silver too. The unglazed (biscuit) porcelain figures and vases invented at Vincennes around 1750 were inedible and therefore more permanent versions of such rococo extravagance. Other materials were also employed. The Portuguese Count d'Aveiro ordered from the Paris goldsmith Abraham-Nicolas Cousinet in 1757-8 a *surtout*

*P*orcelain, marble, mirror and gilt-bronze *surtout*. The remnant of the elaborate table centrepiece made for the banquet held in the newly opened Opera House at Versailles on 16 May 1770, for the wedding of the Dauphin (later Louis XVI), and Marie Antoinette. The table decoration consisted of the colonnade and an arrangement of biscuit sculptures, including putti emblematic of the Seasons, vases on columns, fountains spouting water, mythological figures (including a *Venus aux belles fesses*) and a sculpture of Louis XV after Pigalle. The colonnade was only loaned by the Sèvres factory for the banquet, and was afterwards reduced in size and sold to the dealer Madame Lair, who fitted it with garlands of flowers and small vases. The watercolour by Jean-Michel Moreau le Jeune of the banquet given by Madame du Barry for Louis XV at Louveciennes in 1771 shows a centrepiece with domed trellis work, which is either this one or another made from the remainder of the components.

consisting of a set of silver-gilt figures in the style of Boucher's Beauvais tapestry cartoons, and the Swiss banker Jean-Frédéric Perregaux, established in Paris at the end of the eighteenth century, owned table ornaments in the form of antique temples, made of marbled wood or cardboard, which recall the famous columned *surtout* created by Sèvres for the wedding of the Dauphin, the future Louis XVI, to Marie Antoinette in 1770.

Meals in such surroundings were served according to a ritual evolved at the court of Louis XIV, and known as *service à la française*. Each of the three or more courses consisted of a number of different dishes placed in their containers in patterns around the centrepiece. The dishes remained static, and a guest was expected to be within reach of several at once. Guests were provided with a plate and a *couvert*, or set of fork, spoon, knife and salt-cellar. It was customary to bring one's own servants to go round the table and collect food from the various dishes, and to go to the sideboard to collect a glass of wine. When the Comte and Comtesse du Nord attended a banquet given in their honour by the Prince de Condé at Chantilly in 1782, no fewer than three servants were in attendance upon each guest. It is hardly surprising that such extravagance was regarded as impractical, and that in reaction the fashion was introduced, largely by Louis XV, of dining without servants in smaller and more comfortable surroundings. In his *Tableau de Paris* of 1788, Mercier castigated the practice of asking servants every time guests wanted a drink: "You rich people should place decanters and bottles on the table." This fashion was partly responsible for the change in room use and distribution which took place in the middle of the eighteenth century and which resulted in the familiar room arrangement of today.

# TABLE SILVER

The practice of making large and elaborate silver dinner services of unified design had become firmly established in France by the beginning of the eighteenth century, and such sets became fashionable throughout Europe. Components of many of these survive to this day, but they were the preserve of the ultra-rich, and most people made do with scaled-down versions, often accumulating sets over many years. These could comprise all the components necessary for the dining table and sideboard. Linen damask tablecloths, some with elaborate patterns, were used to cover dining tables, which were not intended to be visible. The oval *terrines*, for soup, and the round *pots à oille*, for stew, were the largest components, and were often placed in pairs on their stands in the centre of tables instead of *surtouts*. A variety of round, oval, square and rectangular dishes and stands, some with covers, were used to form the patterns required by the *service à la française*, along with sauce-boats, mustard pots and *porte-huiliers* (cruets). The *couverts* were placed around the matching plates on the edge of the table. For evening meals, candlesticks and candelabra are found in large numbers among services. The great Orlov service, ordered from Paris in 1770 by

*S*ilver-gilt *chocolatière* and *réchaud* by Henri-Nicolas Cousinet, from Marie Leczinska's *nécessaire*, Paris, 1729. The arms were removed at the revolution.

Catherine the Great for her lover, Count Gregory Orlov, comprises no fewer than forty-eight candlesticks and sixty candelabra. Other components were intended for use on the sideboard; these are the *seaux* for cooling bottles and decanters of various sizes, as well as those for glasses, known as *seaux crénelés* (called monteiths in English) because of the indentations in their borders which held the stems of glasses while the bowls were immersed in crushed ice.

# THE TOILETTE

The *toilette* provided the other great excuse for extravagant silver. Traditionally given to a bride, this was a set of fitments for the dressing table, and could comprise a staggering variety of different objects, such as a mirror, candlesticks, pots for make-up and scent, boxes for jewellery, powder and *mouches* (beauty-spots), brushes, *nécessaires* for

sewing, writing or making hot chocolate, ewers and basins, *écuelles* and trays for snuffers or gloves. Silver was not the only material used for such sets; the *marchands-merciers* could supply them in mounted porcelain, enamel or lacquer; one delivered by Delaroue to the Garde-Meuble in 1751 was entirely covered in gold and silver brocade, including the frame of the mirror; it was provided with a cloth (the origin of the word *toilette* is *toile* or cloth) of the same material, as well as with a folding table of walnut. The reign of Louis XV saw the appearance of the *table de toilette*, a marquetry table with fitted drawers and compartments containing all the elements mentioned above. These were not necessarily designed for travelling; much more probably they

*T*oilet service by Sebastien Igonet, Alexis Loir, Antoine Lebrun and Etienne Pollet. Commissioned by the Portuguese Duc de Cadaval, Paris, 1738-9. The decoration is mostly executed in low relief, respecting the utilitarian nature of this nevertheless extremely lavish set.

*T*ankard, Chinese porcelain with gold and silver-gilt mounts and glass liner, Paris, 1729-30. Probably among the purchases made by Charles-Albert, Elector of Bavaria, in Paris in the 1730s. Inventoried in Munich in 1747 and now preserved in the Residenzmuseum, Munich.

the shine of silver (sometimes called *argent blanc* by opposition) was appreciated for its own sake. The *bronzier* Pierre Gouthière gilded silver (and bronze) so finely for François-Thomas Germain that the latter was moved to claim in 1766 that he was himself responsible for bringing the technique back into fashion.

Because it was extremely difficult and costly for an outsider to become a *maître-orfèvre*, the craft remained a traditional one, passing from father to son for several generations. Thus many of the great gold- or silversmiths of the eighteenth century were the sons and grandsons of those who had been responsible for the extravagances of the reign of Louis XIV. This was the case of Thomas Germain (1673-1748) and his son François-Thomas, who stand out among the silversmiths of the eighteenth century on account of the originality and quality of their work.

Thomas was the son of Pierre Germain, a silversmith who had participated in Louis XIV's silver furniture. He learnt drawing in the studio of the painter Bon Boullogne and went to Rome in 1688; he may perhaps have been intending to become a painter or an architect. His architectural proposals for the church of Saint-Louis-du-Louvre, and his designs for the crimson and gold silk hangings destined for the Salon de Mercure in the Grands Appartements at Versailles show his competence in fields other than silver. Germain returned to Paris in 1706 and was soon employed by the most prestigious clients, becoming one of the three Orfèvres et sculpteurs du Roi in 1720. He executed in 1726 the *toilette* of the young Queen, Marie Leczinska, and from 1727 made a number of the components of the most prestigious group of precious

were used to store the components when not in use.

The purpose of the *toilette* could be extremely varied. It would have been inconvenient to use every single part of the really elaborate ones every day, but the various elements were employed for a large range of daily pastimes, such as breakfast or other snacks, sewing, washing or applying make-up. They formed a sometimes significant part of a bride's dowry, and may have been arranged on the dressing table and around the bedroom when a lady received visitors elegantly but informally in the morning. Like table silver, a variety of components might be assembled over the years, and could serve as a display of wealth. Madame de Pompadour's *toilette* became as much a court ritual as Louis XV's *Lever*, but Dufort de Cheverny informs us that she used the excuse of sitting at her *toilette* to defuse formality in her presence. Dufort adds that she received foreign ambassadors thus seated, except, of course, the Papal Nuncio.

# THE MAKERS

Like the other guilds, gold- and silversmiths suffered under their own set of quaint antiquated rules, including hallmarking requirements with all the attendant verifications. For example, pieces had to be taken to the hallmarking office twice, when they were started, and when they were finished. Large-scale gold objects were practically never made, silver-gilt (*argent doré* or *vermeil*) being successfully used instead, but

*P*ainting of a *seau*, a soup tureen, two dishes and two views of a candlestick by François Desportes, 1737-43. These objects belonged to Louis XV. A similar tureen survives by Nicolas Besnier, one of the three Orfèvres du Roi, and it is likely Besnier was the maker of the one shown here. The figures on the stem of the candlestick are identical to those visible on a candlestick on a shelf in the famous portrait of Thomas Germain and his wife by Largillière, now in the Gulbenkian Foundation, Lisbon.

metal objects of the eighteenth century (alas, long since melted), the solid gold service (*vaisselle d'or*) of Louis XV, including in 1736 an *écuelle* and its stand, and, in 1747, shortly before his death, the pair of gold *girandoles* of five branches, each on a rococo base with the Royal arms and four putti holding the stems. These stood in Louis XV's bedroom at Versailles, on the great commode by Antoine-Robert Gaudreaus with gilt-bronzes by Jacques Caffiéri. The Lisbon earthquake of 1755 destroyed the other vital part of Thomas's work, executed for the King of Portugal, and which his son François-Thomas was to replace.

Juste-Aurèle Meissonier held the post of designer to the Royal household and may have provided drawings to be executed by Germain; in the book of Meissonier's collected engravings, a *cuvette*, a candelabrum and a nef are specifically stated to be for the King, and the inventory taken after Germain's death in 1748 records a set of these engravings in his possession. Louis XV had forced the goldsmiths' guild to make Meissonier a *maître-orfèvre* without the usual formalities, and the lack of surviving pieces bearing his stamp probably indicates that he was mainly a designer, a fact confirmed by his role in the supply of silver to the Duke of Kingston in the 1730s; he produced the designs, subcontracted the manufacture, but sold the pieces himself to the Duke. He was of course entitled to do so by virtue of his status as a guild member, and he proudly engraved the tureens with the words *Fait par I. A. Meissonier Architectte*. In 1741, when Tessin tried to obtain fashionable designs for silver to send back to Sweden, he found that "the goldsmiths either won't show them, or want to sell their ideas too expensively," and he was obliged to resort to drawing actual pieces surreptitiously in private houses.

An exuberant *rocaille* movement pervades much of Thomas Germain's surviving work. Asymmetry, a rococo characteristic visible most clearly in Meissonier's designs, was used by Germain and other silversmiths of the first half of the eighteenth century for large

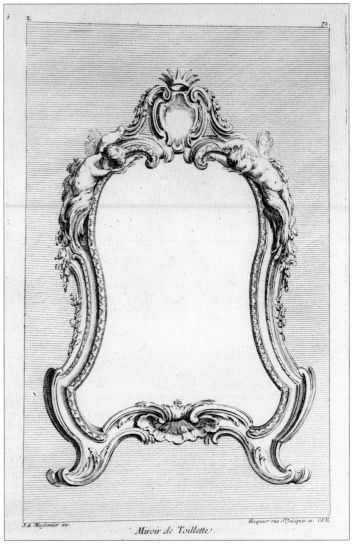

*D*esign for a *miroir de toilette*, perhaps for the now lost mirror of Marie Leczinska, executed in silver-gilt by Thomas Germain in 1726. Engraving by Huquier, plate 28 of Juste-Aurèle Meissonier's *Oeuvre*.

*F*our salts, two with covers, by Edmé-Pierre Balzac, Paris, 1747. Salts such as these were placed on tables beside each of the guests as part of the *service à la Française*.

sculptural pieces such as wine coolers, *surtouts* and candelabra, with bold rockwork, leafy scrollwork and animal or aquatic motifs in high relief, exquisitely chased and stippled. For such pieces, which were designed to be seen and not handled, the adoption of the rococo style was fluent and complete by the second half of the 1720's. Hunting became a favourite theme for heavily sculptural silver during this period; the *surtout* made by Jacques Roettiers for the Duc de Bourbon in 1736 represents a stag hunt and a wolf caught in a trap, with wild boars' heads in the four corners. Roettiers may have designed it himself; he had studied at the Académie Royale de Peinture et de Sculpture before being apprenticed to Thomas Germain and to Nicolas Besnier, another Ofrèvre du Roi, whose daughter he married in 1734.

Silversmiths who produced lesser objects, or those for everyday use, tended to be more traditional, and the shapes and decoration of Louis XIV silver continued well into the 1740s, with a gradual relaxing of established formal patterns; moulded borders became wavy, engraving or matting created subtle contrasts of surface, lambrequins were replaced by bulrushes, and shallow or simulated gadrooning enveloped the entire surfaces of objects both flat and in the round. The lid of a silver-gilt *écuelle* of 1733-4 by Thomas Germain in the Louvre bears an early example of this: simulated spirally swirling gadrooning, executed in very low relief with contrasting surfaces indicated by a high polish or stippled *ciselure*. Candlesticks generally retained the traditional baluster shape on a spreading foot, at first of octagonal section, with symmetrically applied rococo cartouches, but gradually a round section became more common, and the foot assumed a wavy outline. The stems of cutlery were outlined with a double reeding, and the end might be decorated with a shell.

Thomas Germain's son, François-Thomas (1726-91) followed in his

*T*ray by François-Thomas Germain, Paris, 1750. Trays of this sort formed part of *toilettes*, and spaces for two *gobelets* (beakers) can clearly be seen. Even at the height of the rococo style, Germain still employed classical details such as the bound wreath around the rim.

father's footsteps both in his style and as supplier to the French as well as to foreign courts, and his membership of the Académie de Saint Luc in addition to that of the goldsmiths' guild confirms that he too was more than a simple craftsman. He worked in gilt-bronze, and proudly signed some of his work in this medium, including a set of four wall lights made for the *appartements de parade* at the Palais-Royal in 1756, perhaps to designs provided by the architect Pierre Contant d'Ivry. Two sets of silver objects supplied to Louis XV illustrate the variety of his

*S*ilver-gilt teapot and sugar-bowl by Jean-Baptiste de Lens, Paris 1732-3.

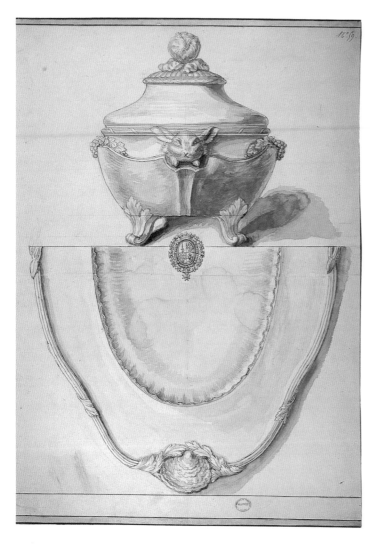

production: two cooking pots (*marmittes* [sic]) on a tripod, one fitting inside the other, with ebony handles and knops, were stated to be for making broth *au bain marie*; while a mill (*moulin*) was for roasting coffee. Both of these were delivered in early 1754, within a few days of the Vincennes *bleu céleste* service, and it is probable that they were for the King's very personal use in the *petits cabinets* at Versailles. The Nabob of Golconda was perhaps the most exotic of Germain's foreign clients, and he may have been the first silversmith to execute pieces in the neoclassical style. Germain's downfall came as a result of the strict regulations of the goldsmiths' guild, which forbade members to enter into partnerships with anyone except fellow goldsmiths. In 1765, plagued by the perennial eighteenth-century problem of late- or never-paying customers, he formed a partnership with financiers, and the guild forced him into bankruptcy as a result.

Both Germains collaborated with their colleagues in the execution of large orders. That this practice became widespread is confirmed by the many dining services and *toilettes* which are the work of more than one goldsmith (see page 226). The famous service originally ordered by the Comte de Toulouse (and now known as the Orléans-Penthièvre service) for which Thomas Germain supplied pieces as early as 1728,

*D*esign from the Sèvres factory archives for a tureen and stand (possibly for rabbit stew) of the 1750s, with the arms of Henry-Léonard-Jean-Baptiste Bertin, one of Louis XV's ministers. Clearly a silver design which Bertin may have wanted Sèvres to copy in porcelain.

RIGHT
*T*ea-kettle and stand by François-Thomas Germain, the stand 1756-7, the kettle 1762-3. One of Germain's early ventures into neoclassicism, the stand displays a fluent understanding of *goût grec* motifs. The kettle, on the other hand, is in an exotic style which found as much favour during the neoclassical epoch as it had during the rococo.

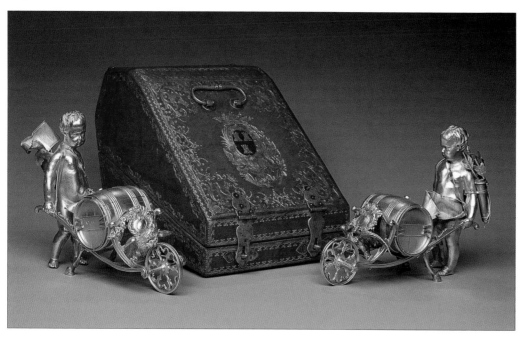

*P*air of mustard-pots by Antoine-Sébastien Durand, Paris, 1750-51. The arms on the fitted case confirm the identity of the original owner – Madame de Pompadour.

received supplementary components in the 1750's from Edmé-Pierre Balzac and Antoine-Sébastien Durand, in a *rocaille* style as exuberant as that of the original pieces. Agents such as Bonnet, working for foreign princes, were able to coordinate goldsmiths' work; naturally foreigners always expressed anxiety lest their pieces should be out-of-date. Bonnet was instructed by Dutillot in 1760 that Monseigneur's tureens should be "of a shape in the latest fashion".

Unlike most of his colleagues, Edmé-Pierre Balzac (b. 1705) did not originate from a family of goldsmiths, and was forced to resort to complicated and expensive means to become a *maître*. His workshops were situated in the Pont-au-Change quarter in Paris, close to the hallmarking office and to most of his colleagues. In addition to an extensive and splendid production, he was a technical innovator. His machine for the manufacture of plates and dishes without the use of solder for border decoration was honoured by a certificate from the Académie des Sciences in 1756, while his cutlery-making machine appears to have required ten years of research. He too experienced difficulties, and this despite being the largest producer of silver in Paris in the late 1760s, being responsible for one-twelfth of the total weight sent for hallmarking. He produced all types of objects, unlike many of his colleagues who specialized in particular pieces, such as goblets, cutlery or *nécessaire* fittings.

Classical features had managed to survive the onslaught of the rococo upon silver, with details such as rosettes, bound wreaths and Vitruvian scrolls continuing to be employed, so that when in the early 1760s the fashion for classicism returned in a purified form goldsmiths were ready to respond, in some cases with designs which appear to owe more to Louis XIV baroque than to Ancient Greece.

*P*air of silver-gilt candlesticks by Louis-Joseph Lenhendrick, Paris, 1762.

*S*ilver-gilt plate by L. A. Horning, Strasbourg, 1775.

The Orlov service, largely made by the Roettiers family in the early 1770s, has been considered to derive its inspiration from silver made for Louis XIV, which, although it had long been melted, may have been known through drawings in the Louvre workshops. The *seaux à bouteilles*, for example, are of strong baroque vase shape, nearly identical to Louis XIV's silver orange-tree tubs, known today from Gobelins tapestries. Jacques-Nicolas Roettiers made other pieces in this style, and the pair of dishes in the Metropolitan Museum in New York come from a service similar to Orlov's, but more elaborate (see right).

Paradoxically, the more excessive manifestations of the *goût grec* had much in common with the baroque. The silversmiths of the second half of the eighteenth century were to evolve a style which, although it used neoclasssical detail with great fluency, managed to restrain it and impart to it a great deal of the lightness and elegance which had made the rococo so popular. Features such as ribbon-tied laurel or flower garlands, symmetrically arranged stiff-leaf foliage and friezes with low relief or engraved leafy scrollwork were used with restraint, often in bands enclosed by mouldings or engraved borders.

While the gradual spreading-out of wealth in the second half of the eighteenth century led to a greater demand for simple silver, which in

*O*ne of a pair of low covered dishes by Jacques-Nicolas Roettiers, Paris, 1775-6. From a service bought in 1794 by the American Gouverneur Morris, during his stay in Paris as ambassador of the new American republic. He may have obtained it from the Comtesse d'Angiviller, whose husband had been Directeur des Bâtiments during Louis XVI's reign. Covered dishes formed part of the regular components of services, but these are unusual, flattened versions of the tureens. The service bears a strong resemblance to the Orlov service, also by Roettiers; the Orlov *seaux*, for example, are decorated with the same remarkable ivy garlands as these dishes.

*O*ne of a pair of *seaux crénelés* (monteiths) by Robert-Joseph Auguste, Paris, 1779-80. From one of the services ordered by Catherine the Great. The crenellations have been given a neoclassical treatment.

*S*auceboat, partly gilded, by Jean-Baptiste-François Cheret, Paris, 1762. This object, with its naturalistic foliage, is a late example of the rococo style.

turn was responsible for encouraging makers such as Balzac to adopt industrial manufacturing processes, the continued requirements for more refined silver resulted in the creation of large numbers of incredibly lavish services for foreign princes. The survival of many of these provides the most eloquent testimony to the genius of men such as Antoine-Sébastien Durand, Jacques-Nicolas Roettiers, Louis-Joseph Lenhendrick, and the last and greatest, Robert-Joseph Auguste, who reigned as Orfèvre ordinaire du Roi from 1778 to the revolution.

Not one piece of Auguste's work for Louis XVI is known to survive, but components of the huge services ordered by Catherine the Great for her provincial capitals were sold by the Soviet government in the 1920s and are now in Western museums. From 1775-6, Count Creutz commissioned Auguste to produce a service of such grandeur that after his return to Sweden he eventually had to sell it to his sovereign in 1781. The shafts of the candlesticks are decorated with three addorsed female terms and drapery in high relief, while the tureens, shaped like vases on their large stands with gadrooning punctuated by rosettes, have handles

in the shape of intertwined putti whose legs become a frieze of raised foliate scrollwork, interrupted by low-relief plaques in solid gold, said to be by Pajou and commemorating Gustav III's *coup d'état*.

Unlike many of the other crafts of the eighteenth century, the art of the goldsmith was practised with astonishing fluency by a number of provincial makers, in Strasbourg (see page 233) and Toulouse for example, and some of their production shows all the skill and elegance of the finest Paris work. Toulouse saw the rise of the Samson family,

*P*latinum and blue glass sugar-bowl, inscribed *Platina Janety Fecit 1786*. The Paris silversmith Marc-Etienne Janety, who pioneered the use of platinum in the late eighteenth century, made a speciality of sugar-bowls, salts and mustard-pots with glass liners, some of which have open-work garlands of flowers. The mythological scenes decorating the bowl, shown in detail on the right, are taken from seventeenth-century engravings.

who worked in a bold rococo style as well as concurrently producing work of restrained and elegant proportions.

Silver and gold were occasionally employed as mounts for porcelain, hardstones or lacquer in the tradition of the seventeenth century, although gilt-bronze had become far more common. A new fashion of the neoclassical era was the use of liners in blue glass fitted in openwork salt-cellars and mustard-pots. The goldsmith Jean-Nicolas Bastin ordered from Sèvres in the early 1780s a number of pieces of porcelain in *bleu céleste* or green with gilt outlines, which he intended to mount in silver-gilt. These included mustard-pots, salt-cellars with one, two or three compartments, eggcups and cruet stands. A mustard-pot and two

*P*air of candelabra by Antoine Bouillier, Paris, 1787.

*J*asper bowl on two-colour silver-gilt foot by Jacques Kirstein, Strasbourg, 1787.

salt-cellars in *bleu céleste* with mounts incorporating rams' heads and garlands of flowers, which survive in the Wallace Collection, may have formed part of a larger set of this type owned by Louis XVI.

When the Comte de Stahremberg, Maria Theresa's ambassador to Paris, left the Hôtel de Soyecourt in 1766, among the items offered for sale were two Meissen tureens and their stands, described as "made from the designs of Germain and mounted by him in silver". Rock crystal was also especially popular, and several ewers and basins with gold mounts have been recorded, including one given to the Ottoman Sultan by Louis XV in 1742. The example in the Wallace Collection, with mounts by Jean Gaillard of 1727-32, may well be the one mentioned in Madame de Pompadour's inventory, and Mademoiselle Laguerre, a member of the chorus at the Opera whose chief claim to fame was to have been caught *in flagrante* in a box with a judge during a rehearsal, owned a rock-crystal *déjeuner* mounted with silver-gilt serpents and tulips, which was included in her sale in 1782.

# APPENDIX ONE

Extracts from some letters written by Madame Huguet de Grafigny, while staying with Voltaire and his mistress Madame du Châtelet at Cirey in December 1738. The letters are addressed to Monsieur Devaux, who held the post of *lecteur* at the Court of King Stanislas Leczinski in Lorraine.

His [Voltaire's] small wing is so closely connected to the house, that the door is at the foot of the grand staircase. There is a small *anti-chambre*, the size of your hand, followed by a small, low-ceilinged bedroom covered in crimson velvet; an alcove of the same has a gilt fringe; this is the winter upholstery. There is little material on the wall, but mostly panelling, on which are charming paintings; looking-glasses, very fine lacquer corner cupboards; porcelains, Oriental figures, a clock supported by Oriental figures of unusual shape, an infinity of objects in this taste, expensive, refined, and so clean you could kiss the floor . . . This leads into the small gallery, which must be no more than thirty or forty *pieds* (9.7-12.9 m) in length. Between the windows are two very fine small sculptures, on pedestals of Indian [meaning Oriental] lacquer: one is the Farnèse Venus, the other Hercules. The side opposite the windows is divided into two cupboards; one with books, one with scientific instruments; between the two, a stove in the wall, which makes the air as warm as in the spring; in front is a tall pedestal, on which is a large putto shooting an arrow: this is not finished; a carved alcove is being made to hide the stove. [FOOTNOTE The inscription at the base of this putto is as follows: *Qui que tu sois, voici ton maître; Il l'est, le fut, ou le doit être*]. The gallery is panelled and painted light yellow. Clocks, tables, desks, you can be sure nothing is lacking. Beyond is the dark room, which is not ready yet; neither is the one where he is going to put all his instruments: that is why they are all still in the gallery. There is but one sofa, and no comfortable chairs, that is to say, the small number of chairs are fine, but they are sparsely upholstered; physical comfort is obviously not his vice. The panelling frames very fine Indian [meaning Chinese] papers; the screens are of the same; there are tables with screens, porcelains, everything is of a highly refined taste.

Sa petite aile tient si fort à la maison, que la porte est au bas du grand escalier. Il a une petite anti-chambre grande comme la main; ensuite vient sa chambre, qui est petite, basse et tapissée de velours cramoisi; une niche de même avec des franges d'or; c'est le meuble d'hiver. Il y a peu de tapisserie, mais beaucoup de lambris, dans lesquels sont encadrés des tableaux charmants; des glaces, des encoignures de laque admirables; des porcelaines, des marabouts, une pendule soutenue par des marabouts d'une forme singulière, des choses infinies dans ce goût-là, chères, recherchées, et surtout d'une propreté à baiser le parquet . . . On passe dans la petite galerie, qui n'a guère que trente ou quarante pieds de long. Entre ses fenêtres sont deux petites statues fort belles, sur des piédestaux de vernis des Indes: l'une est cette *Vénus Farnèse*, l'autre *Hercule*. L'autre côté des fenêtres est partagé en deux armoires; l'une de livres, l'autre de machines de métaphysique; entre les deux, un fourneau dans le mur, qui rend l'air comme celui du printemps; devant, se trouve un grand piédestal, sur lequel est un *Amour* assez grand qui lance une flèche: cela n'est pas achevé; on fait une niche sculptée à cet Amour, qui cachera l'apparence du fourneau. [FOOTNOTE Voici l'inscription qu'il y avait au bas de cet Amour: Qui que tu sois, voici ton maître; / Il l'est, le fut, ou le doit être.] La galerie est boisée et vernie en petit jaune. Des pendules, des tables, des bureaux, tu crois bien que rien n'y manque. Au-delà est la chambre obscure, qui n'est pas encore finie, non plus que celle ou il mettra ses machines: c'est pour cela qu'elles sont encore toutes dans la galerie. Il n'y a qu'un seul sopha et point de fauteuils commodes, c'est-à-dire, que le petit nombre de ceux qui s'y trouvent sont bons, mais ce ne sont que des fauteuils garnis: l'aisance du corps n'est pas sa volupté, apparemment. Les panneaux des lambris sont des papiers des Indes forts beaux; les paravents sont de même; il y a des tables à écrans, des porcelaines, enfin tout est d'un goût extrèment recherché.

## SHE VISITS MADAME DU CHÂTELET'S APARTMENT

Voltaire's is nothing compared to this one. Her bedroom is panelled and painted light yellow, with pale blue mouldings; an alcove of the same, framed with delightful Indian [Chinese] paper. The bed is in blue moiré, and everything matches so that even the dog basket is yellow and blue, like the chair frames, writing desk, corner cupboards and secretaire. The looking-glasses with silver frames, everything is wonderfully polished. A large door, glazed with looking-glass, leads to the library, which is not yet finished. Its carving is as precious as a snuffbox: nothing is as beautiful. There will be looking-glasses, paintings by Veronese, etc. One side of the alcove is a small boudoir; you fall on your knees when you go in. The panelling is blue, and the ceiling has been painted and lacquered by a pupil of Martin, who has been here for the last three years. All the small panels have paintings by Watteau; these are the Five Senses; then two Fables by La Fontaine, *Le Baiser pris et rendu*, of which

Celui de Voltaire n'est rien en comparaison de celui-ci. Sa chambre est boisée et peinte en vernis petit jaune, avec des cordons bleu pâle; une niche de même, encadrée de papiers des Indes charmans. Le lit est en moiré bleu; et tout est tellement assorti que, jusqu'au panier du chien, tout est jaune et bleu: bois de fauteuils, bureau, encoignures, secrétaire. Les glaces et cadres d'argent, tout est d'un brillant admirable. Une grande porte vitrée, mais de glace-miroir, conduit à la bibliothèque, qui n'est pas encore achevée. C'est une sculpture comme une tabatière: rien n'est joli comme tout cela. Il y aura des glaces, des tableaux de Paul Véronèse, etc. D'un côté de la niche est un petit boudoir; on est prêt à se mettre à genoux en y entrant. Le lambris est en bleu, et le plafond est peint et verni par un élève de *Martin*, qu'ils ont ici depuis trois ans. Tous les petits panneaux sont remplis par des tableaux de *Watteau*: ce sont les cinq Sens; puis les deux contes de

I had the engravings, and *Les Oies de Frère Philippe*. Ah! what paintings! The frames are gilt, and pierced to show the panelling. There are the Three Graces, beautiful and as pretty as the mother of little putti. There is a chimneypiece diagonally in the corner, and corner cupboards by Martin, with beautiful objects on them, including an amber desk-set which the Prince of Prussia sent him with some poems: I'll tell you about that later. The only furniture is a large armchair covered with white taffeta, and two matching stools; for, by God's grace, I haven't seen a *bergère* in the entire house. This divine boudoir has an exit through its only window, on to a charming terrace with a splendid view. On the other side of the alcove is a divine *garderobe*, paved with marble, with blue-grey panelling, and the prettiest engravings. Finally, even the muslin curtains on the windows are embroidered with exquisite taste. No, there is nothing so beautiful in this world!

## SHE DESCRIBES HER OWN BEDROOM

It is the length and height of a large hall, with draughts coming in through a thousand slits around the windows, and which I will try to block if I live that long. This huge room has only one window, divided into three, as in the old days, with six shutters. The whitewashed panelling only partly remedies the sad effect of little light and no view . . . The tapestry has large figures, but I don't know who they are and they are rather nasty. There is an alcove covered with very expensive-looking dress material, but unpleasant because ill-arranged. There is nothing whatever to say about the chimneypiece . . . Old-fashioned armchairs, a chest of drawers, the only table is the bedside table, but in atonement a beautiful lacca povera dressing table. That is my bedroom, and I hate it . . . I have a *cabinet* with printed cotton, which does not prevent me seeing the light through the corners. I also have a very nice little *garderobe*, not upholstered, also full of draughts to match the rest . . . I have to say that apart from the apartments of the lady and Voltaire, everything is disgustingly awful.

The *appartement des bains*. Ah! how enchanting is this place! the *antichambre* is the size of your bed, the *chambre de bain* is covered with glazed tiles, apart from the floor which is marble; there is a *cabinet de toilette* of the same size, with light celadon green panelling, bright, divine, beautifully carved and gilt; furniture on the right scale, a small sofa, delightful small armchairs, similarly carved and gilded, corner cupboards, porcelains, engravings, paintings and a dressing table; finally the ceiling is painted. The bedroom is richly decorated, the same as the *cabinet*; there are looking-glasses and amusing books on lacquer stands. All of this seems to have been made for Lilliputians: no, nothing is as beautiful! this spot is delightful and enchanted! If I had a suite such as this, I would ask to be woken up during the night to see it . . . The chimneypiece is no bigger than a normal armchair, but it is a jewel you could put in your pocket.

*Lafontaine, Le Baiser pris et rendu* dont j'avais les deux estampes, et *Les Oies de Frère Philippe*. Ah! quelles peintures! Les cadres sont dorés et en filigrane sur le lambris. On y voit trois Graces, belles et aussi jolies que la mère des tendres Amours. Il y a une cheminée en encoignures, des encoignures de *Martin*, avec de jolies choses dessus, entre autres une écritoire d'ambre que le prince de Prusse lui a envoyé avec des vers: nous parlerons de cela ailleurs. Pour tout meuble, un grand fauteuil couvert de taffetas blanc et deux tabourets de même; car, grâce à Dieu, je n'ai pas vu une bergère dans toute la maison. Ce divin boudoir a une sortie par sa seule fenêtre, sur une terrace charmante et dont la vue est admirable. De l'autre côté de la niche est une garderobe divine, pavé de marbre, lambrissée en gris de lin, avec des plus jolies estampes. Enfin, jusqu'aux rideaux de mousseline qui sont aux fenêtres sont brodés aven un goût exquis. Non, il n'y a rien au monde de si joli!

C'est une halle pour a hauteur et la largeur, où tous les vents se divertissent par mille fentes qui sont autour des fenêtres et que je ferai bien étouper, si Dieu me prête vie. Cette piece immense n'a qu'une seule fenêtre coupée en trois, comme du vieux temps, ne portant rien que six volets. Les lambris, qui sont blanchis, diminuent un peu la tristesse dont elle serait, en égard au peu de jour et au peu de vue. . . . La tapisserie est à grand personnages à moi inconnus et assez vilains. Il y a une niche garnie d'étoffe d'habits très-riches, mais désagréables à la vue par leur assortiment. Pour la cheminée, il n'y a rien à en dire. . . . Des fauteuils du vieux temps, une commode, une table de nuit pour toute table, mais en récompense une belle toilette de découpure. Voila ma chambre, que je hais beaucoup. . . . J'ai un cabinet tapissé d'indienne qui n'empêche pas de voir l'air à travers les coins des murs. J'ai une très-jolie petite garderobe sans tapisserie, fort à jour aussi, afin d'être assortie avec le reste. . . . Au demeurant, tout ce qui n'est point l'appartement de la dame et de Voltaire est d'une saloperie à dégoûter.

L'appartement des bains Ah! quel enchantement que ce lieu! l'antichambre est grande comme ton lit, la chambre de bain est entièrement de carreaux de faïence, hors le pavé qui est de marbre; il y a un cabinet de toilette qui est de même grandeur, dont le lambris est vernissé d'un vert céladon clair, gai, divin, sculpté et doré admirablement; des meubles à proportion, un petit sopha, de petite fauteuils charmants, dont les bois sont de même façon, toujours sculptés et dorés; des encoignures, des porcelaines, des estampes, des tableaux et une toilette; enfin le plafond est peint, la chambre est riche, et pareille en tout au cabinet; on y voit des glaces et des livres amusans sur des tablettes de laque. Tout cela semble être fait pour des gens de Lilliput: non, il n'y a rien de si joli! tout ce séjour est délicieux et enchanté! Si j'avais un appartement comme celui-là, je me serais fait réveiller la nuit pour le voir . . . la cheminée n'est pas plus grande qu'un fauteuil ordinaire, mais c'est un bijou à mettre en poche.

241

# APPENDIX TWO

The following list has been compiled from two documents that record the activities of suppliers to the Garde-Meuble de la Couronne in 1785. Entitled *Registres de Factures. Comptes ouverts avec les fournisseurs*, they provide, in considerable detail, information about the sort of requisites ordered on a regular basis by the largest and most elaborate household in France in the eighteenth century. They are preserved in the Archives Nationales, Paris (0¹ 3603 and 0¹ 3604). Original spellings have been retained.

ARSON, *md. foureur* (furrier), supplied bearskin rugs.

ARTHUR, *md. de papier peint* (wallpaper merchant), supplied paper *tentures*, including one of Chinese paper on canvas, screens, two portable closets to be hung with paper, panels of arabesque paper for a boudoir, the Queen's *garderobe* to be hung with paper, paper for various rooms, including for ceilings, *5 rouleaux tontisse cramoisy* (5 rolls of crimson flock paper) and six-leaf screens of blue and white paper.

AUGUSTE, *md. orfevre* (goldsmith), supplied silver and silver-gilt for the dining room, including tureens, dishes, tea caddies and coffee pots, as well as decorative or useful objects, such as candelabra, candlesticks and gaming chips.

VE. BARDOU (*Veuve*: widow), *peintre-doreur* (painter and gilder), painted seat furniture *en blanc verni* (in white, varnished).

BAUDIN, embroiderer, embroidered bed hangings and joined a border of a carpet.

BELLANGER, *tapissier-rentrayeur* (upholstery repairer), repaired old tapestries and Savonnerie seat covers.

BEURTAUX, *tourneur* (turned wood specialist), supplied and repaired chairs with straw seats, rods for sedan chairs, cots, ladders and pulleys.

BOUCHER, *md. mercier* (mercer), supplied different types of toiles, including *cholettes, d'Alençon, polizeau, de Laval* and *cingale* in several colours, including white, blue and green.

BOULARD, *menuisier* (carpenter), supplied or repaired chairs, beds, and screens, prior to upholstery.

BOUVIER, *md. brossier* (brush merchant), supplied sponges, brooms, hearth brushes, feather dusters and bellows.

BROCHANT, *md. de draps* (linen merchant), supplied *draps de Sedan* and *de Berry* ("Sedan" and "de Berry" linen).

CAPIN, *tapissier* (upholsterer), provided window curtains, upholstered chairs and beds. Some were matching sets with the same material for the window curtains, chairs and bed, including pillows, bedsteps, folding screen and firescreen. Materials used include *Gros de Tour* (heavy woven silk), *Pekin peint* (painted silk), *Perse, Bazin* and *fleuret vert*. He also lined drawers with *maroquin et chamoy* (morocco and chamois leather), provided dust covers for chairs and recovered mattresses.

CARANDA, clockmaker, cleaned and repaired clocks, and supplied clock keys.

CARDIN, *peintre* (painter), painted *Pekin* (silk) and other upholstery material. Provided several designs for upholstery, the design for the embroidery of a daybed and three cushions, and repaired painted upholstery.

CHATARD, *peintre-doreur*, painted and gilded old and new seat furniture and beds, gilded the iron rods of a *cousinière* (mosquito net) and painted *chancelières* (foot warmers) to look like mahogany.

COURBIN, *serrurier* (locksmith), supplied locks, and ironwork for blinds, ladders and beds.

DAGUERRE, *bijoutier* (this word means jeweller, but we would call him a *marchand-mercier*), supplied a console table (probably mahogany) with a marble top.

DELACOUTURE, *md. de toile cirée* (oilcloth merchant), supplied painted linen hangings and oilcloth.

DONNEBECQ, *plumassier* (feather merchant), supplied and cleaned feathers for bed crestings, including 120 feathers for the King's bed.

DUFOURNY, *md. linger* (textile merchant), supplied textiles including *gaze d'Italie* and *mousseline double*, also *piqué anglais pre. qualité.*

DUPERRON, *md. tabletier* (dealer in small furniture, including games tables and accessories), supplied accessories for games, including *1 garniture de trictrac complette* (complete fittings for a backgammon table), *2 garnitures de billes avec la carambole* (two sets of billiard balls) and *12 tableaux de loto Dauphin avec 2 Dauphins* (12 lotto boards with fittings). He also provided silk and ivory flags, as well as silvered candle nozzles, to fit into the holes in the tops of backgammon tables.

FIZELIER, *franger* (trimmings merchant), supplied edging materials, such as braid, *chenille* and *crette*. Also supplied pulls for various purposes, including bells, curtains and the mobile panels of firescreens, cords for chandeliers and lanterns, tassels, ribbon, laces for mattresses and finials for bed crestings (including one of cabbage shape).

GERVAIS, *bosselier* (embosser), supplied 16 bellows.

GUILLAUME, leather merchant, supplied blue, green, yellow and red morocco leather, as well as lamb and chamois leather.

GUILLAUMOT, *poelier* (tinsmith), supplied various brass objects, including candlesticks, snuffers, saucepans, moulds and tanks. Also iron objects including firedogs with egg-shaped finials, tongs and shovels, and pipes. Repaired and retinned *la batterie de cuisine du Roy*.

HAURÉ supplied furniture of all types, including beds, chairs, screens (before upholstery), some case furniture (but not veneered), and some gilt-bronze objects, such as wall lights and chenets. One design is included, a terracotta model of a bedframe and its canopy. He also acted as a repairer. Hauré's role as supplier of miscellaneous objects is seen in such entries as *1 marbre bleu pour un secrétaire* (one blue marble top for a secretaire), *48 boulons de ployants dorés* (48 gilt nuts for folding stools) and *4 mains de cuivre de couleur* (4 varnished brass handles).

VE. HAYET, *md. de toile* (linen merchant), supplied toile de Jouy and material for borders.

HENRIOT, *md. de soye* (silk merchant), supplied *damas vert à palmes*.

Ve. Langlois, *md. de laine* (wool merchant), supplied blankets of wool and cotton.

Le Dreux, *md. mercier*, supplied upholstery materials including horsehair, nails, tacks, hammers, screwdrivers, webbing, various textiles including fustian and ticking, also clock rope.

Leleu supplied *3 tables de jeu dont 2 de wigt* (3 games tables, including 2 for whist).

Masson et Hippe, *paulmier* (suppliers of sports goods, the name derives from the French for real tennis, *jeu de paume*), transported a billiard table from La Muette to Saint-Cloud, and supplied cues and a *bistoquet*.

Mayeux, *md. de galon* (braid merchant), supplied edging materials including gold and silver braid, chandelier cords and tassels.

Michel, *md. de soie* (silk merchant), supplied textiles including *Gros de Tour, velours d'Utrecht* and moquette.

Nau, *md. de soye*, supplied textiles including *Gros de Naples*, damask, *taffetas d'Angleterre, velours à la Reine, moëre* and satin.

Papillon, *doreur* (gilder), supplied gilt nails and brass rings (perhaps for curtains).

Ve. Parmentier supplied *moëre bleüe sur fil*.

Paulus et Reverard, *md. mercier*, supplied ribbon, silk thread (by the weight), braid and pins.

Petit, *md. miroitier* (glass merchant), supplied small looking-glasses in red frames, toilet mirrors of various sizes and loose mirror glass.

Prieur, *gainier* (fitted case maker) supplied fitted cases for *pots à oilles*, terrines, dishes and *écuelles*, and bags and morocco cases for plates.

Riezner, *ébéniste* (cabinetmaker), supplied furniture in walnut and mahogany, including tables, screens, secretaires and commodes.

Robert, *md. de papier peint*, supplied *papier velouté* (flock paper), a screen covered in paper, paper stuck to a canvas backing and paper for several rooms, including a *garderobe*, a *salle à manger* and an *antichambre*. He also papered a ceiling.

Samuseau, *doreur*, supplied *10 cadres de fer en 2 battants a mettre en couleur d'eau* (10 double iron frames, *en couleur d'eau* may mean they were to be varnished). The frames could have been for double doors or windows.

Sené l'aîné, *menuisier* (chairmaker), supplied a bed and chairs.

Sené le jeune, *menuisier* (chairmaker), supplied chairs.

Touchard, *sellier* (saddler), supplied one sedan chair with gilt panels, and repaired another.

Trompette, *menuisier* (carpenter), supplied ladders and folding tables.

# CITATION OF SOURCES

Titles cited in shortened form are given in full below. Any not included here will be found in the Bibliography. Original spellings have been retained.

Antoine, Michel, *Louis XV*, Fayard, Paris, 1989

Bastide, Jean-François, *Contes de M. de Bastide*, two vols., Louis Cellot, Paris, 1763 (vol. II: *La Petite Maison*)

Bimont, Jean-François, *Principes de l'art du Tapissier*, Lottin l'Aîné, Paris, 1770

Biver, Comte Paul, *Histoire du Château de Bellevue*, Librairie Gabriel Emault, Paris, 1933

Blondel, Jacques-François, *Traité de l'architecture dans le goût moderne: De la distribution des maisons de plaisance et de la décoration des édifices en général*, two vols., Paris, 1737-8 (all references are to vol. II)

Briganti, Chiara, "Documents sur les arts à la Cour de Parme au XVIIIème siècle", *Antologia di Belli Arti*, 1977: 380-401

Burkard, Suzanne (ed.), *Mémoires de la Baronne d'Oberkirch sur la Cour de Louis XVI et la société française avant 1789*, Mercure de France, Le Temps retrouvé, Paris, 1989

*Dictionnaire de l'Académie Française*, Paris, 1776 (5th edn.)

Guicciardi, Jean-Pierre (ed.), *Mémoires de Dufort de Cheverny – la Cour de Louis XV*, Perrin, Paris, 1990

Havard, Henri, *Dictionnaire de l'ameublement et de la décoration depuis le XIIIe siècle jusqu'à nos jours*, four vols., Maison Quantin, Paris, 1889

*Lazare Duvaux's livre-journal*, two vols., Louis Courajod, Paris, 1873 (vol. I: introductory essay, vol. II: *livre-journal*)

Proschwitz, Gunnar von (ed.), *Tableaux de Paris et de la Cour de France, 1739-42, lettres inédites de Carl Gustav, comte de Tessin*, Acta Universitatis Gothoburgensis, Jean Touzot, Goteborg and Paris, 1983

Rathery, E. J. B. (ed.), *Mémoires et journal du marquis d'Argenson*, nine vols., Société de l'Histoire de France, Paris, 1859-76

## 1. CLIENTELE

**p11** "Architectural drawings . . ." (On ne peut amuser le Roi absolument que de dessins d'architecture). See *Louis XV*: 513

**p13** "Louis XVI has simple tastes" (Louis XVI a des goûts simples). *Baronne d'Oberkirch*: 161

**p13** "I found them beautiful . . ." (Je les trouvai beaux et moins ornés que ceux de la Reine). Ibid.

**p15** The Swedish King was enthralled (c'était un véritable enchantement). See Scott, Barbara, "Gustav III's Love of Paris", *Apollo*, November 1970: 350-57

**p19** . . . with the intention of helping the Lyon silk weavers, who were suffering from lack of work (soutenir des manufactures de Lyon qui manquent d'ouvrage). See *Louis XV*: 515

**p19** "Come straight away to thank the King . . ." (Venez incontinent remercier le Roi qui vous a nommé Contrôleur de ses bâtiments. Cette place est comme celle de Pétrone: vous devez être l'arbitre des élégances, & encourager les beaux-arts. Mais pour cela vous serez obligé de les étudier, sans croire ces petits flatteurs qui assiègent les gens en place, & les louent effrontément des bonnes qualités qu'ils n'ont pas). *Lettres de Madame la Marquise de Pompadour, 1746-52*, London, 1776. Reprinted Librairie Bleue, Paris, 1985: 109

**p23** "Have you heard that I have just bought the Hôtel d'Evreux? . . ." (Savez-vous que j'ai acheté l'Hôtel d'Evreux? Car il faut bien que j'aie une maison dans Paris: mais je vais le faire abattre, & en bâtir un autre plus à mon goût. On se moque partout de la folie de bâtir: pour moi je l'approuve fort, cette prétendue folie, qui donne du pain à tant de misérables: mon plaisir n'est pas de contempler de l'or dans mes coffres, mais de le répandre.) Ibid.: 73

**p27** "have you any ideas . . ." (avez-vous quelque idée pour décorer un peu cette Toilette angloise?) Eriksen, Svend, "Some Letters from the Marquis de Marigny to his Cabinet-maker Pierre Garnier", *Furniture History, The Journal of the Furniture History Society*, 1972: 82

**p27** "ebony and gilt-bronze furniture . . ." (les meubles en ébenne et bronze sont beaucoup plus nobles que les meubles en acajou surtout dans une bibliothèque qui est blanche et or.) Ibid.: 83

**p27** "a bronze by Le Lorrain . . ." (un bronze par Le Lorrain, représentant Andromède attachée au rocher). *Lazare Duvaux*, vol. I: 233-61

**p27** "two commodes in marquetry . . ." (deux commodes de marqueterie avec ornements de cuivre doré faites par Boule). Ibid.

**p27** "a tortoiseshell coffer . . ." (un coffre d'écaille fait en Angleterre, garni de lames de cuivre avec un pied de bois sculpté & doré). Ibid.

**p27** "two cupboards of lacquer . . ." (deux armoires de lacq en relief, avec figures & fruits de pierre de larre). Ibid.

**p27** "A small lacquer *vide-poche* table . . ." (une petite table en vide-poche de laque avec un dessus de porcelaine de France). Ibid.

**p27** "a pot-pourri vase of antique lacquer" (un pot-pourri d'ancien laque). Ibid.

**p29** "a vase of antique porcelain" (une urne d'ancienne porcelaine). Ibid.

**p29** "a small vase of antique green porcelain . . ." (une petite urne de porcelaine verte ancienne d'une très belle couleur & très-bien montée). Ibid.

**p29** "in the middle, an alabaster vase . . ." (au milieu, un vase d'albâtre sur un pied de cuivre doré; deux bouteilles à petits goulots & lézard d'ancienne porcelaine, & deux boîtes d'ancien laque rouge sur leur pieds de cuivre doré). Ibid.

**p29** "These two bottles have belonged to the Duc de Tallard . . ." (Ces deux bouteilles ont appartenu à M. le Duc de Tallard et à M. de Julienne, et elles viennent de M. de Boisset; on les a vues aussi garnies de pied et collet de vermeil richement travaillé, ce qui caractérise combien les pièces d'élite en cette agréable porcelaine étoient estimées). *Le Cabinet du duc d'Aumont*, auction catalogue, P. F. Julliot fils & A. J. Paillet, 12 December 1782, lot 203. See Parker, James (intro.), *Le Cabinet du Duc d'Aumont. A Facsimile Reprint of the 1870 Edition (with an Introduction by Baron Charles Davillier) Recording the Auction of 1782*, Acanthus Books, New York, 1986: 109n

**p29** "the most eccentric . . ." (l'homme le plus original et le plus sale de France). *Baronne d'Oberkirch*: 214

**p 30** "borrowed from la Deschamps" (empruntée de la Deschamps). See *Diderot et l'art de Boucher à David, les Salons 1759-1781*, exhibition catalogue, Hôtel de la Monnaie, Paris, 1984-5: 137

**p30** "fine porcelain from Sèvres . . ." (belles porcelaines de Sèvres et autres, flambeaux de vase d'albâtre et de porcelaine céladon, montés en bronze doré d'or moulu sur des colonnes de marbre, figures et groupes de marbre, de terre cuite et de biscuits de Sèvres, baromètres, thermomètres, seaux, verrieres). See Benabou, Erica Marie, *La prostitution et la police des moeurs au XVIIIème siècle*, Perrin, Paris, 1987: 332

**p30** "Mélite . . . utterly forgot that she was in a *petite maison* . . ." (Mélite . . . oublia réellement qu'elle étoit dans une Petite Maison, & qu'elle y étoit avec un homme qui avoit parié de la séduire par ces mêmes choses qu'elle contemplait avec si peu de précaution, & qu'elle louoit avec tant de franchise). *La petite maison*: 77

**p30** "apprenticed here [in Paris] . . ." (apprenti icy chez celui du Roy dans la rue Clery). *Comte de Tessin*: 275

**p31** "the house is magnificently furnished . . ." (la maison est meublée magnifiquement, des meubles anciens et des Vernis Martin admirables). *Baronne d'Oberkirch*: 211

**p31** "we stayed there two hours . . ." (nous y restames deux heures et nous n'en avons pas vu la moitié). Ibid.: 212

**p32** "A mirror and its pair ..." (Un miroir, et son pendant, de Quattorze pieds de haut ... des Paliniers pesant plusieurs marcs d'argent et portant des flambeaux. ... Une table a Douze couverts en Argent, ouvrage du fameux Germain, et, comme tout ce qu'il fait d'un prix ridicule... Une Jatte avec son bassin de Christail de roche montés en or et sur le Couvercle une Hyacinthe Orientale grosse comme le poing ... Plusieurs tapis de la Savonnerie). *Comte de Tessin*: 328

**p33** "the riches of the sea" (les richesses de la mer). *Registres des Présents du Roi*, 1742, Ministère des Affaires Etrangères, Paris, MD 2059

**p33** "These carnival embassies ..." (Ces Ambassades de Carneval sont dispensieuses et de nulle utilité réelle). *Comte de Tessin*: 331

**p33** "send me the measurements ..." (Il s'agiroit de me faire tenir les mesures des places dans ma nouvelle maison, ou vous jugeriés a propos de mettre des certaines Decorations, comme Trumeaux, Comodes, Tables de marbres, encognures, Dessus de portes, Lits en niche etc ... Faittes moi la grace de me dire la mesure de la Tapisserie qu'il Y faudrait pour le cours, la hauteur et le nombre des pieces). Ibid.: 97

**p33** "we will have to decide ..." (il faudra, s.v.p se regler pour la hauteur des Cheminées que je voudrois de marbre pour etre plutot ruiné). Ibid.: 111

**p33** "I was wearied to death ..." Butterfield, L. H. (ed.), *The Diary and Autobiography of John Adams*, Cambridge, Mass., 1961

## 2. DESIGNERS, GUILDS AND DEALERS

**p38** "everything fine and tasteful ..." (tout ce qui s'est fait à Paris de précieux et de recherché pendant cet espace de tems a été conduit par lui ou soumis à son examen). See *De Dugourc à Pernon*, exhibition catalogue, Musée Historique des Tissus, Lyon, 1990-91: 101

**p38** to have painted on canvas (sur la toile, sur le bois, le verre et sur le marbre, par les moyens les plus ingénieux). See *Le Faubourg Saint-Germain. La Rue du Bac*: 50

**p40** "May I suggest ..." (J'ose vous proposer ... un jeune homme sculpteur qui dessine l'architecture ...; il connoit le genre du bâtiment et du meuble très bien, modèle en terre et en cire – comme il exécute, travaille le pierre et le stuc dans une occasion). *La Cour de Parme*: 387

**p42** "Design for a clock ..." (Project d'une boîte de pendule où se voient les Portraits du Roi et de la Reine que la Renommée présente à la France). Guiffrey, Jules, *Histoire de l'Académie de Saint Luc*, Société de l'Histoire de l'Art Français, Paris, 1915. Reprinted, twenty-four vols., F. de Nobele, Archives de l'Art Français. Recueil de documents inédits. Nouvelle période 1907-1969, Paris, 1970, vol. IX: 109

**p45** "I have saved the Infant ..." (Jay épargné sur les ouvrages dont jay été chargé plus de 3 mille francs a l'infant par les soins immenses que je me suis donné pour faire chercher et aller chercher moi-même dans les faubourgs éloignés ... les ouvriers les plus parfaits, parce que ces gens-la, charmés d'etre paiés comptant contre la coutume des marchands qui leur font supporter de très longs credits, me donnaient a grand marché ce que javois souvent achetté le double chez ceux de cette ville qui ont la grande vogue comme Lebrun, Migeon, Hebert et des autres, réputations qu'ils doivent a ces meme ouvriers que jay scu employer a bon compte). *La Cour de Parme*: 382

**p45** "A small square glazed lantern ..." (Une petite lanterne de glace carrée, à berceau, avec quatre petits bustes de porcelaine sur les angles, ornée de branchages dorés d'or moulu, & fleurs de Vincennes, avec le cordon de soie en blanc et bleu garnie de ses houppes). *Lazare Duvaux*, vol. II, no. 1213

**p47** "it was impossible to get near his shop ..." (on ne pouvait approcher de son magazin, tant il y avait de monde). *Baronne d'Oberkirch*: 306

**p49** "To mounting in gilt-bronze ..." (La garniture en bronze doré d'or moulu de deux urnes de porcelaine céladon, modèles faits exprès par Duplessis). *Lazare Duvaux*, vol. II, no. 1810

**p49** "the finest Vincennes flowers" (les plus belles fleurs de Vincennes). *La Cour de Parme*: 389

**p49** "An extremely large ..." (Un très grand magot presque de grandeur naturelle venant de Chine et habillé en étoffe). See Wildenstein, Georges, "Simon-Philippe Poirier, fournisseur de Madame du Barry" *Gazette des Beaux-Arts*, 1962, 2: 373

**p49** "A Chinese instrument ..." (Un instrument chinois, espèce d'orgue, pour attacher au bras dud. magot). Ibid.

**p49** "During the summer ..." (L'été il courroit et furetait dans les pais étrangers, et l'hyver, de retour à Paris, il convertissoit ses breloques en beaux deniers). Heidner, Jan, *Edmé-François Gersaint, neuf lettres au comte Carl Gustav Tessin 1743-1748*, Archives de l'Art Français, Société de l'Histoire de l'Art Français, Paris, 1984: 187

**p49** "nothing is as beautiful ..." (rien n'est joli et brillant comme cette boutique). *Baronne d'Oberkirch*: 172

## 3. STYLES AND INFLUENCES

**p53** "the subjects are too serious ..." (les sujets sont trop sérieux ... il faut qu'il y ait de la jeunesse mêlée dans ce que l'on fera). See *Louis XV*: 517

**p53** "the Chinese craze" Watson, Sir Francis and Whitehead, John "An Inventory Dated 1689 of the Chinese Porcelain in the Collection of the Grand Dauphin, son of Louis XIV, at Versailles", *Journal of the History of Collections*, 3, no. 1, 1991: 15

**p53** "when she drinks coffee ..." (quand elle boit du café ses femmes de chambre sont obligées de s'habiller en turc, elle-même s'habille de même; quand elle boit du thé, c'est le costume indien qu'on revêt). See Ronfort, Jean-Nérée and Angarde, Jean-Dominique, "Le maître du bureau de l'Electeur", *L'Estampille-L'Objet d'Art*, January 1991: 63

**p54** "Never in my life ..." (Je n'ai de ma vie fait un souper plus gai et plus aimable). *Dufort de Cheverny*: 317

**p56** "it was he who invented ..." (ce fut lui qui imagina le contraste dans les ornements). Blondel, *Traité de l'architecture*

**p56** "His taste was unfortunately imitated ..." (Ce goût fut malheureusement imité par la multitude des artistes; et ceux-ci, n'ayant ni son génie ni ses talents, ont produit un nombre infini de chimères et d'extravagances). Ibid.

**p56** "practically worthless ornamental designs" (dessins d'ornements assez misérables). Henry, C. (ed.), *Charles-Nicolas Cochin, Mémoires inédits*, Société de l'Histoire de l'Art Français, Paris, 1880: 140

**p59** "an unruly genius ..." (un génie sans règle et de plus gâté en Italie). Ibid.

**p59** "We have been freed ..." (On est sorti de l'esclavage auquel l'ancien usage carrés ou rondes, avoit assujeti ... depuis quelques années on a introduit plus de vivacité et moins de sécheresse dans les ornemens: je n'entends pas parler de ceux que produit le déreglement de l'imagination mais de ceux qui tiennent le milieu entre la stérilité des anciens siècles & la fécondité de celui-ci). Blondel, *Traité de l'architecture*

**p70** "he was the first ..." (le premier, il donna l'exemple d'employer les genres Arabesques et Etrusque). See *De Dugourc à Pernon*, exhibition catalogue, Musée Historique des Tissus, Lyon, 1990-91: 101

**p70** "elaborate banners covering the walls ..." (riches bannières formant tapisserie à la façon des Arabes). See Benabou, Erica Marie, *La prostitution et la police des moeurs au XVIIIème siècle*, Perrin, Paris, 1987: 334

## 4. DISTRIBUTION OF ROOMS

**p73** "The character ..." (L'on peut juger du caractère du maître de la maison, ... par la manière dont elle est disposée, ornée & meublée). See Eleb-Vidal, Monique and Debarre-Blanchard, Anne, *Architectures de la vie privée – Maisons et mentalités XVIIe – XIXe siècles*, Archives d'Architecture Moderne, Brussels, 1989: 45

**p73** "nowhere in Paris ..." (nul lieu dans Paris ni dans l'Europe, n'est ni aussi galant, ni aussi ingénieux). *La Petite Maison*: 48

**p73** "It is of circular shape ..." (Il est de forme circulaire, voûté en calotte, peinte par Hallé; les lambris sont imprimés couleur de lilas, & enferment de très-belles glaces; des dessus de porte, peints par le même, représentent des sujets galans. La sculpture y est distribuée avec goût, & sa beauté est encore relevée par l'éclat de l'or. Les étoffes sont assorties à la couleur du lambris … Le jour finissoit; un Nègre vint allumer trente bougies, que portoient un lustre & des girandoles de porcelaine de Seve, artistement arrangées, & armées de supports de bronze dorés). Ibid.: 53-4

**p73** "This room is of square shape …" (Cette pièce est de forme quarrée et à pans; un lit d'étoffe de Péquin jonquille, chamarré des plus belles couleurs, est enfermé dans une niche placée en face d'une des croisées qui donnent sur le jardin: on n'a point oublié de placer des glaces dans les quatres angles. Cette piece d'ailleurs est terminée en voussure qui contient dans un quadre circulaire, un tableau où Pierre a peint, avec tout son art, Hercule dans les bras de Morphée, réveillé par l'Amour. Tous les lambris sont imprimés couleur de soufre tendre. Le parquet est de marqueterie mêlée de bois d'amaranthe & de cedre; les marbres, de bleu turquin. De jolis bronzes & des porcelaines sont placés avec choix & sans confusion, sur des tables de marbre en console, distribuées au-dessous de quatre glaces.) Ibid.: 57-8

**p73** "The walls are entirely lined …" (Toutes les muralles en sont revêtues de glaces, & les joints de celles-ci, masqués par des troncs d'arbres artificiels, mais sculptés, massés & feuillés avec un art admirable. Ces arbres sont disposés de manière qu'ils semblent former un quinconce: ils sont jonchés de fleurs, & chargés de girandoles dont les bougies procurent une lumière graduée dans les glaces … l'on croit être dans un bosquet naturel, éclairé par le secours de l'art. La niche où est placée l'ottomane, espèce de lit de repos qui pose sur un parquet de bois de roses à compartimens, est enrichie de crépines d'or mêlées de verd, & garnie de coussins de différens calibres … la menuiserie & la sculpture en sont peintes d'une couleur assortie aux différens objets qu'elles représentent, & cette couleur a encore été appliquée par Dandrillon, de manière qu'elle exhale la violette, le jasmin & la rose.) Ibid.: 59-60

**p76** "Marble, porcelain and muslin …" (Le marbre, les porcelaines, les mousselines, rien n'y a été épargné. Les lambris sont chargés d'arabesques exécutés par Perot, sur les desseins de Gilot, & contenues dans des compartimens distribués avec beacoup de goût: des plantes maritimes montées en bronze par Caffieri; des pagodes, des crystaux & des coquillages entremêlés avec intelligence, décorent cette salle dans laquelle sont placées deux niches, dont l'une est occupée par une baignoire, l'autre par un lit de mousseline des Indes, brodée & ornée de glands en chaînettes. A côté est un cabinet de toilette dont les lambris ont été peints par Huet, qui y a représenté des fruits, des fleurs & des oiseaux étrangers, entremêlés de guirlandes & de médaillons dans lesquels Boucher a peint en camayeus, de petits sujets galans, ainsi que dans les dessus de porte. On n'y a point oublié une toilette d'argent par Germain; des fleurs naturelles remplissent des jattes de porcelaine gros bleu, rehaussées d'or; des meubles garnis d'étoffe de la même couleur, & dont les bois sont d'aventurine appliqués par Martin, achèvent de rendre cet appartement digne d'enchanter … cette pièce est terminée dans sa partie supérieure par une corniche d'un profil élégant, surmontée d'une campane de sculpture dorée, qui sert de bordure à une calotte surbaissée, contenant une mosaïque en or, & entremêlée de fleurs peintes par Bachelier). Ibid.: 63-5

**p76** "with a marble bowl …" (garni d'une cuvette de marbre à soupape, revêtue de marqueterie de bois odoriférant, enfermée dans une niche de charmille feinte, ainsi qu'on l'a imité sur toutes les muralles de cette pièce, & qui se réunit en berceau dans la courbure du plafond, dont l'espace du milieu laisse voir un ciel peuplé d'oiseaux. Des urnes, des porcelaines remplies d'odeurs sont placées artistement sur des pieds d'ouche: les armoires masquées par l'art de la peinture, contiennent des crystaux, des vases, & tous les ustensiles nécessaires à l'usage de cette pièce). Ibid.: 69

**p76** "This *cabinet* is panelled …" (Ce cabinet est revêtu de laque du plus beau la Chine; les meubles en sont de même matière, revêtu d'étoffe des Indes brodée; les girandoles sont de crystal de roche, & jouent avec les

plus belles porcelaines de Saxe & du Japon, placées avec art sur des culs-de-lampes dorés d'or couleur). Ibid.: 75

**p76** "walls with stucco …" (des murs revêtus de stuc de couleurs variées à l'infini, lesquelles ont été appliquées par le célèbre Clerici. Les compartiments contiennent des bas-reliefs de même matière, sculptés par le fameux Falconet, qui a représenté les fêtes de Comus & de Bacchus. Vassé a fait les trophées qui ornent les pilastres de la décoration. Ces trophées désignent la chasse, la pêche, les plaisirs de la table & ceux de l'amour. De chacun d'eux, au nombre de douze, sortent autant de torchières portant des girandoles à six branches). Ibid.: 80-81

**p76** "the table plunged into the kitchens …" (la table se précipita dans les cuisines qui étoient pratiquées dans les souterrains, & de l'étage supérieur elle en vit descendre une autre qui remplit subitement l'ouverture instantanée faite au premier plancher, & qui étoit néanmoins garantie par une balustrade de fer doré). Ibid.: 80

**p76** "was covered with heavy green silk …" (est tendue de gourgouran gros verd, sur lequel sont placées avec symmétrie les plus belles estampes de l'illustre Cochin, de Lebas, & de Cars. Elle n'étoit éclairée qu'autant qu'il le falloit pour faire apercevoir les chef-d'oeuvres de ces habiles Maîtres. Les Ottomanes, les Duchesses, les Sultanes y sont prodiguées). Ibid.: 86

**p81** "The first room upon entering a building …" (La pièce du bâtiment qui s'offre la première à ceux qui entrent, et qui sert de passage pour aller aux autres pièces). *Dictionnaire*

**p81** "is used to convey an idea …" (sert à donner une grande idée de la magnificence des Appartements). Blondel, *Traité de l'architecture*

**p81** "tapestries should be hung …" (on doit y poser sur un lambris d'appui de belles Tapisseries, … On met dans les dessus de porte des Tableaux qui peuvent avoir quelque rapport avec les inclinations ou les emplois du Maître, & l'on peut placer entre les Fenêtres, des Tables de marbre avec des pieds dorez). Ibid.

**p84** "normally larger and more elaborately decorated …" (ordinairement plus grande et plus ornée que les autres … On appelle aussi Salon, une pièce qui ne sert ni de cabinet, ni de chambre à coucher, ou l'on peut se réunir). *Dictionnaire*

**p84** "it is for these rooms …" (ce sont les pièces que l'on s'attache d'embellir le plus richement que l'on peut). *La Cour de Parme*: 387

**p88** "twenty footmen who watch you …" (vingt valets qui regardent ce que vous vous mettez dans la bouche). See Franklin, Alfred, *La vie privée d'autrefois. Arts et métiers. Modes, moeurs, usage des Parisiens du XIIe au XVIIIe siècle. Les repas,* Plon, Paris, 1889: 110

**p88** "this happens either in the country …" (ce qui se pratique soit aux maisons de campagne, soit aux petits soupers particuliers du Roi à Versailles, à cause de la difficulté du service). Ibid.

**p88** "should have a parquet floor …" (il est bon qu'elle soit parquetée, & que les murs en soient revêtus de Menuiserie peinte en blanc et ornée de Sculptures dorées). Blondel, *Traité de l'architecture*

**p88** "one should be careful to arrange chairs …" (c'est une attention qu'il faut avoir, de pratiquer des sièges dans une pièce à peu près selon la quantité du monde que sa destination doit attirer, afin de n'être pas dans la nécessité d'y apporter un nombre de sièges étrangers qui défigurent l'ordonnance et la distribution des meubles mobiles, tels que sont les tables de marbre, les torchières, banquettes). Ibid.

**p90** "A room of much greater length …" (Pièce d'un bâtiment beaucoup plus longue que large, ou l'on peut se promener à couvert). *Dictionnaire*

**p90** "it must be elaborately decorated" (elle doit être très-décorée). Blondel, *Traité de l'architecture*

**p91** "A retiring room …" (Lieu de retraite pour travailler, ou converser en particulier, ou pour serrer des papiers, ou les livres, pour mettre des tableaux ou quelque autre chose de précieux). *Dictionnaire*

**p91** "nothing must be neglected …" (on ne doit rien négliger pour en rendre la décoration enjouée et galante. C'est là que le génie peut prendre l'essor et s'abandonner à la vivacité de ses caprices au lieu que, dans les appartements de parade, il doit se resserrer dans les règles les plus exactes de la bienséance et du bon goût). Blondel, *Traité de l'architecture*

# 5. ARCHITECTURAL DECORATION

**p97** "nothing is as fine . . ." (rien n'est si beau pour le travail, ni rien n'est plus triste pour l'effet; deux cent bougies y sont pour rien, le vernis noir et les glaces mangeroient une fois d'avantage. Aujourd'huy il n'y a que les couleurs claires à la mode et surtout le jaune et le Celadon). *Comte de Tessin*: 225

**p107** "painted with Indian fruits . . ." (peint en fruits et plantes des Indes sur un fond jaune). See *Le Faubourg Saint-Germain. La Rue Saint-Dominique. Hôtels et Amateurs*: 104

**p107** The *Almanach des Artistes* . . . See *Lazare Duvaux*, vol. I: 302

**p107** "We are unlucky . . ." (Nous sommes malheureux en miroirs; j'ay bien grondé l'emballeur, mais cela ne nous rend pas notre glace). *Comte de Tessin*: 191

**p108** even the King had to make do with imperfect mirrors (Le roy luy meme n'a pas de glaces sans défauts). *La Cour de Parme*: 390

**p108** Le Camus entreated his readership not to expect perfection (ne croyez pas trouver de glaces parfaites; celles qui ont le moins de défauts sont les plus belles . . . ) Mézières, Nicolas Le Camus de, *Le guide de ceux qui veulent bâtir*, two vols., Paris, 1781, vol. II: 153

**p108** His practical advice . . . (les plus belles [glaces] doivent se mettre à la portée de la vue & dans les endroits les mieux éclairés). Ibid.

**p108** . . . mirrors are quite delightful (très-séduisans), castigates them as being pointless (cause de stérilité) when they surround a room so entirely that all they reflect is the person standing in it (la figure de ceux qui s'y mirent). See *Lazare Duvaux*, vol. I: 303

**p109** Dufort de Cheverny described such a system . . . *Dufort de Cheverny*: 317

**p109** "Our stay at Bellevue . . ." (Le voyage de Bellevue n'a point été agréable. Il a fait une fumée continuelle dans les appartements). *Marquis d'Argenson*, vol. VI: 295

**p109** a small chimney sweep going up the chimney (Savoyard qui monte dans une cheminée). Guiffrey, Jules, *Histoire de l'Académie de Saint Luc*, Société de l'Histoire de l'Art Français, Paris, 1915. Reprinted, twenty-four vols., F. de Nobele, Archives de l'Art Français. Recueil de documents inédits. Nouvelle période 1907-1969, Paris, 1970, vol. IX: 448

**p113** The description of the *salon* . . . See *Lazare Duvaux*, vol. I: 302

**p113** "I was led into a stuccoed dining room . . ." (on me mène dans la salle à manger décorée en stuc, avec un énorme poêle de faience surmonté d'une figure de femme du plus beau modèle, noire comme de l'ébène, posée comme la Vénus de Médicis et drapée de même. Frappé de la beauté des contours, je m'approche et pose la main sur la plus belle croupe possible; la mollesse des chairs me fait retirer la main avec effroi: c'était une Négresse, chose que je n'avais jamais vue, qui, avec la liberté de son pays, vint me sauter au cou et me rendît stupéfait pendant longtemps). *Dufort de Cheverny*: 149

# 6. FURNITURE

**p118** . . . unless one looks carefully, the two can often be confused (si l'on y fait pas attention, on prend souvent l'un pour l'autre). Bimont: 10

**p119** "so as to provide space . . ." (pour y trouver la sculpture dans la mace du bois). See Eriksen, *Delanois*: 38

**p119** "with frames carved and painted green . . ." (les bois sculptés et peints en vert à moulures dorées). *Bellevue*: 287

**p119** "finely and carefully recarved . . . to revive it" (bien reparé avec soin . . . pour le faire revivre). See Eriksen, *Delanois*: 38

**p119** "on account of the considerable amount of time . . ." (eu egard au temps considérable des Repareurs, Doreurs, consommation et double employ de l'or attendu leurs grandes richesses et délicatesses des ornements). Ibid.

**p123** "the King can lie down and rest his head" (le Roi puisse s'y étendre et reposer sa tête). *Archives de la Maison du Roi*, Archives Nationales, Paris, 0¹ 3427

**p139** "If you really must work . . ." (Si l'on est obligé de travailler . . . on écrira pour cet effet sur un pupitre exhaussé en s'appuyant sur un tabouret qui le soit aussi). Tronchin, Henri, *Théodore Tronchin*, Plon, Paris and Künding, Geneva, 1906: 392

# 7. GILT-BRONZE

**p145** "He has a lot of bronzes for sale . . ." (Il a beacoup de bronzes à vendre pour servir à la décoration des appartements, soit en girandoles, en bras de cheminées, feux et flambeaux de toute espèce et toute grandeur ornés avec figures. . . et des boîtes de pendules toutes prêtes à recevoir des mouvements). See Watson, Sir Frances, "The Paris Collections of Madame B., part II, French Eighteenth-century Objects of Art", *The Connoisseur,* February 1964: 74

**p145** "four crystal candelabra with porcelain flowers" (4 girandoles de cristal avec des fleurs de porcelaine). *La Cour de Parme*: 390

**p145** "life-size female figures . . ." (figures de femmes de grandeur naturelle, portant chacune des branches de lys, à cinq bobèches formant torchères). Duc de Choiseul sale, auction catalogue, A. J. Paillet, Paris, 18 December 1786, lot 208

**p145** "white marble vases . . ." (vases de marbre blanc portant des branchages de lys pour former de belles girandoles à cinq lumieres; ils sont aussi garnis de têtes de béliers, bandeau à postes avec guirlandes de fruits & feuillages, le tout porté sur un socle rond; le stuc imitant le granit). Ibid., lot 206

**p151** "Fire-irons with four polished iron rods . . ." (Une Grille à quatre branches de fer poly de 22 pouces de profondeur, ornée sur le devant d'une chasse d'ours, et de sanglier, de bronze doré d'or moulu, avec pelle, pincettes et tenailles, aussi de fer poli, à boutons dorez, et surtous de fer blanc doublez de revêche). *Journal du Garde-Meuble*, 1754, Archives Nationales, Paris, 0¹ 3316

**p158** "They have only been given a gold colour . . ." (Ils ne sont qu'en couleur d'or, attendu la trop grande dépense; les personnes qui les auront pourront en toute sûreté les faire dorer d'or moulu). Description of lot 1 of the furniture in Cressent's first auction of his stock and collection, in 1749. See Ballot, M. J., *Charles Cressent, sculpteur, ébéniste, collectionneur*, Société de l'Histoire de l'Art Français, 1919. Reprinted, twenty-four vols., F. de Nobele, Archives de l'Art Français. Recueil de documents inédits. Nouvelle période 1907-1969, Paris, 1970, vol. X: 196

# 8. PORCELAIN

**p166** "The porcelains are considered as the masterpieces of our factory . . ." (Les porcelaines sont regardées comme un chef-d'oeuvre de notre manufacture et servent à décorer les cheminées dans les superbes cabinets de Monseigneur le Dauphin et de Madame la Dauphine). See Stryienski, Casimir, *La mère des trois derniers Bourbons, Marie-Josèphe de Saxe et la cour de Louis XV*, Plon, Paris, 1902: 88

**p166** "an uncomfortable and affected appearance . . ." (un air gêné, contraint et affecté qui leur ôte de la grâce; . . . je préfère la porcelaine d'ici et je voudrais qu'on l'imitât en Saxe). Ibid.: 338

**p167** "relief moulded like those from Japan" (en relief comme celles qui viennent du Japon). See Chavagnac, Comte X. de and Grollier, Marquis de, *Histoire des Manufactures françaises de porcelaine*, Alphonse Picard et Fils, Paris, 1906: 32

**p167** "Tree trunks, for making candelabra" (Troncs d'Arbres, pour faire des Girandoles). Ibid.

**p168** "The Chantilly service . . ." (Le service de Chantilly est pour les secondes tables, tout le monde trouve cette porcelaine plus agréable que celle des Indes et chacun veut en avoir. Cette manufacture sest relancé, je ne scait trop si elle se pourra soutenir, pour faire mon service ils ont pris de nouveaux moules fait a limitation du modèle de Seve qui leur ont beaucoup coutté). *La Cour de Parme*: 396

**p170** "in imitation of natural flowers" (à l'imitation des fleurs naturelles).

*Extrait des Registres du Conseil d'Etat* (Confirmation of Privileges of 1745 and 1748), 17 April 1749, Archives Nationales, Paris, 0¹ 2059

**p171** naturally coloured branches (branchages vernis imitant la nature). *Lazare Duvaux*, vol. II, no. 226

**p172** "Outlandish taste is the hallmark of mediocrity . . ." (Le goût de l'extraordinaire est le caractère de la médiocrité . . . Revenez au jasmin, à la jonquille). See *Diderot et l'art de Boucher à David, les Salons 1759-1781*, exhibition catalogue, Hôtel de la Monnaie, Paris, 1984-5: 128

**p174** "He [Louis XV] made us unpack his beautiful blue, white and gold service . . ." (Il nous occupa à déballer son beau service bleu, blanc et or, de Vincennes, que l'on venait de renvoyer de Paris, où on l'avait étalé aux yeux des connaisseurs. C'était un des premiers chefs-d'oeuvre de cette nouvelle manufacture de porcelaines qui prétendait surpasser et faire tomber celle de Saxe). From the Duc de Croÿ's memoirs. See Verlet, Pierre, *Louis XV, Un moment de perfection de l'art français*, exhibition catalogue, Hôtel de la Monnaie, Paris, 1974: 291

**p180** "French [Sèvres] porcelain . . ." (La porcelaine de France s'est placée à côté de la Bijouterie, des Glaces et des autres ouvrages d'art qui distinguent dans toutes les Cours de l'Europe ce qui sort de la main des Français. La porcelaine de Chine n'a plus dans le Royaume cette supériorité exclusive qui nous ruinoit et nous mortifioit). Le Comte d'Angiviller, report for the *Comité des finances*, 28 August 1783, Archives Nationales, Paris, 0¹ 2060

**p183** "the private establishments . . ." (les établissements particuliers qui ont profité des découvertes de la manufacture de Sèvres, ont dans l'espace de vingt ans, rendu l'usage de la Porcelaine françoise plus commun sur nos tables que ne l'étoit pour nos Pères il y a cent ans l'usage de la fayence). Ibid.

**p183** "a selection of new pieces of Clignancourt . . ." (un assortiment de pièces nouvelles en porcelaine de Clignancourt, comme garnitures de cheminées, déjeuners, pendules, flambeaux, vases, carafes à oignons, etc. garnis de bronze doré au mat). See *Dictionnaire de l'ameublement*, vol. IV, column 481

# 9. LACQUER, TÔLE AND WALLPAPERS

**p186** "An old cabinet of antique lacquer . . ." (Un vieux cabinet de laque ancien, sans tiroirs ny autres ornements, . . . les deux côtés et le dessus en vieux laque). Guiffrey, J. J. (ed.), *Inventaires . . . de J.-F. Oeben après sa mort*, Société de l'Histoire de l'Art Français, Paris, 1899, vol. XV. Reprinted, F. de Nobele, Nouvelles Archives, 3ᵉ série (suite), Paris, vol. XIV: 336

**p186** "a magnificent twelve-leaf screen . . ." (un magnifique paravent de laque de 12 feuilles, assez épaisses pour être refendues et former la boiserie complète d'un cabinet). See *Dictionnaire de l'ameublement*, vol. IV, column 99

**p186** "behind the screen in the *salon de compagnie*" (derriere le paravent dans le salon de compagnie). Ibid., vol. IV, column 101

**p188** "Choice pieces are extremely hard to find . . ." (Les morceaux de choix sont de même extrêmement rares à trouver, particulièrement quand ils sont anciens. Ils sont quelquefois portez à des prix qui étonnent, même en Hollande). See Whitehead, John and Impey, Oliver, "Les Laques du Japon dans les Arts Décoratifs aux 17e et 18e siècles", *Connaissance des Arts*, February 1988: 87

**p189** "however accomplished the gold painting . . ." (quoique finis que soient les desseins en or qui se font en Chine sur les pièces de vernis, ils ne sont pas comparables au belles pièces de vernis du Japon). Père d'Incarville, *Mémoire sur le vernis de la Chine*, Mémoires de l'Académie Royale des Sciences, Paris, 1760

**p189** "There is no comparison between the finest Japanese lacquer . . ." (Il n'y a nulle comparaison à faire, du plus beau laque du Japon avec le plus beau qui se soit jamais fait en Chine. Ce dernier, même, au jugement des connaisseurs, n'a pour eux aucun attrait). See Whitehead, John and Impey, Oliver, "Les Laques du Japon dans les Arts Décoratifs aux 17e et 18e siècles", *Connaissance des Arts*, February 1988: 87

**p190** "A corner cupboard . . ." (Une Encognure de Vernis de Martin, fond vert, ceintrée et bombée, representant sur le guichet fermant a clef, un chinois assis sur un tapis, jouant d'une maniere de guitare, à côté duquel est un enfant tête nue; Le tout dans un cartouche de Mozaïque fond d'or, avec son dessus de marbre brèche violette . . . portée sur un pied separé . . . verni et doré dans le goût de l'Encognure . . . Une Tablette à trois Séparations, de semblable vernis fond vert et ouvrage de la Chine). *Journal du Garde-Meuble*, 1738, Archives Nationales, Paris, 0¹ 3312

**p192** "with raised decoration in the Japanese and Chinese style" (en relief dans le goût du Japon et de la Chine). See Vial, Henri, Marcel, Adrien and Girodie, André, *Les artistes décorateurs du bois*, two vols., Bibliothèque d'Art et d'Archéologie, Paris, 1912, vol. II: 16

**p192** "commode in light green lacquer . . ." (commode de vernis de petit vert de Martin . . . ayant des camayeux dans les cartouches fond jaune). Ibid., vol. II: 60

**p192** "mirror frame . . . with gold and aventurine lacquer" (cadre d'un miroir, verni . . . en or et aventurine). *Lazare Duvaux*, vol. II, no. 599

**p192** "Have you been to Martin's . . ." (Avez-vous été chez Martin voir mon nouveau carrosse, comme vous l'aviez dit? Je lui ai défendu de le gâter par des peintures lascives que les honnêtes gens ne sauraient voir sans rougir). *Lettres de Madame la Marquise de Pompadour, 1746-52*, London, 1776. Reprinted Librairie Bleue, Paris, 1985: 56

**p193** The *Sieur* Gosse . . . See Jacquemart, Albert, "Une Manufacture de Laque à Paris, en 1767", *Gazette des Beaux Arts*, 1861, 1: 310

**p193** "At the sign of Fame . . ." (A la Renommée Rue St. Jacques, vis-à-vis la Fontaine St. Severin, Langlois, Marchand, tient Magazin des véritables Papiers des Indes de toutes grandeurs, à Figures, Païsages, Fleurs et à Oiseaux, pour garnir les Appartements de Maîtres; Cabinets de Toilette; Dessus de Portes, Paravents et Ecrans, les accomode de la dernière propreté; de très jolies Feuilles pour les plateaux de Dessert; les papiers veloutés en laine hachée, et peints d'Angleterre, pour imiter les Tentures, en velours d'Utrecht, Damas, Satins, Moires, Pékins, Perses, Indiennes de toutes façons; Papiers imitant les vrais carreaux de Fayance pour garnir les Garderobes et Cabinets de bains; Papiers peints pour lambris formant des Panneaux de toutes grandeurs, et généralement toutes sortes de petits Papiers peints à la main, pour Tapisserie; Papiers en marbre les plus recherchés, pour les Salles à manger, Garderobes et Cheminées, que l'on accomode en compartiments; Papiers en écaille et en bois de rapport de différentes couleurs, pour imiter la Marqueterie; Papier d'or fin pour encadrer les Dessins; etc. A Paris 1772). See Clouzot, Henri and Follot, Charles, *Histoire du papier peint en France*, Moreau, Paris, 1935: 35

**p195** "The Chinese . . ." (Ils ont à la Chine une espèce de papier fort singulier . . . comme si c'étoit une étoffe tricotée). Papillon, Jean-Michel, *Traité historique et pratique de la gravure en bois*, two vols., Paris, 1734-66

**p195** "we do not yet know exactly how it is made" (on ne scait pas encore positivement comme il se fait). Ibid.

**p195** "foliage, English green ground . . ." (rinceaux, fond vert anglois, feuilles d'acanthe, oves, perles, rubans). *Bellevue*: 344

**p195** "toile factory, in the style of gilt leather . . ." (manufacture de toiles, dans le goût des cuirs dorés, à fleurs dorées et argentées et à desseins de toutes couleurs). See *Dictionnaire de l'ameublement*, vol. I, column 1060

**p195** "with panels and Turkish and Persian figures" (à panneaux et personnages Turcs et persans). *Journal du Garde-Meuble*, 1752, Archives Nationales, Paris, 0¹ 3315

# 10. TEXTILES

**p199** on the point of collapse . . . Guiffrey, Jules (ed.), *Le duc d'Antin et Louis XIV. Rapports sur l'administration des Bâtiments*, Académie des Bibliophiles, Paris, 1869

**p202** "Borders can be applied . . ." (On peut mettre des bordures à ses pièces ou les enquadré avec des bordures doré, si l'on ne veut point de bordures en tapisserie). *La Cour de Parme*: 393

**p206** Madame de Genlis ... See Entwistle, E. A., *A Literary History of Wallpaper*, B. T. Batsford Ltd., London, 1960: 32 (the date of 1760 given for this remark is probably incorrect.)

**p210** "the principal flowers ..." (les maîtresses fleurs se mettent dans les milieux de la tapisserie, & à portée de la vue). Bimont: 11

**p210** "the principal flower panel ..." (il est très-essentiel que la fleur principale soit dans le dossier). Ibid.: 12

**p210** "two stripes of the same colour ..." (qu'il n'y ait pas ensemble deux rayures d'une même couleur). Ibid.: 13

**p210** the work can only be as good ... (Il dépend, au reste, du Bourgeois de faire plus ou moins de dépense pour les ornemens.) Ibid.: 14

**p214** "three different [sets] ..." (trois autres ... d'hiver, de printems et d'été). *La Cour de Parme*: 381

**p214** "the more one contemplates this room ..." (plus on examine cette chambre, plus on la trouve magnifique). See *Soiries de Lyon, commandes royales au XVIIIème siècle*, exhibition catalogue, Musée Historique des Tissus, Lyon, 1988-9: 52

**p214** the shaped backboard was enriched ... (dossier chantourné enrichy de feuilles et ornemens de broderie d'or relevée). *Journal du Garde-Meuble*, 1754, Archives Nationales, Paris, 0¹ 3316

**p214** a white satin quilt (un couvrepied de satin blanc). Ibid.

**p217** "it is a masterpiece ..." (c'est un chef-d'oeuvre des Arts que l'on exerce dans la Ville de Lyon). See *Soiries de Lyon, commandes royales au XVIIIème siècle*, exhibition catalogue, Musée Historique des Tissus, Lyon, 1988-9: 60

**p219** "painter on textiles in the Indian style" (peintre sur étoffes imitant celles des Indes). Guiffrey, Jules, *Histoire de l'Académie de Saint Luc*, Société de l'Histoire de l'Art Français, Paris, 1915. Reprinted, twenty-four vols., F. de Nobele, Archives de l'Art Français. Recueil de documents inédits. Nouvelle période 1907-1969, Paris, 1970, vol. IX: 421

**p219** for placing on the floor (n'est propre qu'à faire des tapis de pieds). Bimont: 7

**p219** moquette, with a crimson, green and white mosaic pattern (moquette: à mosaique cramoisi, verte et blanche). Babeau, Albert, "Le mobilier des loges de la reine", *Bulletin de la Société de l'Histoire de Paris*, 28,

1901: 103

**p219** "a canopy bed ..." (un lit en baldaquin de toile Indienne fond sablé à bouquets rouges). *Journal du Garde-Meuble*, 1752, Archives Nationales, Paris 0¹ 3315

**p219** "Painted toiles ..." (Les Toiles peintes de toute espèce servent à faire de beaux meubles, sur-tout pour la campagne). Bimont: 9

**p219** "six armchairs ..." (six fauteuils en tapisseries à remplir, avec les laines qu'il faut, le dessein imite le damas uni). *Comte de Tessin*: 269

**p219** "design of drapery and cartouches" (dessein draperie et à cartouches). *Bellevue*: 367

## 11. SILVER

**p224** "five pieces of mirror glass ..." (5 pièces de glaces sablées et garnies de groupes et vases de fleurs naturelles). *Journal du Garde-Meuble* (Rambouillet papers), 1784, Archives Nationales, Paris, 0¹ 3444

**p224** "marvellous mechanism" (mécanique admirable). See Fleury, Comte, *Louis XV intime et les petites maîtresses*, Plon, Paris, 1899: 85

**p224** "The centre was a river ..." (Le milieu en étoit une rivière qui a coulé pendant tout le repas avec une abondance intarissable. Son cours étoit orné de petits batteaux ... Le jeux des diamans ... faisoit croire qu'on étoit dans un palais de fées). Ibid.

**p224** "You rich people ..." (Riches, mettez carafons et bouteilles sur la table). See Franklin, Alfred, *La vie privée d'autrefois. Arts et métiers. Modes, moeurs, usage des Parisiens du XIIe au XVIIIe siècle. Les repas*, Plon, Paris, 1889: 111

**p227** she used the excuse ... (pour éviter toute étiquette, elle était à sa toilette). *Dufort de Cheverny*: 97

**p228** "the goldsmiths either won't show them ..." (les Orphèvres en sont ou jaloux, ou mettent leurs idées à trop haut prix). *Comte de Tessin*: 224

**p233** "of a shape in the latest fashion" (d'une forme à la dernière mode). *La Cour de Parme*: 397

**p239** "made from the designs of Germain ..." (faits sur les dessins du S. Germain et montés en argent par le même). See *Le Faubourg Saint-Germain. Rue de l'Université*: 90

# BIBLIOGRAPHY

Bibliographies in the books mentioned here will point the way to further reading, in book and article form, as well as original documents. Other works that may be of interest are given in the Citation of Sources.

Badin, Jules, *La manufacture de tapisseries de Beauvais depuis ses origines jusqu'à nos jours*, Société de Propagation des livres d'Art, Paris, 1909

Bellaigue, Geoffrey de, *The James A. de Rothschild Collection at Waddesdon Manor. Furniture, Clocks and Gilt bronzes*, Office du Livre, Fribourg, 1974

Brédif, Josette, *Toiles de Jouy. Classic Printed Textiles from France 1760-1843*, Thames and Hudson, London, 1989

Cordey, Jean, *Inventaire des biens de Madame de Pompadour*, Société des Bibliophiles Français, Paris, 1939

Publications of the Délégation à l'Action Artistique de la Ville de Paris and the Société d'Histoire et d'Archéologie du VIIe Arrondissement, 1980-90:
    *Le Faubourg Saint-Germain. La Rue de Grenelle*, exhibition catalogue, Galerie de la SEITA, Paris, 1980
    *La Rue de Lille*, exhibition catalogue, Institut Néerlandais, Paris, 1983 and *L'Hotel de Salm, Palais de la Légion d'Honneur, Rue de Lille*, exhibition catalogue, Musée National de la Légion d'Honneur et des Ordres de Chevalerie, Paris, 1983 (one catalogue for both exhibitions)
    *Le Faubourg Saint-Germain. La Rue Saint-Dominique. Hôtels et Amateurs*, exhibition catalogue, Musée Rodin, Paris, 1984

    *Le Faubourg Saint-Germain. Palais-Bourbon, Sa Place*, exhibition catalogue, Institut Néerlandais, Paris, 1987
    *Le Faubourg Saint-Germain. Rue de l'Université*, exhibition catalogue, Institut Néerlandais, Paris, 1987
    *Le Faubourg Saint-Germain. Le Quai Voltaire*, exhibition catalogue, Musée National de la Légion d'Honneur et des Ordres de Chevalerie, Paris, 1991 (catalogue published 1990)
    *Le Faubourg Saint-Germain. La Rue du Bac*, 1990 (collection of essays)

Diderot, Denis and d'Alembert, Jean, *Encyclopédie, ou dictionnaire raisonné des sciences, des arts et des métiers...*, Braison, David, Le Breton, Durand, Paris, 1751-77

Eriksen, Svend, *The James A. de Rothschild Collection at Waddesdon Manor. Sèvres Porcelain*, Office du Livre, Fribourg, 1968

—— *Louis Delanois, menuisier en sièges*, F. de Nobele, Paris, 1968

—— *Early Neo-classicism in France*, Faber and Faber, London, 1974

Eriksen, Svend and Bellaigue, Geoffrey de, *Sèvres Porcelain. Vincennes and Sèvres 1740-1800*, Faber and Faber, London, 1987

Fenaille, Maurice, *État général des Tapisseries de la manufacture des Gobelins depuis son origine jusqu'à nos jours, 1600-1900*, M. M. Fenaille, Paris, 1903-23

Feray, Jean, *Architecture intérieure et décoration en France, des origines à 1875*, Berger-Levrault, Caisse Nationale des Monuments Historiques et des

Sites, Paris, 1988

*La Folie d'Artois,* Château de Bagatelle exhibition catalogue, Paris, 1988

Gauthier, Serge (pref.), *Les porcelainiers du XVIIIe siècle français,* Hachette, Paris, 1964

Impey, Oliver, *Chinoiserie. The Impact of Oriental Styles on Western Art and Decoration,* Oxford University Press, London, 1977

Kimball, Fiske, *The Creation of the Rococo Decorative Style,* Dover Publications, New York, 1980

Mabille, Gérard, *Orfèvrerie française des XVIe, XVIIe et XVIIIe siècles,* Musée des Arts Décoratifs and Musée Nissim de Camondo, catalogue raisonné of the collections, Paris, 1984

*Merveilles des châteaux de l'Île-de-France,* Hachette, Paris, 1963

Nocq, Henry, *Le poinçon de Paris, répertoire des maîtres orfèvres de la juridiction de Paris, depuis le Moyen-Âge jusqu'à la fin du XVIIIe siècle,* H. Floury, Paris, 1926-31

Ottomeyer, Hans and Proschel, Peter, *Vergoldete Bronzen. Die Bronzearbeiten des Spätbarock und Klassizismus,* Klinkhardt & Biermann, Munich, 1986

Paget Toynbee, Mrs. (ed.), *The Letters of Horace Walpole, 4th Earl of Orford. . . ,* sixteen vols., Clarendon Press, Oxford, 1903-5, plus *Supplement,* 1925

Pallot, Bill G. B., *L'art du siège au XVIIIe siècle en France,* ACR Gismondi, Paris, 1987

Plinval de Guillebon, Régine de, *Paris Porcelain 1770-1850,* Barrie & Jenkins, London, 1972

Pons, Bruno, "Un collaborateur de Chalgrin: François-Joseph Duret (1729-1816), sculpteur en ornements et sculpteur figuriste. Son livre-journal de 1767 à 1806", *Bulletin de la Société de l'Histoire de l'Art Français,* 1985: 138-78

——— *De Paris à Versailles, 1699-1736. Les sculpteurs ornemanistes parisiens et l'art décoratif des Bâtiments du roi,* Association des Publications près les Universités de Strasbourg, Strasbourg, 1986

——— "Le château du duc d'Antin, Surintendant des Bâtiments du roi, à Petit-Bourg", *Bulletin de la Société de l'Histoire de l'Art Français,* 1987: 55-91

Pradère, Alexandre, *French Furniture Makers. The Art of the Ébéniste from Louis XIV to the Revolution,* Philip Wilson, London, 1991

Préaud, Tamara and d'Albis, Antoine, *La porcelaine de Vincennes,* Adam Biro, Paris, 1991

Savill, Rosalind, *The Wallace Collection Catalogue of Sèvres Porcelain,* The Wallace Collection, London, 1988

*La table d'un roi. L'orfèvrerie du XVIIIe siècle à la Cour du Danemark,* exhibition catalogue, Musée des Arts Décoratifs, Paris, 1987

Thornton, Peter, *Authentic Decor: The Domestic Interior, 1620-1920,* Weidenfeld & Nicolson, London, 1984

Verlet, Pierre, *French Furniture and Interior Decoration of the Eighteenth Century,* Barrie & Rockcliff, London, 1967

——— *Les bronzes dorés français du XVIIIe siècle,* A. and J. Picard, Paris, 1987

——— *The James A. de Rothschild Collection at Waddesdon Manor. Savonnerie,* Office du Livre, Fribourg, 1982

# PICTURE CREDITS

National Trust)
**108** Pierpont Morgan Library, New York. Gift of the Fellows, #1966.8, f.70
**109** Rosenberg & Stiebel, New York
**110-111** Private collection/photo J. M. Tardy
**112** Agence Top, Paris
**113** Hazlitt, Gooden & Fox, London
**114-115** Calmann & King Archives
**116** Calouste Gulbenkian Foundation Museum, Lisbon (detail of page 127)
**117** Christie's, Monaco sale, 7 December 1989, lot 116
**118** Private collection, Paris
**119 above** Musées de la Ville de Strasbourg
**119 below** Sotheby's, Monaco Roche Guyon sale, 6-7 December 1987, lot 109
**120-121** Bibliothèque Nationale, Paris
**122 left** Collection of the Earl of Rosebery at Dalmeny House, West Lothian
**122 right** Sotheby's, London sale, 24-25 November 1988, lot 125
**123 above** From Goodwood House, Chichester, by courtesy of the Trustees
**123 below** Bowes Museum, Barnard Castle, Co. Durham, #FW359
**124** Christie's, Monaco sale, 18 June 1989, lot 188
**125** Alexander & Berendt, London
**126 above** Collection of the Earl of Rosebery at Dalmeny House, West Lothian
**126 below** ©1985 Sotheby's Inc, New York sale, 4 May 1985, lot 306
**127** 88×64 cm. Calouste Gulbenkian Foundation Museum, Lisbon, #262-A
**128 above** Sotheby's, Monaco sale, 24-25 June 1984, lot 3125
**128 below** Sotheby's, Monaco sale, 24-25 June 1984, lot 3236
**129** Private collection, England
**130** Cobbe Collection of Historical Keyboard Instruments, Hatchlands Park, Surrey
**131** Quirinale Palace, Rome/photo De Antonis
**132 above** Ader Picard Tajan, Paris sale, 18-19 March 1981, lot 249
**132 below** Collection of the Earl of Rosebery at Dalmeny House, West Lothian
**133** The Marquess of Tavistock and the Trustees of the Bedford Estate, Woburn Abbey
**134** Secretaire, circa 1776-7, veneered with tulipwood, satinwood, amaranth, and ebony on oak carcass, set with soft paste porcelain plaques, gilt-bronze mounts, enamelled metal, 107.3×101×35.5 cm. The J. Paul Getty Museum, Malibu, #81.DA.80
**135 above** Private collection, England
**135 below** The Marquess of Tavistock and the Trustees of the Bedford Estate, Woburn Abbey
**136** Musée National du Château de Versailles ©RMN Paris
**137** The Marquess of Tavistock and the Trustees of the Bedford Estate, Woburn Abbey
**138-139** Private collection
**140-141** Private collection/photo J. M. Tardy
**142** Musée National du Château de Versailles ©RMN Paris
**143** Ader Picard Tajan, Paris sale, 22 November 1987, lot 226
**144** Residenz Munich, Schatzkammer

**145** Private collection, USA
**146 above** Bibliothèque Nationale, Paris, #12471 HD 64 RES FT 4 F°36
**146 below left** The Wernher Collection, Luton Hoo, Bedfordshire
**146-147** Jonathan Harris, London
**147 right** Ashmolean Museum, Oxford
**148 left** The Marquess of Tavistock and the Trustees of the Bedford Estate, Woburn Abbey
**148 right** From the Palace at Pavlovsk, courtesy Aurora Art Publishing, Leningrad
**149** From the Palace at Pavlovsk, courtesy Aurora Art Publishing, Leningrad
**150 above** Pair of firedogs, circa 1735, gilt-bronze, 35.9×38.1×24.4 and 32.3×38.7×22.6 cm. The J. Paul Getty Museum, Malibu, #71.DF.114.1-2
**150 below** Bowes Museum, Barnard Castle, Co. Durham, #FW44
**151 left** Attributed to Pierre Gouthière, firedog, circa 1780, gilt-bronze, enamel panels, 39.7×37.9×13.9 cm. The J. Paul Getty Museum, Malibu, #62DF1.1
**151 right** Collection of the Earl of Rosebery at Dalmeny House, West Lothian
**152** Private collection/photo J. M. Tardy
**153** By Permission of the Trustees of the Victoria & Albert Museum, London, #172&A-1879
**154** Sotheby's, London sale, 24-25 November 1988, lot 114
**155** Reproduced by permission of the Marquess of Bath, Longleat House, Warminster, Wiltshire
**156 left** From the Palace at Pavlovsk, courtesy Aurora Art Publishing, Leningrad
**156 right** Pelham Galleries, London
**157** The Marquess of Tavistock and the Trustees of the Bedford Estate, Woburn Abbey
**158 left** Schloss Fasanerie, Eichenzell, Germany
**158 right** Private collection
**159** Musée National du Château de Versailles, #V.5251 ©RMN Paris
**160** Musée National de Céramique, Sèvres, #MNC 25234 ©RMN Paris
**161** Private collection, USA
**162-163** Photo J. M. Tardy
**164** Ader Picard Tajan, Polo Collection, Paris sale, 30 May 1988, lot 6
**166 above** Private collection/photo J. M. Tardy
**166 below** Antique Porcelain Company, London
**167 above** The J. Paul Getty Museum, Malibu, #82.DE.167.1-5
**167 below** Christie's, London sale, 30 September 1991, lot 88
**168 above** Private collection/photo J. M. Tardy
**168 below** Private collection, London
**169 both** Private collection, England
**170 above** The Carnegie Museum of Art, Pittsburgh. Alisa Mellon Bruce Fund and John Berdan Memorial Fund and gift of Thomas W. Rassieur, #88.6a,b
**170 below** Ader Picard Tajan, Monaco sale, 11 November 1985, lot 55
**171 above** Collection of the Earl of Rosebery at Dalmeny House, West Lothian

**171 below** Private collection/photo J. M. Tardy
**172** The Walters Art Gallery, Baltimore, #48-9 1796
**173** ©The Frick Collection, New York
**174 above** The Marquess of Tavistock and the Trustees of the Bedford Estate, Woburn Abbey
**174 below** Bowes Museum, Barnard Castle, Co. Durham, #X.1271
**175 above** British-American Tobacco PLC, London
**175 below** From Goodwood House, Chichester, by courtesy of the Trustees
**176 above** The Trustees of the Firle Estate Settlement, Sussex
**176 below** The Marquess of Tavistock and the Trustees of the Bedford Estate, Woburn Abbey
**177** The Marquess of Tavistock and the Trustees of the Bedford Estate, Woburn Abbey
**178 above** Private collection/photo J. M. Tardy
**178 below** Private collection, England
**179** National Trust Photographic Library/ photo Roy Fox
**180-181** Christie's, London sale, 17 June 1987, lot 70
**182** Private collection, London
**183** Christie's, London sale, 3 July 1989, lot 45
**184-185** Bibliothèque Nationale, Paris
**186 above** Ader Picard Tajan, Paris sale, 9 December 1981, lot 312
**186 below** Musée du Louvre, #M.R.380-85 ©RMN Paris
**187** Château de Compiègne/photo Hutin
**188 above** The Wallace Collection, London, #F109
**188 below** By Permission of the Trustees of the Victoria & Albert Museum, London, #1049-1882
**189** Musée des Beaux Arts, Tours/photo Arsicaud
**190 above** Musée du Louvre, #OA 8170 ©RMN Paris
**190 below, 191** Musée du Louvre, #OA 11.292 ©RMN Paris
**192** Musée Carnavalet, #937/62 751/31 142/ 170/Photothèque des Musées de la Ville de Paris
**193** Spink & Son Ltd, London
**194** Étude Daussy-Ricqlès, Paris sale, 25 April 1990, lot 65
**195** National Trust Photographic Library
**196-7** From Goodwood House, Chichester, by courtesy of the Trustees
**198** Savonnerie panel, *Spring*, circa 1717, 2.90×2.20 m, and chairs. The Cleveland Museum of Art, John L. Severance Fund, #52.14 & 47.184-185
**200 left** Screen of three panels (one of a pair), circa 1714-40, wool thread, wood frames, 273×193.2 cm. The J. Paul Getty Museum, Malibu, #83.DD.260.1
**200 right** Manufacture Nationale de Sèvres, #IV.49/photo J. L. Charmet
**201** Formerly Alexander & Berendt, London
**202-3** S. Franses Collection, London
**204 left** Sotheby's, Monaco sale, 14-15 June 1981, lot 69

**204-5** Formerly S. Franses Collection, London
**206-207** ©1986 Sotheby's Inc, New York sale, 1 November 1986, lot 138
**207 right** Collection of the Earl of Rosebery at Dalmeny House, West Lothian
**208** Rosenberg & Stiebel, New York
**209** C. John, London
**210** Manufacture Nationale de Sèvres, #IV.44/photo J. L. Charmet
**211** Spink & Son Ltd, London
**212-13** Château de Compiègne/photo Hutin
**214** Spink & Son Ltd, London
**215** Spink & Son Ltd, London
**216 both** Spink & Son Ltd, London
**217** Château de Compiègne/photo Hutin
**218** Musée de l'Impression sur Étoffes, Mulhouse, #M.I.S.E.959.6.1
**220-221** Private collection/photo J. M. Tardy
**222** A. F. Desportes, *Buffet d'Orfèvrerie*, 1727, oil on canvas, 261.6×187.3 cm. The Metropolitan Museum of Art, New York. Bequest Mary Wetmore Shively in memory of Henry L. Shively M.D. 1964, #64.315
**224** Musée National du Château de Versailles, #Umb 14 295 ©RMN Paris
**225** Musée du Louvre, #OA 9598 ©RMN Paris
**226** Duc de Cadaval toilet service, 1738-9, silver. ©The Detroit Institute of Arts, Gift of the Elizabeth Parke Firestone Collection Fund, #53.177-53.192
**227 above** Residenz Munich, Schatzkammer
**227 below** Manufacture Nationale de Sèvres, on loan to Compiègne/photo Hutin
**228 above** By Permission of the Trustees of the Victoria & Albert Museum, London #E.211-1967
**228 below** S. J. Phillips, London
**229 above** F.-T. Germain, tray, 1750, silver, 3.8×21.9×20 cm. The J. Paul Getty Museum, Malibu, #71.DG.78
**229 below** By Permission of the Trustees of the Victoria & Albert Museum, London, #4246-1856 & 4271-1857
**230 above.** Manufacture Nationale de Sèvres/photo J. L. Charmet
**230 below** Calouste Gulbenkian Foundation Museum, Lisbon, #287 A/B
**231** Museu Nacional de Arte Antiga, Lisbon
**232** Musée des Arts Décoratifs, Lyon/photo Studio Basset
**233** S. J. Phillips, London
**234** J.-B. Cheret, sauceboat, 1762, silver and silver gilt, 12.1×14.3×19.8 cm. The J. Paul Getty Museum, Malibu, #71.DG.76
**235 above** Silver, 18.5×31.75 cm. The Metropolitan Museum of Art, New York. Gift of Mrs Robert R. Livingston, #1973.318 abc
**235 below** Musée du Louvre, #OA 10370 ©RMN Paris
**236-237** Platinum with blue glass, 13.3×17.78 cm. The Metropolitan Museum of Art, New York. Purchase, gift of Mrs A. L. Garbat, Manya Garbat Starr, and Jullian A. Garbat by exchange, and Harris Brisbane Dick Fund by exchange, #1974.164a-c
**238** S. J. Phillips, London
**239** Partridge Fine Arts, London

# INDEX